International Socialism 124

Autumn 2009

Contributors

Ian Birchall is working on a biography of Tony Cliff which is due to appear next year.

Simon Behrman is doing postgraduate research in law and has recently written in this journal on classical music.

Michael Bradley organises the industrial work of the Socialist Workers Party.

Claire Ceruti is editor of the South African magazine *Socialism from Below*.

Katherine Connelly is a member of the PCS union and is currently writing a political biography of Emmeline Pankhurst.

Gareth Dale lived in Potsdam in 1989. He has written three books on East Germany: *Between State Capitalism and Globalisation*, *Popular Protest in East Germany, 1945-1989* and *The East German Revolution of 1989*.

Neil Davidson is a senior research fellow at the University of Strathclyde where he is working on the impact of neoliberal globalisation on ethnic and class identity.

Adam Fabry is currently researching Hungary and international political economy from 1989 at Brunel University.

Christakis Georgiou is a member of the NPA in France and is associated with the magazine *Que faire?* He is currently researching French capitalism and European integration.

Owen Hatherley is the author of *Militant Modernism*. He writes on political aesthetics for a variety of publications and at http://nastybrutalistandshort.blogspot.com

Christian Høgsbjerg is undertaking research for his thesis on C L R James.

Peyman Jafari is a member of the International Socialists in the Netherlands. He is a PhD candidate at the University of Amsterdam and the International Institute of Social History.

Charlie Kimber has written regularly for the journal, most recently on the state of class struggle in Britain.

Andrew Kliman is the author of *Reclaiming Marx's "Capital": A Refutation of the Myth of Inconsistency* and teaches economics at Pace University in New York.

John Molyneux is the author of *Marxism and the Party* and *What is the Real Marxist Tradition?* Much of his writing can be found at http://johnmolyneux.blogspot.com

Oliver Nachtwey is a researcher in the department of sociology at the University of Jena.

David Renton is a barrister working in London and a member of the executive of the Haldane Society of Socialist Lawyers.

Wishful thinking

"The Recession Is Over".[1] That is the message with which much of the media has chosen to mark the anniversary of the collapse of Lehman Brothers and the transformation of the credit crunch into the worst economic crisis since the 1930s. Governments looking for votes have been quick to take up the message. "We are on the road to recovery," Gordon Brown told the TUC in September.

The message is deceptive. Recession, in the purely technical sense of a continuing fall in economic output, has stopped in some countries—for the moment at least—but the wider crisis has a long way to go. Little of the output lost in the recession has yet been made up (as figure 1 shows). Eurostat reports that it actually continued to fall in the eurozone in June and July.[2] Claims that the banks are restored to health are preposterously premature: the Moody's rating agency forecasts further losses for British banks over the next few years of at least £130 billion, a figure which it says could rise to £250 billion. The vast government expenditures undertaken at the height of the panic a year ago must somehow be recouped. And all the forecasters assume rising unemployment for at least the next 12 months. The economic, social and political repercussions of the crash will be with us for the foreseeable future.

1:     Front page headline, *Daily Telegraph*, 9 September 2008.
2:     *Financial Times*, 15 September 2009.

Fears for the future appear in the same financial pages that head-line the supposed turning point. Nouriel Roubini is not alone in warning "there is a big risk of a double-dip recession"[3] nor is the National Institute for Economic and Social Research alone in expecting a period of stagnation now, with "output rising in some months and falling in others".[4]

Figure 1: UK economic output
Source: GFC Economics

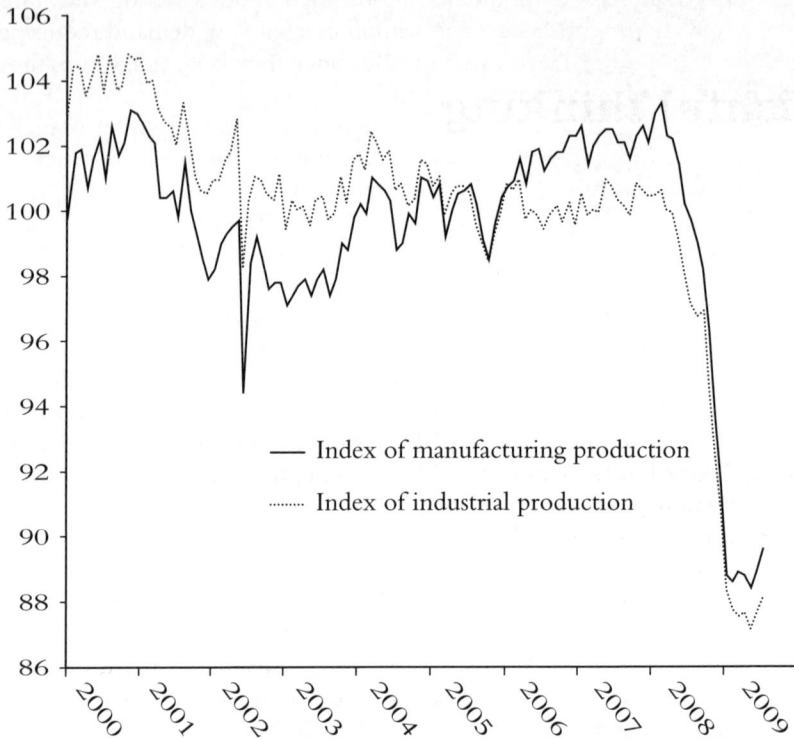

The total collapse of the financial system a year ago was prevented not by its supposed dynamism, but by states replacing private debt with govern-ment debt, which has now risen to levels never seen before in peacetime.

3: *Financial Times*, 7 September 2009.
4: *Financial Times*, 8 September 2009.

Further state expenditures were then needed to prevent a complete collapse in the markets for industrial and commercial capitalists.

In Western Europe and North America stimuli such as "cash for clunkers" schemes, which pay people to replace old cars, are behind much of the limited revival in industrial output. But they have not raised industrial investment—a precondition for self-sustaining recovery.

What is more, the limited recovery in output is exaggerated in the statistics. Fear of a terrible slump led firms to cut back to a minimum their stocks of raw materials, components and finished goods awaiting sale. This meant they were caught short when stimuli created new demand requiring a quick burst of restocking to catch up. But once they have caught up, they can be expected to operate at a reduced level.

In China the stimulus has taken the form of encouraging provincial and local government to undertake a massive upsurge in infrastructure spending (roads, railways, airports, dams) to compensate for lost export markets, while loosening controls on bank lending. Bank lending has risen 30 percent. And here the effect *has* been to raise industrial investment—also by 30 percent. This has raised raw material prices elsewhere in the world but cannot act as a locomotive pulling the world economy forward since Chinese imports have, in fact, continued to contract and the country's economy, which contributes just 8 percent to global output, is simply not big enough.

Most importantly, the reliance on stimuli has raised a huge question for each national component of the system: how long should governments keep the stimuli going?

States have had to turn to borrowing to cover the combined cost of the bank rescues, the stimuli and the huge loss in tax revenues caused by the recession. But they cannot do so indefinitely without eventually damaging their credit ratings. This is causing deep, sometimes bitter, debate among those who advise them. On one side are those who contend that the only way to avoid dangerous inflationary consequences is to start reducing borrowing now by cutting public expenditure. On the other are those who warn that doing this too soon will push the system back into deep recession, with even hardened neoliberals such as Martin Wolf of the *Financial Times* warning that "the extreme fragility of the private sector" means that "premature monetary and fiscal tightening could cause another economic downturn".[5]

These are not mere intellectual arguments. They reflect the pressures

---

5:   *Financial Times*, 9 September 2009.

faced by different capitalist interests. There are those who have benefited from the stimuli and those who have not. There are governments that have spent more on the stimuli, like the US, and those that have spent less, like Germany. And there are those that are going to start cutting back on spending in the near future—with Britain due to take the lead early next year—and those that fear they will suffer from this. Adding to the contradictory pressures are the banks that were saved by government handouts a year ago and now feel reinvigorated enough to demand that the same governments follow their diktats.

The cutters are winning. The centre-right parties openly accept the logic of cuts. European social democrat and Labour parties, looking for votes, have tried to avoid speaking of cuts, but are now shifting their tone. In the US the Republicans are beginning to feel they can gain the support of conservative Democrats in Congress by going on the offensive. And even in China, where the level of government borrowing is less of a problem, there are fears that cuts to the stimulus package are necessary to stop it creating a speculative bubble, even though Premier Wen Jiabao warns that the "foundations of recovery are not stable. We cannot afford the slightest relaxation or wavering".[6]

Whatever happens globally, attempts at deep cuts are inevitable in Britain. All three mainstream parties are drawing up their own plans for after next spring's election. Gordon Brown's admission at the TUC that he plans cuts simply makes public a policy his government has been privately committed to since April. This in turn has given further confidence to those who want to prepare the ground for the biggest cuts since the Second World War. When Liberal Democrat leader Nick Clegg spoke in September of "savage cuts" he was articulating what the Tories and key New Labour figures such as Peter Mandelson and Alistair Darling really want.

The pressures on states to cut back on public expenditure are rooted in the problems that led to the crisis. We have argued in this journal that the financial bubble and bust were symptoms of a deeper malaise for capitalism. Its partially successful attempts to raise profitability to the level needed to sustain accumulation could only be achieved by cutting the share of output going to workers. That left a gap in markets for finished goods which was plugged by growing consumer indebtedness.

The stimuli are, in effect, attempts to use government spending (and borrowing) to replace private debt-fuelled spending. Capitalists everywhere fear that a failure to deal with the rising state debt will lead to

---

6: *Financial Times*, 26 August 2009.

either inflation or tax rises that will cut into profitability, so they are caught between supporting cutbacks to guarantee profitability and opposing them lest they damage markets. The easiest way for capitalists based in any state to deal with the dilemma is to rely on other states—and other capitalists—to pay for the stimuli. But that in turn feeds into the recurrent and sometimes bitter wrangling between states, of which small but significant symptoms are the US tariffs on Chinese tyres and the Chinese arrest of Australian RTZ executives.

There are two conclusions to draw from all this. First, the crisis, in the sense of the global economy being in a mess, is far from over. Second, the attempts by governments to find an "exit strategy" will lead to continued tensions within and between states and to a concomitant weakening of the ideological messages that capital as a whole would like to convey.

We may have seen the end of the beginning of the crisis; we haven't yet seen the beginning of the end.

Left behind?

The derisory message of a four-page piece by journalist Andy Beckett in the *Guardian*'s *G2* supplement in mid-August was that the far left had missed "the political opportunity presented by the financial crisis".[7] And there are a good number on the far left who think the *Guardian* was right. Tariq Ali, for instance, concludes, in an informative interview in *Socialist Review*, that "the mood in Europe is very right wing. The fact that the bank bailouts in Britain have excited very little anger is a sign of the times".[8]

Certainly anyone who expected instant revolution last autumn has been proved wrong. François Sabado of the New Anticapitalist Party (Nouveau Parti Anticapitaliste, NPA) in France has accurately summed up the balance sheet of the European elections in June:

7: *Guardian*, 17 August 2009. See also the reply by Alex Callinicos, *Guardian*, 21 August 2009. The article was written after a brief visit to the Socialist Workers Party's summer Marxism festival.
8: Tariq Ali interviewed by Judith Orr, *Socialist Review*, September 2009.

Progress for the right flanked by the extreme right; a collapse of social democracy; a rise in the votes of the Green parties; the maintenance without any new advance of radical left, whether left reformist or anticapitalist except in Portugal and Ireland.[9]

But such honest accounting does not justify anyone sliding back into the miserabilism which much of the Marxist left internationally has been prone to for at least two decades.

The social, political and ideological consequences of economic crisis rarely work themselves out immediately. Often there is a considerable lag. The devastating political impact of 1929, for instance, was not fully felt until 1933-6. Any great crisis has contradictory effects. On the one hand it shatters the ideological—and sometimes the political—unity of the ruling class. Each section blames other sections for the severity of its losses and, in doing so, throws into question many of the old methods by which they have collectively maintained their hegemony over the rest of the population. And it does so as the effects of the crisis cause rapidly growing, if uneven, levels of popular bitterness.

At the same time the crisis, by destroying jobs, closing down workplaces and creating widespread insecurity, removes immediate focuses for that bitterness by weakening the confidence of workers in their capacity to struggle collectively.

So sudden explosive and insurrectionary moods are by no means the automatic product of every crisis. This was something Leon Trotsky spelt out almost 90 years ago as a leader of the Communist International coming to terms with a failed uprising in central Germany:[10]

> The political effects of a crisis (not only the extent of its influence but also its direction) are determined by the entire existing political situation and by those events which precede and accompany the crisis, especially the battles, successes or failures of the working class itself prior to the crisis. Under one set of conditions the crisis may give a mighty impulse to the revolutionary activity of the working masses; under a different set of circumstances it may completely paralyse the offensive of the proletariat and, should the crisis endure too long and the workers suffer too many losses, it might weaken

---

9: François Sabado, "Après les Résultats des Elections Européennes", *Imprecor* 551–552, http://orta.dynalias.org/inprecor/article-inprecor?id=743
10: The "March Action" of 1921.

extremely not only the offensive but also the defensive potential of the working class.

Under such circumstances groups which are severely hit can turn to the most radical ideas and methods, while the majority of workers put their faith in reformist leaders to ward off the worst effects of the crisis: "The longer the crisis lasts the more it threatens to nourish anarchist moods on the one wing and reformist moods on the other".[11]

But the lack of an immediate class-wide response was not the end of the matter for Trotsky. The underlying bitterness created by the crisis would persist and so could provide the fuel for explosions of class struggle the moment it seemed that united action could succeed.[12]

That was how it was to be with the crisis of the 1930s. It was not until the fifth year of the crisis, 1934, that upsurges of resistance in France, Spain and the US opened a new cycle of left advance. This would suggest that while there are lessons to learn from developments over the past year, they provide only a limited insight into what is to come.

Different paths

The political impact of the crisis has varied immensely from country to country. In the US there was a swing by workers towards Barack Obama, in the Baltic states spontaneous riots, in Ireland huge protests over budget cuts, in France three big one-day strikes, in Greece the Athens riots and in Hungary the mass mobilisations of the far right against the Roma. Only in Iceland was the left actually able to channel the popular mood into bringing down the government.

These enormous differences in response had much to do with the varying impact of the crisis on people's material conditions. While in Ireland, the Baltic states and Hungary there were enormous, immediate onslaughts on employed workers and people on benefits, in Germany, Britain and France government stimulus packages blunted the immediate material impact on important groups of workers, with small increases in benefit payments and reductions in mortgage interest payments in Britain, and subsidies for employers to keep workers in their jobs in Germany.

On top of this trade unions' responses differed. In countries where

11: Leon Trotsky, "Flood Tide", www.marxists.org/archive/trotsky/1924/ffyci-2/06.htm
12: See, for instance, Leon Trotsky, "Report on the World Economic Crisis and the New Tasks of the Communist International", www.marxists.org/archive/trotsky/1924/ffyci-1/ch19b.htm

they were tied, formally or informally, to ruling social democratic or Labour parties they did their utmost to blunt resistance—with the main British union leaders telling people when the crisis broke last year to put their faith in Gordon Brown and even left union leaders calling off action over pay. By contrast, where the centre-right has been in power the union leaders have called limited action, albeit half-heartedly, and provided some focus for class anger. Hence the one-day general strikes or days of action in France, Greece and Ireland.

We have examined the apparently dismal situation that prevailed in Britain through last winter and the early spring in previous issues of this journal.[13] But even in countries where the trade union leaderships did provide focuses for struggles, these had their limitations. As two activists in the NPA in France write:

> There was the possibility of a general struggle with millions of strikers and demonstrators out on the days of action of 29 January, 19 March and 1 May, as well a tough strike against redundancy plans in the private sector just as the public sector was in struggle (higher education, hospitals, the power industry).

> Yet the union leaders still succeeded in paralysing the development of the struggles so that there was no follow through after the demonstrations of 1 May. Each sector was left to fight in isolation from the others. The elections were now disconnected from the perspective of struggle, and the crisis of social democracy was confirmed without translating itself into a significant advance for the NPA.[14]

Similar things could be said about developments in Ireland or Greece. But nowhere is this the end of the matter. In Britain, as Michael Bradley and Charlie Kimber explain in this journal, there are very important signs of a new mood of militant resistance among some groups of workers which may spread in a way which we have not seen for many years. It is not pre-ordained that this will happen. The outcomes of particular battles can be crucial—and the role socialists play in trying to generalise the new and militant methods of struggle can be a decisive factor. In France:

13: See, in particular, Charlie Kimber, "In the Balance: The Class Struggle in Britain", *International Socialism* 122, www.isj.org.uk/?id=529

14: Leila Soula and Rodolphe Juge, *Que Faire*, August-October 2009. *Que Faire* is published by a network of NPA activists who share many of our analyses.

Our side is putting up resistance and doing so quite well. The generalisation of the struggles has been paralysed but the movement has not suffered a frontal defeat. The example of the Continental tyre firm shows that the most determined struggles get the best results. July, a month not very favourable for mobilisations, saw a multiplication of struggles with a hard character in Michelin, Nortel, SKF, JLG, New Frais and Simmons.[15]

The combination of weakened hegemony and popular bitterness means that ruling classes are still wary about going fully on the offensive. Martin Wolf expresses some of their fears in an article on "the resurgence of finance":

Financiers are back to their high-earning ways, while tens of millions of people have lost their jobs, economies are far below potential and public sector debt is exploding upwards. It is little wonder that bonus-bashing is on the menu.[16]

This underlay fears of the possible resurgence of support for the Left party (Die Linke) in Germany in federal elections set to take place while this journal was at the printers.

Other factors that are not immediately economic add to their worries. Afghanistan is rapidly rising up the political agenda. What was presented only a year ago as the "good war" has very rapidly morphed into "the war which could be lost". There are already warnings that this could damage the Obama presidency as he wrestles to get Congressional support for his health policy:

Having on the campaign trail championed the war as worth fighting the president now has to decide how committed he really is to the conflict. His choice boils down to sending more troops or scaling back on US goals. It comes at a time when he is being assailed for alleged weakness over domestic policy and when his own popularity and that of the war is on the slide.[17]

Zbigniew Brzezinski, one of the architects of US foreign policy from the 1970s to the 1990s, warns, "Washington is in danger of becoming bogged down in an escalating war".[18] US worries are not helped by the

---

15: Leila Soula and Rodolphe Juge, *Que Faire*, August–October 2009.
16: *Financial Times*, 8 September 2009.
17: *Financial Times*, 8 September 2009.
18: *Financial Times*, 8 September 2009.

reaction of its European Nato allies, who formally endorse the war but—with the exception of Britain—are not keen for their own troops to be in the firing line. There were even worries as we went to press that the issue would play a role in the German general election. All these factors add to the tensions within and between the governments that are supposed to be working out an "exit" strategy for the economic crisis.

No one can foresee in detail how these different factors are going to interact. But some things are certain. There is not going to be a smooth and easy re-establishment of global economic stability. That means political and social volatility, with sudden governmental crises, attacks on workers' conditions, eruptions of resistance and, from the other side, repeated attempts to divert bitterness into racial and religious scapegoating—attempts that may in time provoke new forms of resistance.

We have seen small but significant examples of how this could happen in Britain. It was glimpsed in the militant demonstrations and student occupations over Gaza in January and again in the protests against attempts to build on the electoral gains of the Nazi British National Party in the European election. Both of these movements have drawn thousands of mainly young people onto the streets.

The task of the left in this situation is not to bemoan its record over the past year. It is to try to draw together networks of those workers who want to fight back, creating the sinews of solidarity and linking the political, economic and social issues. The outcome of the struggles ahead will shape the political landscape for a long time to come.

Will the sparks flare up?

Charlie Kimber and Michael Bradley organise the Socialist Workers Party's (SWP) industrial work. They spoke to International Socialism about recent developments in the class struggle in Britain

Charlie wrote an analysis in this journal six months ago of what was happening in British industry.[1] The picture was of a potentiality for struggle that was being thrown away as the recession broke out. The result was a lack of resistance to the pain it caused—for instance, the 30,000 redundancies that followed Woolworths going bust or the sacking of workers on short-term contracts at the Cowley car plant. This was a continuation of the record of the previous decade, with a series of struggles being wasted by union leaderships—the post workers' strikes in 2002, the firefighters' strikes in 2002-3, the bus workers' strikes of last year. But the article also implied there was the possibility of change. How would you say the situation has developed in the past few months?

CK: I would say that the potential I tried to identify in that article has to some extent become actuality. I wrote that you could see in the Waterford occupation in Ireland that if a group of workers moved, they could become a focus for a much broader mood inside the working class and potentially kick off a process of contagion of struggle. And I think we have seen that, because it is not just one group of workers who have taken action in recent months. There have been a string of victories won by the most militant methods.

If it had been just the occupation of the Visteon car components plant in north London, or just the success at Linamar in South Wales, or just the Lindsey oil refinery strike, which spread to 20 other construction

1:    Charlie Kimber, "In the Balance: The Class Struggle in Britain", *International Socialism* 122, www.isj.org.uk/?id=529

sites, or just the occupation of the Vestas wind turbine factory on the Isle of Wight, I am not sure they would have had nearly as much influence. The fact that there has been a series of struggles is extremely significant. It means there is a layer inside the working class who now have concrete examples of the potential to fight and the potential to win.

People also know that these victories were won by defying the anti-union laws, by rank and file action, and, in some cases, by action by non-unionised workforces. So there is a radical content to the victories that have been achieved.

The idea of radical struggle has seeped into far wider layers of the working class. So the London bus workers, for instance, kicked off this year's campaign for central pay bargaining by occupying the foyer of the Transport for London building. I don't believe they would have done that six months before. It was because there was something in the air. They knew that other groups of workers had done this. We are seeing a qualitative shift in what is happening. Groups of workers are saying, "We are not prepared to pay for a crisis that is not of our making."

The political impact has been sharp. All of the struggles have raised the question of the anti-union laws. All of them have raised Labour's failure to protect working people in a time of crisis while the bankers get massive help. Vestas, obviously, has raised the question of climate change in a way that would not have been possible through dozens of meetings and thousands of leaflets. Wide layers have begun discussing the question of climate change and more specifically the government's failure to address it.

So you have a wave of struggle that breaks the wall of fear about fighting back against the recession, and in the course of that a whole number of political issues have been raised.

MB: As well as those examples there is also the return of the all-out strike. The Bristol bin workers' dispute was one example, Linamar another. Now we have the dispute at the John Lennon Airport in Liverpool and we have an all-out strike at Tower Hamlets College in east London. Arguments for extensive strike action are being put at London Metropolitan University and in other places.

The pattern in the past was the long drawn out ballot, the one-day strike, the slowly developing campaign. The pace is now changing rapidly. People have been used to pushing and shoving through negotiation, leading to management backing down from redundancies. But employers at places such as London Met and Tower Hamlets College have just wanted to drive job losses through.

Very importantly, all these disputes are on a knife edge, and so direct intervention by socialists can make a difference. In Visteon, Vestas and elsewhere interventions by socialists in the early days made a big difference.

Vestas is a classic example. There was no union there. So in the first few days it was socialists who had discussions with workers about taking action. The union did not come into the dispute until it was four days old, and it was not the union that was supposed to represent the workers there.

A sceptic might say we have been through this before, with struggles that looked as if they would bring about change and then did not—for instance the Magnet dispute and the Liverpool dockers' strike in 1997, or the firefighters' and postal workers' disputes around 2002 and 2003. Are things radically different now?
CK: I think things are radically different to how they were six months ago. That does not mean I think a breakthrough has happened which will inevitably go forward. The elements of the old and new confront one another sharply in the class struggle.

At the same time as the positive examples I have given you, at Corus steel there have been mass redundancies. There was a big demonstration in Redcar and then silence. Almost nothing happened. That's the old method of doing things, if you like. At the Johnnie Walker whiskey plant in Kilmarnock 20,000 marched against job losses, with huge popular support. But the union has been incredibly slow to follow up the demonstration and call action, even though it is completely obvious that the sort of radical action we saw at Visteon would be hugely popular, turn the redundancies into a huge political issue in Scotland and embarrass a multinational company that is still profitable. So there are situations where the old still predominates.

Then you have some disputes where the old and the new occur within the same thing. So in the postal workers' dispute at the moment you have an incredible push from the bottom that forces the union to call a series of local strike ballots and a national ballot. Yet at the same time the union is able to keep the lid on any outbreak of unofficial action—despite management acting in the most provocative manner by sacking people, victimising people, cutting pay and imposing new conditions without consultation.

The old and the new clash on the same picket line. So one postal worker will say, "We need to walk out unofficially," while the next one will say, "No, we have the national ballot coming." There are these new possibilities but the old still exists and weighs like a nightmare on the brain of the living. And the way that is resolved, as Michael says, comes down to leadership, to the arguments that are put, to the networks that are capable of altering the way the argument comes out at the end. It is not preordained, but it does mean there are new opportunities if people can grasp them. One of the greatest dangers is that disputes are fought in 2009 and 2010 using the methods of 2007 and 2008.

I was speaking to a library worker recently about how you would respond to a library closure. In 2007 and 2008 you would have had a consultative ballot, a Unison union official would have said, "You have to do this; you have to do that," maybe you would then have had a strike ballot, and it would have gone on for months. This kind of thing is not only what happened locally, but also nationally, for instance with the civil service workers, the teachers and the university lecturers last year. They were important disputes but were drawn out by these endless ballots. I think in the situation today there is a much greater chance of saying, "They are closing our facility; let's occupy it; or let's have a walk out," or, "If we are going to have a strike, let's have an all-out strike, not a one-day strike." These are the new possibilities if people can grasp them. But they are not preordained.

There was a point in the Visteon dispute where the trade union officials nearly got hold of it and put it at risk.
CK: After a period of time the employers went to court and got an injunction against the occupation and named persons inside it. They did something similar in Belfast, and the Belfast workers simply ignored it. But in Enfield in north London the union officials went into the occupation and said not only would union reps be taken to jail unless they ended the occupation but also special squads of police would wade in—police from the force who had killed Ian Tomlinson on the 1 April demonstration against the G20 summit in the City of London. On that basis they won the majority of the occupation to coming out—although when you spoke to people afterwards, many more said they thought it was the wrong thing to do. But there was not the organisation to put a different argument.

That could have been absolutely deadly for the struggle. Two things sustained it. One was that Belfast stayed in with a continuing occupation. The other was that the Enfield Visteon workers had enough activists and supporters to mount a continuing picket of their plant while coming up with a strategy of preparing to picket out the Ford plant at Bridgend in Wales, which makes engines for the Fiesta—the only model in the entire Ford range making a profit. This was a powerful lever forcing the Ford company to do something about the Visteon workers. At first Ford and Visteon were not going to talk at all. Then the union officials said, "You know they are going to go to Bridgend." Suddenly Ford came to the negotiating table.

It is worth spelling out some of the history of the dispute. It started spontaneously and it was not called by the union leadership. Workers in Enfield heard about the occupation in Belfast and then felt they had to do something.

CK: The key workers who decided to act had been involved in the union, although it was not occasioned by the union. And although the union took their time, they did move to support it.

It was a strange situation. In Belfast one of the leading full-time officials undoubtedly encouraged the occupation. He had been heavily involved in the occupation at Waterford Crystal and seems to have told the Belfast Visteon workers it was time to go in there as well. And it seems that local officials in London were ready for something to happen. You can't explain otherwise why there were Unite union flags all over the plant by the first afternoon of the occupation. All that is true.

But it is also true that the union officials were useless at supporting it. So the only thing that sustained it through the first 48 hours was the arrival of local socialists with messages of support, but also physical, concrete things—food, sleeping bags, water. All these things were provided essentially by SWP members and others. Had they not done that, I am not sure the occupation would have survived. It was socialists who took people from the occupations to speak at union conferences, such as that of the teachers, and to leaflet the Ford plant at Dagenham. That got across the idea right from the start that it was not just going to be about simply sitting in the plant, but also going out and winning solidarity from Ford workers.

You spoke about the enormous impact of these struggles. But if you read the Financial Times *or the* Guardian, *let alone the* Sun *or the* Daily Mirror, *you would not have known about any of the struggles before Vestas.*

MB: You would have known about Lindsey.

Lindsey was a contradictory dispute, wasn't it?

MB: It was a messy situation at the beginning of the year. The slogan "British jobs for British workers" had a strong influence, summed up by the demonstration at Staythorpe where people at the front chanted, "What do we want? Foreigners out!"

But as well as that the strike raised the question within the working class of unofficial action. And the dynamic of the second wave of action a couple of months later was different. That was triggered by the sacking of scores of union activists and then the sacking of the hundreds of workers who struck in their support. The dominant feeling then became one of class solidarity. It is clear that the arguments that were put up inside the movement against the slogan "British jobs for British workers" had an enormous impact. Everyone now says the slogan was wrong. It is difficult to find anybody among the leadership who claims it was a good slogan. The press were looking around for it in the second stage of the struggle but found it hard to find it. That doesn't mean it's missing from the construction industry now as an argument or that it can't blow up again. But the main lesson for people inside the trade union movement is that you can break the anti-union laws. Lindsey and Vestas have had a huge impact through the media. People on picket lines talk about the Lindsey dispute.

The trade union bureaucracy's position on the breaking of the anti-union laws is also interesting. The front page of the *Reporter*, the paper that goes out to Unite union reps, has got Vestas, Visteon and Lindsey down as great victories. This is a nod and a wink to thousands of Unite members that it is all right to break the anti-union laws. Yet this is taking place at the same time as in the bus industry the union is calling off disputes across the country at different stages because of the threat of legal action—in Sheffield, Chester and London. But their position means you can raise the question of breaking the union laws in a way you couldn't do in the past, when you were seen as crazy for doing so.

So in the Lindsey dispute you had a first stage which was clearly directed against foreign workers—even though some people on the left, like the Socialist Party and Seumas Milne in the Guardian, *denied this, while the Communist Party seemed to support banning foreign workers, describing them getting jobs as "social dumping". In that situation a section of the left—the SWP, the head of the civil service workers' PCS union Mark Serwotka, and so forth—waged a big propaganda campaign against the slogan. And you are saying that this itself influenced the situation in the second round of the dispute and people began to see it more clearly in class terms.*
MB: By the time of the second dispute we had won the argument in important sections of the class. So the GMB union conference voted to reject the "British jobs for British workers" slogan. So did the conferences of the biggest teaching union the NUT, and the lecturers' UCU. It means we won an argument among people—but that does not mean the argument has gone away.

The most militant people to fight, in Visteon and Vestas, had little or no traditions of industrial action. And both groups were faced with the closure of their entire plant and did not have a lot to lose. What problems do we face when we try to translate that into other groups of workers who are fighting over specific grievances?
CK: There is clearly a difference between being offered £45,000 to go quietly compared with when you get nothing. It is easier to win an

argument with those being offered nothing. However, fewer and fewer people are being offered those big pay-offs to go—and not just in the private sector but in the public sector too. There is a big struggle coming in the civil service as the government attempts to slash what's called the "compensation scheme"—the amount people get when they are made redundant. It is clearly the prelude to mass redundancies, the opening shots in a war that's coming after next year's general election. Also more and more people are relearning the lesson that what looks like quite a lot of money does not last long, because you can't just go and pick up another job.

So it is not only in the cases that people are offered nothing that you can put the argument for militant resistance. The majority of the Vestas workers were going to get some redundancy money—not vast amounts but some. The people at Lindsey put their jobs on the line. This is an industry in which a blacklist exists and they could have been finished. It was only solidarity that managed to keep their jobs.

The difficult cases are the big national disputes or where the union bureaucracy have a strong hold. There will be an argument inside the PCS civil service union about how to react to the attack on their compensation scheme. Arguing for quick action will be more difficult because of the way in which union bureaucracies work. And there are cases like Corus and Johnnie Walker where the union is in control and the rank and file is weak.

As the examples spread you get a growing number of people who know about the disputes, collect money for them, go to meetings on them—a core within the working class who catch on to the idea of what is happening and what is possible. It is this group that is driving for more militant forms of action. It is not that the whole of the working class has shifted, but a serious core of people is being created around each of these disputes—of thousands and tens of thousands of people who know what happened at Vestas, Lindsey, etc—and their numbers are growing.

They are going to come up against the methods of the bureaucracy and it will not be an easy process. Every day there is a battle over this question. That is why we need socialist militants and socialist politics but also a wider group of people who form around these disputes to keep in touch with each other and create networks to confront the bureaucracy.

Vestas was a quite small group of workers—about 600 in three factories—in a part of the country which many socialists would think of as industrially and politically backward. How did we get an occupation there?
MB: Our first reaction to the news of the closure of the Isle of Wight plant was to go though the classic model—to find out from Unite's regional

official if the place was unionised. He said it wasn't. There might have been some union members in the plant but the union was not in contact with them. There had been attempts to unionise before but the Isle of Wight was anti-union and people who might join had been intimidated, and so on.

Then some other socialists sent some young people down there from a climate camp to spend a week or so banging out leaflets and calling a public meeting. Most of the hundred or so people at the meeting did not like it, but one of our young people got talking to some of them, and we went down to meet five of them in a pub. We took some of our pamphlets on the occupation of Visteon down with us—at one stage this was the most popular publication in the high street on the Isle of Wight. After that there were a series of meetings, some in pubs and one in a hall, where the idea of occupation was bandied about. People were going to try to go for it through the classic method by which you agitate inside the factory, with leaflets going into the factory, and then on a certain day call everyone together on the shopfloor and vote on occupying. But people learnt that the management were ready to deal with that, and a number of people decided just to go in to occupy the place.

The way the argument for occupation was won relied on the big picture; it wasn't simply a "bread and butter" question. We said you have to fight over jobs, and the climate change angle will hit the headlines and you will make a huge stir.

For the first three or four days of the occupation there was no union involvement at all. People asked me what union should they join and I said Unite was meant to represent them. But while Unite did nothing, people got talking to local members of the RMT rail and seafarers' union and, after a couple of days, the RMT leaders. The RMT general secretary, Bob Crow, came down and did a big speech in support, and the place was mobbed out with RMT flags and membership forms.

The occupation has transformed things politically down there. This was an area of poor union organisation, low pay and bad conditions. Now contacts between union activists on the island must be better than in most places in the country. The factory next door to Vestas has clearly been scared to lay off workers as it wanted to so long as the Vestas dispute is going on. Almost the entire population of the island know what's going on. At various times the occupation has been the dominant political factor on the island.

The experience bears out all the stories you hear about how people shift in struggle. Young workers who started off saying they were not interested in politics have now reached the stage where they know the differences between the different political groups and what they are arguing.

Politically, the issue is still huge, even though the factory is closed and people are looking for work. If you want a dispute which summarises the argument why political trade unionism is a key factor, Vestas is it. It sums up as well the argument about the role of individuals and socialists. If people had just sat back in the traditional way, waiting for something to happen, Vestas would never have erupted.

There are lots of situations at the moment where whether people decide to fight or not is on a knife edge. Since the 1970s most people don't have experience of situations where socialists can intervene to such an effect and so people tend to stand back from doing so.

In the SWP we have had an argument against the orthodoxy of the industrial relations establishment and much of the left since at least the end of the miners' strike in 1985. They said neoliberalism and globalisation have destroyed the capacity of workers to fight, and unions don't matter any more. By contrast we have argued that there is a tradition in the British working class of trade unionism, that there is a minority in every workplace that have been in unions, but that the union bureaucracy do not take the initiative, while the left gets trapped in a miserabilism that stops them taking initiatives. Then there is the question of general political ideas. I feel it must make a difference if you are occupying a factory not just to protect your own particular job, however important that is, but also as part of saving the world. The key lesson we have to learn from these disputes is raising the wider questions, that is, the need for political trade unionism.

CK: That is true. But there is a slight danger of drawing the conclusion from Vestas that you can only get away with militant struggle if there is some socially useful thing that you are occupying over. That will be true for large elements of the public sector, which is an important thing to stress. But even when it is not at all obvious that what you do is particularly socially beneficial—in the case of Johnnie Walker you would be occupying a whisky bottling plant—you would be asking, "Why should we be paying for the crisis?" If you have that clearly as the slogan on which you are launching your campaign, then you can get support. There is such a strong feeling about the bankers, the bailouts, the MPs' expenses scandal. People don't buy the argument any more that everything has to be profitable.

The minority in the class with some level of militancy and consciousness feel more confident now. Saying we can fight, and here's Visteon and here's Vestas and here's Lindsey, is much easier than simply saying we ought to fight. That was the difficulty at Cowley. There were not those clear examples of what could be done. Were the Cowley sackings to happen now, someone would probably say we can fight because Visteon and Vestas did.

MB: Even if you talk about the public sector, if you don't take issues up politically then things can go wrong. The campaign a year ago about teachers' pay did not talk about the question of the needs of children and so on. It was all about the retail price index. And the moment the crisis broke the left collapsed, unable to put the arguments for continued struggle. The successful campaigns about jobs are always the ones that talk about the bigger picture. So part of the reason there has been a fight at Tower Hamlets College is that there was a campaign over the teaching of English to those from an immigrant background, which drew in parents and the local population. So the issue today does not seem like that of supposedly well paid lecturers wanting to keep their jobs in the recession.

Looking forwards we are faced with two big issues. One is the attack on pensions in the private sector. We are still waiting for a serious fight on this. The other is the cuts that are coming in the public sector, beginning already with serious attacks in higher education and, more slowly and beneath the surface, in health.

CK: It may well be that local government pensions come under attack before the election—and there will be job cuts in local government. And the dispute in the civil service will be a big test. Whether there will be struggles over private sector pensions, we cannot tell yet.

MB: Unless you can persuade a layer of people to fight in a different manner they will be ritually slaughtered. That is what is going on at the moment in some parts of higher education, with huge cuts going through and people not responding at the right level.

CK: Two points I want to make. The ruling class are quite weak in a lot of these disputes. They often talk hard, but in truth they are not as confident because they are not used to any real resistance. The second phase of the Lindsey dispute threw the employers into complete disarray. They did not know what to do about it. Ford was similarly discomforted by this relatively small group of workers at Visteon. The government, given its general weak state, would not be able to stand up to serious resistance. That is an important point to take into consideration.

The other thing is the role of things like the demonstration to the Labour Party conference and the Right to Work Conference. These are focuses for the core of people I spoke about who are getting more and more aware of the potential for resistance.

Die Linke and the crisis of class representation

Oliver Nachtwey

The European radical left is characterised by its lack of synchronicity.[1] We can see decline, regroupment and regeneration happening almost simultaneously, and so far no role model for a successful left has emerged.[2] The fate of the left in Italy, which a few years ago was a centre of regeneration, shows how hope can be transformed into disappointment. In Britain the split in Respect has destroyed the opportunity to build a visible left party for years. Besides the Nouveau Parti Anticapitaliste (New Anti-capitalist Party) in France, which has still to prove itself, the most successful product of left regeneration in Europe so far has been Die Linke (The Left) in Germany. Nevertheless, it is often seen as a new more or less reformist organisation which (this is the implicit conclusion) will soon revert to adaptation, de-radicalisation and participation in government.[3] This perspective, which concentrates on the programmatic orientation of the party, underestimates Die Linke's significance for class representation, its internal and external dynamism, and its political openness in a period of global turbulence.

1:   This article was translated by Einde O'Callaghan. It was written before the state elections in Thuringia and Saarland on 30 August 2009 and the federal elections on 27 September 2009.
2:   Callinicos, 2008.
3:   Sabado, 2009; Fülberth, 2008.

The transformation of social democracy

The starting point for the emergence of Die Linke was the partial decline of social democratic hegemony in the labour movement, which had reached its highpoint during the period of the Red-Green coalition government.[4] The decline began with an election victory. The decisive reason for the success of the Social Democratic Party (Sozialdemokratische Partei Deutschlands, SPD) and the Greens in the federal election in 1998 was the desire for more social justice. In the first six months the new Red-Green government honoured its promises. Above all it withdrew various measures introduced by the previous conservative-liberal government.[5] The demographic factor in the 1997 pension reform was postponed, the loosening of job security was revised, the financial contribution to the health service was corrected and the law reducing the right to sick pay was withdrawn. The then chairman of the SPD, Oskar Lafontaine, who was also the finance minister invested with extensive powers, was a vehement advocate of this course. Lafontaine, rather than the chancellor, Gerhard Schröder, seemed to be steering government policy in this period.

However, the Lafontaine era lasted just 163 days. His plans for a European economic policy, stronger regulation of the financial markets and political control over the European Central Bank were scuppered by the resistance of the business elite and chancellor Schröder. In March 1999 Lafontaine resigned from all his positions. After his resignation his demand-oriented course of budgetary expansion was given up in favour of a consolidation policy that withdrew almost all spending increases.[6] Financial policy was no longer a question of "redistribution, but of the competitiveness of the economy".[7]

On 14 March 2003 Schröder announced Agenda 2010, the overture to the "greatest reduction of the welfare state since 1949",[8] which was supposed to secure the long-term competitiveness of the German economy. The greatest controversy was provoked by the Hartz IV law, which developed out of Agenda 2010. This prescribed the amalgamation of unemployment benefit and social security benefit into what was called "unemployment benefit II", worsening conditions for those receiving payments. The measures also reduced the period of eligibility for earnings related "unemployment benefit I" to 12 months from 36 months for unemployed people under 55,

---

4: From 1998 to 2005.
5: Egle, 2006.
6: Zohlnhöfer, 2003.
7: Egle, 2006, p168.
8: Soldt, 2004.

reduced the right of the unemployed to refuse to accept jobs they considered unreasonable and reduced the threshold for job protection. However, the Red-Green government retained the basic institutions of the German welfare state and in other places the role of the welfare state expanded (for instance in childcare).

Something that has not been investigated empirically but which appears self-evident is that Agenda 2010 undermined the self-confidence and combativity of the working class. For them the "shadow of the market" had become significantly greater and more threatening. Reduced job protection and the reduction of unemployment benefit I, which protected standards of living, weakened the readiness of the working class to enter into conflict and so also indirectly weakened the trade unions. This can be seen in the fact that the wage share after the announcement of Agenda 2010 fell drastically from what was already a low level. By the end of the Red-Green coalition the wage share had reached the lowest level for more than 50 years.

Left wing critics often use the term "social liberalism" to characterise the recent transformation of social democracy. The term appears to be imprecise for two reasons. First, it implies that post-war social democracy functioned according to significantly different principles from social democracy today. It is assumed that in the past "politics against markets"[9] was the driving force for social democratic parties but that they have now broken from that. However, a realistic look at the history of European social democracy shows it carried out a contradictory combination of policies.[10] It was a productive regenerator and protector of the market economy, but attempted at the same time to frame the effects of the market and its risks in such a way that they were tolerable for the individual. If you adopt this perspective, then both post-war social democracy and its latest transformation appear in quite another light. Transformed social democracy is not a break with the principles of post-war social democracy, as the term "social liberalism" implies, but its continuation by other means.

In my view it therefore makes sense to speak of "market social democracy".[11] Market social democracy differs qualitatively from anti-statist and anti-redistributive neoliberalism. Keynesian social democracy wanted to limit the powers of the markets but at the same time it wanted to retain them. In market social democracy the relationship has doubly metamorphosed: it is intended to promote the market using the means of the social

9: Esping-Andersen, 1985.
10: Sassoon, 1996.
11: Nachtwey, 2009.

realm and the social is only retained insofar as it supports the effects of the market. Tightening the criteria for unemployment support goes along with "investment" in human capital. This politics aims to increase economic efficiency, but occasionally has redistributive side-effects. Also even in its crudest period the SPD never distanced itself from the German system of worker co-determination because it saw this as contributing to economic growth.

The second problem with the concept of "social liberalism" is that it concentrates too much on the ideological orientation of social democracy and leaves the question of class representation under-exposed. From their very essence social democratic parties are, as Lenin said, "capitalist workers' parties" which integrate the working class into the capitalist system but are also simultaneously in part tied to the articulation of working class interests. They exercise hegemony by "accommodating the interests and tendencies of the groups over which hegemony is supposed to be exercised so that a certain balance of compromise is formed".[12]

For a period the social democratic model was in a position to integrate the working class and above all the trade unions, and it built up longstanding loyalties that continue to have an effect today. The concept of market social democracy assumes that, in a rudimentary form, the SPD continues to be a capitalist workers' party, whereas the concept "social liberalism" implies that it is a bourgeois formation among others. In other words, German social democracy has indeed partially lost its hegemony in the (organised) labour movement but it has not yet completely forfeited its privileged position.

The crisis of class representation
The unions had supported the SPD in the 1998 election campaign but the relationship had been strained for some time. Shortly after the new government took office critical social scientists and trade union officials feared that through its adoption of the "Third Way" the SPD was distancing itself more and more from the labour movement.[13] The unions and social movements mobilised more than half a million people against Agenda 2010 and there was a massive wave of protests in many cities—but they had no influence over the government.

This led to the establishment of a new left formation in West Germany. Independently of each other two initiatives went public in the spring of 2004 and they later united to form Work and Social Justice—the Electoral Alternative (Wahlalternative Arbeit und Soziale Gerechtigkeit,

---

12: Gramsci, 1991, pp1566-1567. Translated from German.
13: Schmitthenner, 1999; Mahnkopf, 2000.

WASG). One component of this came directly out of a split of trade union oriented SPD members in southern Germany, and the other came out of a process of convergence and regroupment involving left wing intellectuals who looked to the labour movement, trade unionists, critics of globalisation, organised socialists and Communists who wanted to create a left party covering all of Germany.[14]

The "united front of reformers",[15] which was supported by all other parliamentary parties—there was literally "no alternative"—and which was unique in post-war history, led to a crisis of representation. More precisely, there was no representation for those who advocated the welfare state arrangements as they had existed up until then—and they formed the great majority.[16] Only the WASG and the Party of Democratic Socialism (Partei des Demokratischen Sozialismus, PDS), which emerged from the former ruling Communist Party in East Germany, criticised the dismantling of the welfare state and were able as a result to distinguish themselves as parties of social justice.

Die Linke was formed out of an electoral alliance of the PDS and WASG. It achieved its first big success in the federal elections on 18 September 2005. It won 8.7 percent of the party list vote, twice the result in the previous election when the PDS, with 4 percent, had failed to get over the 5 percent hurdle for parliamentary representation. In 2005 more than 4.1 million voters gave their vote to the left alliance—2.2 million more than in 2002. Die Linke performed disproportionately well among workers, precisely the group where the SPD lost votes. At the beginning of the 1980s the SPD still took 68 percent of the votes among unionised workers. By 2005 they took just 55 percent (and in the East only 32 percent). The SPD's link to the working class had deteriorated sharply.

The PDS, which had been massively under-represented among workers because of its role in the old East Germany, was, in alliance with WASG, able to register enormous growth among workers. This development continues to this day. Die Linke is strongly represented among workers and the unemployed, as well as among some higher income groups.[17]

There are admittedly also structural reasons for the decline of the SPD votes among workers and the unemployed. In recent decades the industrial working class has experienced a weakening of its traditions and has become

14: Nachtwey, 2007.
15: Walter, 2006, p29.
16: For a detailed account of the attitudes of the German population to the welfare state see Nachtwey and Spier, 2007.
17: Kroh and Siedler, 2008.

culturally less homogeneous. As a result of the relative rise of the service sector and of the number of white collar workers, class conscious voting has declined. But there is also a counter-tendency. The dividing line between blue collar and white collar workers (which is socially and politically constructed in any case) has become blurred because of the increasingly precarious position of the workforce in recent years. For a long time Germany was one of the European countries where class differences were most blunted by a comprehensive welfare state and where there was a relatively high level of upward mobility, but this has now gone into reverse. Poverty, social exclusion and precarity are returning. A new social question is emerging, driven by a finance capitalist production model and the marketisation of the welfare state.[18] It is necessary to count more and more of the white collar workforce as working class. Indeed for the first time in decades self-categorisation as a "worker" is increasing.[19] The resulting social polarisation has broken the old patterns of class representation. The traditional representation of the cleavage between labour and capital[20] has been eroded (but has not yet disintegrated).

While class positions in society are gaining significance, the SPD has increasingly distanced itself from class rhetoric and even more from any form of politics in the interests of the working class. This is leading to a crisis of representation.[21] But the left did not just benefit from the crisis of the SPD. It was also able to take possession of the issue of social justice and to link it through intensive work with the unions and the social movements to the pro-welfare attitudes of the German population. It was thus able to shift the representation of the class in its favour.[22]

The contours of Die Linke

In Die Linke two dissimilar left projects came together. The PDS was anchored in East Germany. In West Germany in the early 1990s it remained confined to limited ultra-left milieus and was only to a limited extent part of the social movements. In some of the eastern *Länder* (state) governments the PDS operated as a reformist organisation with a quite orthodox socialist discourse, which alienated many potential sympathisers through its distance from real activity. In addition, it had only a slight orientation on social, workers' and trade union interests in the West.[23] For many on the left in

---

18: Castel and Dörre, 2009; Lessenich and Nullmeier, 2006.
19: Geissler, 2006; Statistisches Bundesamt, 2006.
20: Lipset and Rokkan, 1967.
21: Vester and others, 2001, p13.
22: Nachtwey and Spier, 2007.
23: On this, see Nachtwey and Spier, 2007.

the West, a passage from West to East did not seem possible and so WASG was founded. WASG understood itself primarily as pro welfare state and not necessarily socialist. While the PDS, a former state party, inherited a culture of ruling or wanting to rule, the trade union left wingers in West Germany in WASG nurtured a culture of opposition which maintained a certain distance from government power.[24]

To use the concepts of mainstream political science, the leadership of the former PDS, particularly in the eastern *Länder* organisations, are office seekers.[25] Their central goal is to obtain government power in order to implement reforms from this position. This government socialism is fundamentally prepared to make compromises and adapts its programmatic principles to appear to the other parties as a suitable coalition partner. The western *Länder* organisations of Die Linke, which at their core consist of the old WASG and count many left wing trade unionists in their ranks, are policy seekers. They are primarily interested in the implementation of pro welfare state reforms. They are more open in their choice of methods and they are not fixated on participation in government. Neither participation in government nor opposition nor a politics of transforming the system are excluded. Thus the two source parties are not mutually exclusive party projects but they pursue different approaches to achieve their goals.

As yet there is no party programme—the "Programmatic Principles", which were accepted in the course of the formal unification in 2007, were drafted as a unification document. They were a classic compromise which did not demand too much of either of the two source parties. No programmatic differentiation was made between anti-neoliberalism and anti-capitalism; indeed even the legitimacy of the pursuit of profit was included.

When two reformist, essentially left social democratic, parties unite into one, what can the result be other than a reformist formation? Historically the success of socialist and social democratic parties has been accompanied as a rule by a process of de-radicalisation.[26] In the case of Die Linke this possibility cannot be excluded but so far it has not happened. On the contrary, Die Linke has developed to the left. It is still a left social democratic, sometimes even socialist, formation but at present most of the vectors of its programme and politics are pointing leftwards. How does this express itself and what are the reasons?

First, the return of the social question in Germany offers a strong

---

24: Schui, 2005.
25: Harmel and Janda, 1994; Koss and Hough, 2006.
26: Przeworski and Sprague, 1986.

sounding board for a left wing party. The recomposition of class representation is still in its early stages and the conflicts not only run between Die Linke and the SPD, but also through the middle of Die Linke itself.[27] A factor temporarily aiding left wing forces in Die Linke is the continuing ostracism of the party at federal level. The prospect of participation in government and the exercise of power is usually a strong lever to "discipline" and domesticate a party. But ostracism from the parliamentary system and the consolidation of a right wing party leadership in the SPD mean that on the federal level Die Linke still (but not forever) has no option of holding power. Oskar Lafontaine, the former chairperson of the SPD who now heads Die Linke, plays a special role here. For the whole of the political establishment he is persona non grata to be fought at all costs.

Lafontaine has not mutated from a left social democrat to an anti-capitalist, but his development is exemplary for a whole cohort of former social democrats and trade unionists who are developing to the left and have now found their home in Die Linke. As an opponent of neoliberalism he rejects cuts in the welfare state on principle, just as he does German participation in wars. He represents a pro welfare state and left Keynesian programme, such as was acceptable in the SPD in the 1970s, advocates the right to have a general strike—something that is forbidden in Germany—and rejects all privatisation of public property. He is first and foremost a vote seeker who uses radical rhetoric in order to pursue several goals at once: raising the party's share of the vote, putting pressure on the SPD and, not least, integrating the left wing parts of the party in order to use these as the backbone of his struggle against the eastern *Länder* organisations, which, because of their adaptation to economic liberalism and the SPD, he perceives as a barrier to the continuing success of Die Linke. "Stop lines" formulated by Lafontaine have provoked great internal debates in the party which have put the Berlin party organisation—the only one still participating in government—under massive pressure to justify itself and led to a split in the party group on the city council in Dresden. The majority of the Dresden party group agreed to the privatisation of the city's housing associations but this was repudiated by the city party, and the minority split off to form a separate group supporting party policy.

The different components that formed Die Linke are reflected within its federal and pluralistic structure. Internally the party is fragmented into various tendencies and groups. The strongest grouping of the right wing is the Forum for Democratic Socialism which draws together advocates of

---

27: In the case of both the SPD and Die Linke we are talking about a party model based on passive, ie parliamentary, representation.

participation in government, primarily but not exclusively from the east. In addition to being open to privatisations and preferring balanced state budgets, this group wants to shift the principled anti-militarist position of Die Linke in favour of military deployments under a UN mandate, rightly seeing that this as one of the main barriers to future government participation. So far, however, they have not been successful within the party on this question. And in the medium term they will lose forces because of the advanced age of the majority of party members in the East, while the western *Länder* organisations are constantly gaining members and significance.

On the other side there are the Anti-Capitalist Left (Antikapitalistische Linke, AKL) and the Socialist Left (Sozialistische Linke, SL) groupings. The former is comprised of Marxist and ultra-left parts of the WASG as well as some old school Marxists from the PDS. SL is characterised primarily by left-Keynesian intellectuals, trade unionists, former social democrats and a few Marxists. The AKL and the SL form the majority in the western organisations and have had an enormous influence in moulding the party in terms of its programme, politics and its personnel. For example, the AKL dominates the organisation in North Rhine-Westphalia, which in population is about as big as all the eastern *Länder* put together. In both left tendencies there are a large number of anti-capitalists who are not revolutionary Marxists but see the transcendence of capitalism as being the result of cumulative reforms and the struggle for reforms. Neither of the left tendencies has consolidated itself and there are various interfaces—particularly in the SL—with the right.

One of the most important milieus in the party consists of former SPD members and the trade unionists. What caused them to change parties was not the betrayal of socialism by the SPD but its betrayal of the welfare state. But it is precisely for this reason that they have a keen sense of what a policy of adaptation hidden behind socialist rhetoric means. Often it is the former social democrats who, despite their left-Keynesian philosophy, distance themselves most sharply from a course of coalition with the SPD and form a bastion against the politics of the eastern organisations. While the former SPD members and the trade unionists are further left than the eastern *Länder* organisations on the redistribution axis, one of their great weaknesses is their neglect of questions such as equal rights, civil rights and individual autonomy. This creates a barrier, particularly with younger members.

However, the largest and fastest growing grouping in the party is the Working Group on Workplaces and Trade Unions which gathers together works council members, trade unionists and rank and file activists. This is symptomatic of the shift in class representation both in the German party spectrum and in Die Linke—in the former PDS trade unionists were rare.

Perspectives in times of a passive revolution

In the 2006 election to the assembly in Berlin, Die Linke lost almost 9 percent because it was part of the governing coalition and had shared responsibility for welfare cuts. So far, however, the party has been successful in a project of reconstituting class representation. The lack of a coalition perspective for Die Linke on the federal level has been a barrier against adaptation. But this can be and will remain only a temporary phenomenon; the differentiation process within the party is in full flow. The greater the success of Die Linke the more the programmatic differences will increase.

So far Die Linke has been a party passively representing the widespread desire for social justice. It articulates the dissatisfaction present in the population but does not shape it in a sustained way. Before the economic crisis Die Linke was able to have a relatively strong influence on the political agenda in Germany and constantly gained acceptance among the voters. Initially the crisis did not play into the hands of the party as many had expected—people are rarely rewarded because they "always said it would happen". The crisis has led to what Gramsci called "passive revolution".[28] Economics and politics are being restructured, among other things, by integrating demands made by the opposition and the trade unions without changing the relationships of power substantially. The conservative newspaper, the *Frankfurter Allgemeine Zeitung*, formulates this concisely:

> [Die Linke's] suggestions have simply disappeared in a flood of previously unimaginable measures and discussions—from the "nationalisation" of banks to debates about tax increases or decreases or the limitation of managers' salaries. Their idea of creating jobs by spending hundreds of billions no longer stands out among the economic stimulus plans, opportunities to work short time and plans for Germany. The analysis of Die Linke does not turn out in practice to be as radical as the criticism of capitalism. Even the dispute within the party about how strongly Die Linke should orient on the state is irrelevant at present: in the crisis the state is the most relevant protagonist until further notice.[29]

In this situation the right wing of the party are warning against a radicalism that it says would not appeal to the voters. They are counting on "pragmatic" solutions that only differ from the proposals of the other protagonists in that they contain a certain social element—and by doing so they strengthen the impact of the passive revolution and take away from

---

28: Gramsci, 1991, pp1243, 1727.
29: Küpper, 2009.

the party its own strategic leeway. What Frank Deppe has written about the role of the trade union leaderships in the crisis is just as valid for Die Linke:

> Political protagonists, their leadership groups and intellectuals who do not link their analysis of the current constellations for action in the crisis with reflection on possible (or probable or desirable) transformation perspectives as a result of the crisis persist in a conceptless pragmatism, cement the "strategic paralysis" of their organisations and thus help (unconsciously, of course) to strengthen their opponents and to accelerate the decline of the power of their own organisations.[30]

Admittedly parts of the left wing of the party tend towards a verbal radicalism without developing an active practice that relates to concrete social struggles—sometimes without even playing a role in these struggles as an independent participant. Here, too, there is a "strategic paralysis" which so far has not been resolved. This is also connected with the fact that many activists see the trade unions as being responsible for economics while the party is responsible for politics. One factor in the strategic paralysis is, therefore, the generally low level of class struggle—which in addition is being held artificially low by state interventions such as the short time working benefit. The trade unions have also not found an adequate response to the crisis yet. It is still an open question whether they will continue with competitive-corporatist strategies or will increasingly take up conflict oriented strategies.[31] If they increasingly adopt the former strategy, this will also have consequences for Die Linke as, alongside rank and file union members, the party contains many full-time officials who tend to support the policies of their union organisations. As long as the level of class struggle remains low the danger will arise that some of the full-time union officials will turn against a "radicalisation" of the party.

The history of the adaptation of left wing parties is rich and long. Despite all these negative examples, there is also another history of left wing parties. When the General Union of German Workers and the Social Democratic Workers Party united to form the SPD in 1875, the programmatic orientation was initially disastrous—Marx's anger at the "Gotha Programme" provides impressive evidence of this.[32] But economic and political circumstances allowed the SPD to develop in the following years into

---

30: Deppe, 2009, p9.
31: Deppe, 2009.
32: Marx, 1962.

a Marxist party. This was to remain only a stage in the history of the SPD. Revisionist forces soon gained the upper hand. But when the USPD split off from the social democrats in 1917 a number of the leaders of the old SPD, for instance Rudolf Hilferding, Karl Kautsky and Eduard Bernstein, were among them. The leaders went back to the SPD and the majority of the members of the USPD united with the revolutionary KPD. History does not repeat itself, but this history shows what dynamic regroupment processes can develop in times of crisis.

References

Callinicos, Alex, 2008, "Where is the Radical Left Going?", *International Socialism 120*, (autumn 2008), www.isj.org.uk/?id=484

Castel, Robert and Klaus Dörre (eds), 2009, *Prekarität, Abstieg, Ausgrenzung: Die soziale Frage am Beginn des 21 Jahrhunderts* (Campus).

Deppe, Frank, 2009, "'Die Große Krise' und die Lähmung der Gewerkschaften", *isw-Report 78*.

Egle, Christoph, 2006, "Deutschland", in Wolfgang Merkel and others (eds), *Die Reformfähigkeit der Sozialdemokratie: Herausforderungen und Bilanz der Regierungspolitik in Westeuropa* (VS).

Esping-Andersen, Gøsta, 1985, *Politics against Markets: The Social Democratic Road to Power* (Princeton).

Fülberth, Georg, 2008, *"Doch wenn sich die Dinge Ändern": Die Linke* (Papyrossa).

Geissler, Rainer, 2006, *Die Sozialstruktur Deutschlands*, fourth edition (VS).

Gramsci, Antonio, 1991ff, *Gefängnishefte* (Argument).

Harmel, Robert, and Kenneth Janda, 1994, "An Integrated Theory of Party Goals and Party Change", *Journal of Theoretical Politics*, volume 6, number 3.

Koss, Michael, and Dan Hough, 2006, "Between a Rock and Many Hard Places: The PDS and Government Participation in the Eastern German Länder", *German Politics*, volume 15, number 1.

Kroh, Martin, and Thomas Siedler, 2008, "Die Anhänger der 'Linken': Rückhalt durch alle Einkommensschichten", *DIW-Wochenbericht 41*, www.diw.de/sixcms/detail.php/100834

Küpper, Mechthild, 2009, "Oskars Schicksalswahl", *Frankfurter Allgemeine Zeitung*, 15 August 2009.

Lessenich, Stephan, and Frank Nullmeier (eds), 2006, *Deutschland: Eine gespaltene Gesellschaft* (Campus).

Lipset, Seymour Martin, and Stein Rokkan (eds), 1967, *Party Systems and Voter Alignments: Cross-National Perspectives* (Free Press).

Mahnkopf, Birgit, 2000, "Formel 1 der neuen Sozialdemokratie: Gerechtigkeit durch Ungleichheit", *PROKLA 121*.

Marx, Karl, 1962 [1875], Randglossen zum Programm der Deutschen Arbeiterpartei, in Karl Marx and Friedrich Engels, *Werke*, volume 19.

Nachtwey, Oliver, 2007, "Im Westen was Neues? Die Entstehungsgeschichte der Wahlalternative Arbeit und Soziale Gerechtigkeit", in Tim Spier and others (eds), *Die Linkspartei: Zeitgemäße Idee oder Bündnis ohne Zukunft?* (VS).

Nachtwey, Oliver, 2009, *Marktsozialdemokratie: Die Transformation von SPD und Labour Party* (VS).

Nachtwey, Oliver, and Tim Spier, 2007, "Political Opportunity Structures and the Success of the German Left Party in 2005", *Debatte*, volume 15, number 2.

Przeworski, Adam, and John Sprague, 1986, *Paper Stones: A History of Electoral Socialism* (University of Chicago).

Sabado, François, 2009, "Building the New Anti-capitalist Party", *International Socialism 121*, (winter 2009), www.isj.org.uk/?id=512

Sassoon, Donald, 1996, *One Hundred Years of Socialism* (New Press).

Schmitthenner, Horst, 1999, "Zum Verhältnis von SPD und Gewerkschaften", in Arno Klönne and others (editors), *Der lange Abschied vom Sozialismus: Eine Jahrhundertbilanz der SPD* (VSA).

Schui, Herbert, 2005, "Gehört die deutsche Linke Zusammen?", *Neue Züricher Zeitung*, 21 December 2005.

Soldt, Rüdiger, 2004, "Hartz IV—Die grösste Kürzung Von Sozialleistungen Seit 1949", *Frankfurter Allgemeine Zeitung*, 30 June 2004.

Statistisches Bundesamt, 2006, *Datenreport 2006*.

Vester, Michael, Peter von Oertzen, Heiko Geiling, Thomas Herman, Dagmar Müller, 2001, *Soziale Milieus im gesellschaftlichen Strukturwandel: Zwischen Integration und Ausgrenzung* (Suhrkamp).

Walter, Franz, 2006, *Die Ziellose Republik: Gezeitenwechsel in Gesellschaft und Politik* (Kiepenheuer & Witsch).

Zohlnhöfer, Reimut, 2003, "Rot-Grüne Finanzpolitik Zwischen Traditioneller Sozialdemokratie und Neuer Mitte", in Christoph Egle and others (eds), *Das Rot-Grüne Projekt: Eine Bilanz der Regierung Schröder 1998-2002* (VS).

1989: how the wall was toppled

1980
August: Polish strikes give birth to Solidarność workers' movement and paralyse regime for 16 months.

1981
December: Military rule and arrests smash Polish workers' movement.

1985
Mikhail Gorbachev becomes leader of the Soviet Union.

1986
May: At the Soviet Communist Congress Gorbachev complains of economic "stagnation" and calls for *perestroika* (economic restructuring) and *glasnost* (opening up of criticism).

1987
The media in the Soviet Union begins exposing social and economic horrors.

November: Romanian general strike and uprising in Brasov crushed by *Securitate* riot police.

1988
March: Massive riots in the Soviet republic of Armenia.

May: Defeated Russian troops begin their withdrawal from Afghanistan.

June: First open discussion at Communist Party congress in Soviet Union since 1928.

June: Hungarian riot police viciously smash up demonstation commemorating execution of Imre Nagy, prime minister during the 1956 Revolution.

August-September: Wave of strikes in Poland. Secret talks between the government and Solidarność leader Lech Walesa.

1989
February-April: Roundtable negotiations between government and opposition in Poland. Agreement on power sharing, free elections and legalisation of Solidarność.

March: Mass demonstrations in Hungary on its national day.

March: A number of ruling party candidates lose in first semi-free elections since the 1920s in the Soviet Union.

March: In Bulgaria the government tries to divert attention from its own failings by campaigning against the Turkish minority.

April: Secret meeting between government and opposition in Hungary.

April: Russian troops massacre protesters in Soviet republic of Georgia.

April: 100,000 students demonstrate in Tiananmen Square in the Chinese capital to mourn death of ousted reformist party leader Hu Yaobang.

May: Demonstrations in Tiananmen Square reach a huge size as Gorbachev visits China. Protests and strikes throughout country. Declaration of state of emergency. The army attempts to enter Beijing to crush the demonstrations but is prevented from doing so by protests.

June: Chinese army massacres students in Tiananmen Square.

June: Solidarność wins 99 percent of seats open for election in Poland.

June: Hungarian regime organises ceremonial reburial of Imre Nagy, opens its border with Austria and agrees with opposition on free parliamentary elections in nine months.

July: Miners' strikes sweep Soviet Union from Ukraine to Siberia.

August: 65,000 East German holidaymakers in Hungary seize chance to cross over to Austria.

August: Two million strong demonstrations for independence in Soviet republics of Latvia, Lithuania and Estonia.

September: People in the East German city of Leipzig hold their first weekly Monday evening demonstrations. The movement spreads across the country.

October: Erich Honecker replaced as East German leader by Egon Krenz.

November: Berlin Wall falls.

November: Bulgaria leader Zhivkov resigns after 35 years in power.

November: Czech police attack demonstration in Prague triggering protests by up to 200,000 people. A two-hour general strike follows.

November: Hungarian party dissolves itself to reform under new name.

December: Czech president Gustáv Husák resigns after 20 years in power.

December: Romanian *Securitate* riot police and army try to smash strikes and riots in city of Timisoara. A rally addressed by the dictator Nicolae Ceausescu turns into a spontaneous uprising, forcing him to flee. Government formed by second ranking members of regime executes Ceausescu and his wife after two-hour public trial.

December: Measures against Turkish minority in Bulgaria annulled after massive protests.

1990
March: East Germany holds its first free election.

July: Demonstrations by young people in Albania. The regime introduces reforms while clinging on to power.

October: East Germany merges with West Germany.

1991
March: Second big miners' strike in Soviet Union.

June: Albanian general strike forces prime minister to resign.

June: Boris Yeltsin wins Russia's presidential election.

August: Attempted coup against Gorbachev. Yeltsin organises demonstrations. Majority of army turns against coup. Ukraine declares independence from Soviet Union and is followed by Moldova, Azerbaijan, Kyrgistan and Armenia.

December: Yeltsin and leaders of the other Soviet republics declare dissolution of Soviet Union.

A short autumn of utopia: The East German revolution of 1989

Gareth Dale

Readers of this journal are unlikely to be participating in the twentieth anniversary celebrations of the "transition to capitalism" in Central and Eastern Europe and it's easy to see why.[1] The expansion of Nato shows that its supposedly defensive purpose—to contain the Soviet Union—was a lie all along. The civic freedoms for which Eastern Europeans took to the streets are in a sickly condition in West and East alike. One review of *The Lives of Others*, a film centred on the surveillance of dissidents by East Germany's secret service (the *Stasi*), remarked upon its "relevance to a world where fundamental civil liberties are increasingly at risk of being undermined". Anti-globalisation protesters in the East German seaside resort of Heiligendamm two years ago could be forgiven for thinking that little had changed since 1989 as they gazed up at the steel wall around the G7 summit and heard the spurious reasons given by police for making arrests.

Political scientist Jennifer Yoder has described the further march of democratisation after the great demonstrations in Czechoslovakia, Romania and especially East Germany in 1989-90 as an "elite-dominated period of institutionalisation" in which the citizenry was demobilised. Many Easterners, according to her research, "perceive that, in place of the old regime, there is a new, post-Communist political class" that appears "as far

1:   Thanks are due to Chris Harman for comments on an earlier version of this article.

removed from the people and their interests as the old Communist elites", and "some Eastern Germans believe not much had changed: it is still 'them up there and us down here'".[2]

Disappointment at democracy has been magnified by socio-economic malaise. As the former dissident Friedrich Schorlemmer put it, "Many people no longer value the wonderful gift of freedom because they say, what use is freedom if they are shut out from their jobs?"[3] In Eastern Germany the unemployment rate has for two decades been roughly double that in the West of the country—and this has been the major factor behind an extraordinarily high emigration rate and a slump in the region's population of 25 percent since 1989.

But 1989 cannot be dismissed as a mere turning of the page, history's analogy to a changing of the guard. At least in East Germany the events were revolutionary in nature. This was so with respect to the character of the mass movements, the crisis from which they emerged, and the toppling of regimes that they effected. In this one can do worse than take Lenin as a guide. He drew attention to three basic preconditions of a revolutionary upheaval: (i) that a country's ruling class be passing through a political crisis that substantially weakens the government and "draws even the most backward masses into politics"; (ii) that an "unusual degree of oppression" felt by the mass of the population contributes to widespread demands for change; (iii) that social movement activity experiences a pronounced upturn. In 1989 the old order became subject to internal scrutiny and serious fracture. Through the resulting "fissures", to quote Lenin, "the indignation of the oppressed classes burst forth".[4]

State capitalism meets the world market

The economies of pre-1989 Russia and Eastern Europe had their own peculiarities but were in certain respects typical of capitalism in its mid-20th century statist phase. The Soviet Union's backwardness in its arms race with the US meant that military priorities were felt with uncommon force, shaping all other subsidiary decisions down to how much investment should be devoted to agriculture.[5] The Soviet-type society has been aptly described as a "war economy",[6] in its relative autarky, emphasis on heavy industry, high savings

---

2: Yoder, 1999, pp207, 20.
3: "Gloom Prevails In Germany", *Guardian*, 10 November 2005.
4: Lenin, 1980, p206.
5: Harris, 1983, p170.
6: Lange, 1969; Callinicos 1991. For earlier treatments of the war-economic character of state capitalist societies see Bukharin, 1982; Cliff, 1964.

ratio, allocation by administrative decision, extensive use of political incentives and ideological appeals to increase productivity, and mobilisation of resources towards an overriding goal. For a time these techniques provided a recipe for successful steep-ascent industrialisation. But global tides began to tilt against the Soviet model, and the worldwide enthusiasm for national economic planning began to ebb. "The era in which the state could protect national capitalism is drawing to an end," noted Chris Harman in 1976.[7]

The 1970s were a pivotal decade for Eastern Europe. In its first phase booming world markets and low interest rates encouraged an explosion in syndicated bank lending to both Eastern Europe and the Third World. States and firms found it easy to borrow. "In today's world only fools don't take up loans," said East German leader Eric Honecker. But his bravado was not to last.[8]

Closer integration with the Western economy was not an irrational gamble but given the poor economic cards held by Eastern Europe's rulers the odds of success were long. Integration exacerbated the Soviet-type economies' vulnerability to fluctuations in global demand and interest rates. Higher levels of trade and debt pulled them into the circuits of world capital over which they exercised little control. Each was gradually "sucked into a chaotic, disorganised, world system", as Harman put it, a process that involved an intermeshing between the economic crises of East and West.[9] East Germany's net indebtedness to the OECD increased during the latter half of the 1970s by more than 20 percent annually.

In the 1980s East Germany and most other East European societies engaged ever more closely with the West. Typically for masters of relatively backward economies, a more or less resentful admiration for aspects of Western capitalism prevailed among functionaries and industrialists. They positively fawned upon the Western business and political leaders with whom they dealt, above all the former Nazi and head of the Krupp steel conglomerate Berthold Beitz, and the arch-conservative politician Franz-Josef Strauss. It was Strauss who, by organising a brace of colossal loans, played the pivotal role in securing East Germany against insolvency. Earning hard currency to service these and other loans became the outstanding economic imperative in the 1980s. By the middle of the decade Western market economies supplied two fifths of East Germany's imports and received almost half of its exports.

7:   Harman, 1976, p31.
8:   Adomeit, 1998, p127.
9:   Harman, 1976, p31.

The westward reorientation created a predicament for East Germany's rulers. Fraught debates arose. Were they to accelerate integration with the global economy or to retreat to centrally-planned autarky? And were they to increase borrowing (and dependence upon Western creditors) or to introduce austerity measures (and risk the wrath of the working class)? Austerity and autarky were the Romanian way, while Poland and Hungary favoured debt and integration. But neither path offered a solution to the gathering crisis, and in most cases, certainly including East Germany, the intra-elite divisions that resulted from this dilemma contributed to a creeping paralysis in the corridors of power.

Solidarność

One country, Poland, had experienced its "1989" almost before the actual year had arrived. The reason for this precocity lies with the militancy of its working class. Whereas Hungary and East Germany were both shaken by a major uprising in the 1950s but experienced relative quiescence thereafter, Poland's minor uprising (1956-7) was followed by a student movement in the late 1960s, then strike waves, protest marches and riots centred in the coastal belt around Gdańsk and Szczecin (1970-1), and a wave of industrial action that affected some three quarters of the country's largest factories (1976). During the next four years something in the order of a thousand strikes took place, and these culminated in the strike wave of summer 1980 from which the Solidarność movement for independent trade unions emerged, and which broke the Communist Party's monopoly of power.[10]

Why was the Polish experience unique? One common explanation refers to the peculiarities of its "national culture". But that is facile. After all, the 1950s uprisings in East Germany and Hungary showed that workers there were every bit as eager and capable, when it came to organising independently of state institutions and innovating tactically, as were their counterparts in Poland. A more serious explanation refers to the greater severity of repression in Hungary and East Germany as compared with Poland where containment of protest was effected mainly through reform. Yet an equally important—and generally neglected—difference was the degree to which in Poland networks of militants succeeded in keeping alive collective memories of protest movements. Thanks to the work of Lawrence Goodwyn, Roman Laba and others, we know that the series of uprisings (1956, 1970-1, 1976 and 1980-1) were no mere litany of disconnected events. Although to outside observers they seemed to erupt

---

10: Ost, 1990; Barker, 1986.

as if from nowhere, in fact each followed months and years of organisation.[11] Even during periods in which levels of industrial activity were low, groups of militants in certain factories and regions succeeded in maintaining contact with one another. Memories of past struggles were kept alive and discussed, and lessons learned. An accumulated memory of strategic knowledge, tactical repertoires and organisational skills came to be embodied in such networks. It was particularly among these groups of militants, who had gained their self-education through self-activity, that class identities were kept alive and those tactics developed and tested, notably the sit-down strike, that were to prove so successful in challenging the regime in 1970-1 and again in 1980-1.[12]

The Solidarność-led revolt of 1980-1 shattered the self-confidence of the Polish ruling class and sent shock waves through Moscow and the capitals of Eastern Europe. Although its leaders based their strategy of "self-limitation" upon an assumption that a more radical challenge to the system would have provoked Moscow to deploy its tanks, Soviet documents reveal that this had in fact been ruled out, with KGB chairman Yuri Andropov flatly stating that "it would be impossible now for us to send troops to Poland".[13] The weakness of the self-limitation strategy did enable the Polish security forces to crush the movement but without landing a knockout blow. Less than seven years were to pass before further rolling waves of strikes and street demonstrations arose in spring and summer of 1988. In a shifting context formed by Mikhail Gorbachev's political opening (*glasnost*) and economic restructuring (*perestroika*) in the Soviet Union, this renewed upsurge of militancy brought home to a divided ruling class the potential for a social explosion and led to the recognition of Solidarność, followed by "round table" talks between regime and opposition.[14]

In two distinct ways Poland in 1988 prefigured the rest of Eastern Europe in 1989. One was that mass collective action forced a divided regime to reform. The other was that the old regime came to learn of the potential advantages of co-opting opposition movements and containing revolt by means of democratisation. In Poland the imposition of painful economic restructuring would proceed so much more smoothly if Solidarność leaders were to propose it. Poland's Communist leader, General Jaruzelski, admitted as much in discussions with his East German counterpart Egon

---

11: Goodwyn, 1991, p205 and elsewhere.
12: Goodwyn, 1991, p83; Zirakzadeh, 1997, pp115-116; Fuller, 1999, pp160-161.
13: Adomeit, 1998, p141.
14: Zebrowski, 1988, pp14-15; Cold War International History Project Bulletin 12-13, 2001.

Krenz in 1989. He advised Krenz in no uncertain terms that the ruling class's economic aims could be advanced by political reform. Democracy could prove to be an indispensable means of selling the pain of market reform to a sceptical population. "As a result of major economic problems," the general said:

> We have had to face difficult experiences. I'm thinking of December 1970 and August 1980. We undertook a series of attempts to reform, but these ended in failure. The obstacle was in each case our population. The Party, the government, was not in a position to win the majority to accept unpopular decisions. However, these decisions, now being carried out by the current coalition government, are being accepted fairly quietly, even though living standards are worsening. Strikes are rare. This shows that the population places greater trust in this form of government.[15]

And with a democratic polity, he added, "we are more likely to receive Western assistance," even if—one can almost hear the sigh—"at present the West has only made promises."

Widening fissures

At the end of 1988 the Soviet Bloc was entering a major crisis, the course of which was not predictable any more than its eventual outcome was inevitable. Gorbachev's project was spinning out of control, beset as it was by economic dislocation and national uprisings—to be followed in summer 1989 by mass industrial action. The alert level for a bloc-wide crisis was raised to "high", as attested by this warning which an adviser passed to Gorbachev in October 1988:

> Now we must reflect on how we will act if one or even several countries become bankrupt simultaneously. This is [a] realistic prospect, for some of them are on the brink of monetary insolvency (Poland, Hungary, Bulgaria, Vietnam, Cuba, GDR)... What shall we do if social instability that is now taking an increasingly threatening character in Hungary will coincide with another round of trouble-making in Poland, demonstrations of "Charter 77" in Czechoslovakia, etc? In other words, do we have a plan in case of a crisis that might encompass the entire socialist world or a large part of it?[16]

15: Archived in BA SAPMO, SED-Parteiarchiv.
16: Georgy Shakhnazarov's Preparatory Notes for Mikhail Gorbachev for the Meeting of the Politburo, 6 October 1988, www.wilsoncenter.org/topics/pubs/New_Ev_EndCW.pdf

To the surprise of all, it was to be trouble-making East Germans who were to spark with Hungarian instability to ignite that "world-encompassing" crisis.

The first weeks of 1989 witnessed a series of remarkable policy shifts, including the recognition of non-Communist parties in Hungary and round table talks in Poland. In May, Hungary began to dismantle the fortifications on its border with Austria. In June the Polish Communist Party relinquished its hold on power. The Kremlin tolerated all of these transformations. The precedent had been set by the Soviet leaders' refusal to invade Poland in 1980; intervention by Soviet forces, they feared, could light the touch paper under Eastern Europe as a whole.

The event that turned the potential for a bloc-wide crisis into actuality was Hungary's loosening of border restrictions. Encouraged by West German promises of aid, Hungary began to dismantle the fortifications on its western border. The act of "unlocking the door" came from above but it was ordinary people who pushed it open. In the course of June and July growing numbers of East German holidaymakers sojourning in Hungary seized the opportunity to cross the Austrian border to the West. It was by no means a risk free enterprise: they had to physically break through the border fence and many received injuries at the hands of Hungarian security forces.[17] But the inability of the East German regime to stop them emigrating was a sign of its deepening crisis and erosion of the aura of toughness that had long surrounded its political leaders.

By September the country was abuzz with political discussion. Conversations in office and factory, school and college, kitchen or bar, revolved around a series of questions that were thrown up by the crisis. Would our friends or colleagues return from their holiday in Hungary? Would the exodus continue to swell? Would all borders be closed? Should we emigrate too? Would political change occur, and if so, what would it involve? "A large body of workers, especially in the factories," the *Stasi* (secret police) informants reported, were "showing a growing tendency to attribute blame for the situation to the Party and state leadership, which is deemed to be incapable of addressing the welter of problems".[18]

Anger at the political leaders was mixed with hope (for change), sadness (at the loss of emigrants) and a sense of foreboding (at the prospect of a military crackdown). For some, the regime's paralysis diminished the fear of repression and sharpened irritation at its intransigence. "The

---

17: Hertle, 1996a, p101.
18: Wolle, 1998, p316.

summer brought me hope, above all," one of my interviewees recalled; "hope that change would come." For the exodus had exposed the regime in its frailty: "When the state's rigid structures began to crumble we knew something was bound to happen. We didn't think about it so clearly, so consciously, but it was clear that the state would have to react, and from a weak position." The populace, she added, "was very aware that the regime was in trouble, and were discussing the politics of the situation more and more".[19]

The changes in the Soviet Union and Poland had already excited a widespread questioning of the existing order, and this process accelerated with the exodus. Discovering and thinking through new questions and debating old ones afresh stimulated a formidable thirst for knowledge. A Leipzig health worker, Marianne Pienitz, wrote to friends in Britain, "Can you believe that I read four East German newspapers every day???!!... It strikes me that we have learned more in the past four weeks than in the last 40 years".[20] People began to alter their perceptions of how their interests might best be pursued, considered what they themselves might be able to do to affect the direction of change and, in some cases, weighed up the possibilities and risks of public protest.

Toppling of a despot

In early October the Honecker regime raised the stakes, closing the border to Czechoslovakia to visa-free travel and ordering the security forces to smash the nascent protest movement. I remember this as a very tense time. On 4 October I attended the first public gathering in Potsdam of the civic rights group "New Forum". The meeting had of necessity been publicised by "whisper propaganda", with only limited support from (illegal) leafleting and flyposting, yet the church was filled to the rafters and so many thousands still remained outside that two or three "sittings" had to be held before the last of the crowds eventually trickled out of the churchyard. Within the atmosphere was thick with feelings of hope but also fear and trepidation. Was the person sitting beside you a *Stasi* employee or informant? Had your face been recognised and would your details be passed to the authorities or to your employer?

The meeting had been called by a church group and began with a prayer, the message of which made a good deal of sense even to the many atheists present: "God enjoins the weak to find solidarity, for only thus will

---

19: Antje Neubauer.
20: Marianne Pienitz to Geoff Brown and Judy Paskell, 25 and 29 October 1989.

they be able to assert themselves in these times." There followed a brief period of singing, a musical prologue that transformed the atmosphere in the hall. The audience relaxed. Fear subsided. It was not the lyrics or the religious temper of the songs, but the sense that the thousands within were no longer individuals anxious at the prospect of sanctions but participants in a common cause who found symbolic expression in our collective voice—and the *Stasi* members present were welcome to sing from our hymnsheet or risk attracting attention by refusing to do so.

In addition to New Forum meetings, three techniques of protest proved decisive. One was rioting. Although the least common form of protest, one riot, which engulfed Dresden railway station for the best part of a day, was the most serious the country had seen since 1953 and served notice to the regime that its repressive policies could backfire. Another protest technique was industrial action. In September and October numerous reports gathered by the *Stasi* attested to the urgency with which economic and political changes were being demanded in the workplaces.[21] Their sources, *Stasi* officers reported, were warning that discussion of industrial action was bubbling in numerous workplaces and that "spontaneous strikes could occur"—and indeed they did, in towns across the south.[22] Bus drivers and health workers were among the strikers in the first week of October, and 600 miners in Altenberg near the Czech border began a go-slow, demanding the reopening of the border. The state leaders must have realised, Bernd Gehrke has written, "that a military crackdown on mass demonstrations in Plauen, Dresden or Leipzig would have sparked strike action that could then only have been halted—if at all—by enacting a state of emergency".[23]

But the most important form of protest was the street demonstration. Three of these were critical. On 7 October, in the Saxon town of Plauen, some 10,000 to 20,000 citizens demonstrated, standing firm in the face of police assaults and forcing the mayor to begin negotiations on political change. In Dresden a similar process unfolded on 8 October. Again the security forces assaulted protesters with little mercy and made numerous arrests. But their attempt to kettle protesters misfired as the police ring itself became encaged.[24] In a reprise of the previous day's drama in Plauen, a senior officer gave an unauthorised order for riot shields to be laid down in order for negotiations to take place.[25] These events were unprecedented in

21: Bastian, 1994, pp33-34.
22: Mitter and Wolle, 1990, p226.
23: Gehrke, 2001b, p253.
24: Bahr, 1990, p129.
25: Friedheim, 1993, p104.

East German history. Demonstrators had forcibly gained an acknowledged place on the streets; local leaders had buckled, losing the will to suppress protests and acceding to requests for dialogue. But the real watershed came on 9 October in Leipzig. On that day a military crackdown was expected. The army was put on alert and extra units from outside Leipzig were brought in to replace a local unit that had mutinied during a demonstration the previous week. In all, tens of thousands of security force members, including mobile police, army, "factory battalions" and *Stasi*, were deployed around the city centre. Many were issued with live ammunition. The interior minister ordered his forces to crush demonstrations using "any means necessary". Lest anyone doubt his seriousness, he was later to brag to his underlings:

> I would prefer to go in there and beat up these hooligans so their own mothers wouldn't recognise them. I was in charge here in Berlin in 1953 [when Soviet tanks crushed a workers' uprising]. Nobody needs to tell me what those counter-revolutionary scum get up to. I went to Spain as a Young Communist and fought against the scoundrels, the fascist rabble.[26]

Although Leipzigers were aware of the signs portending a bloodbath, attendance was four times that of the previous week. As evening approached all four city centre churches filled to overflowing. The 10,000 to 20,000 in and around the churches were joined by 50,000 to 90,000 more to form the biggest demonstration in the country's history. It was a tremendous physical presence. And it acted calmly and peacefully: those present were keenly aware of the dangers of provoking the security forces.

After a tense standoff the security forces were pulled back; the firing of live ammunition was prevented and a bloodbath avoided. The decision to hold fire may have resulted in part from an awareness of signs of vacillation and dissent in the security forces, and was certainly influenced by the uncertainty and paralysis that had spread through the apparatuses of power over preceding months. Critical here was the lack of support given to Honecker, or to the application of hardline tactics, by the Kremlin. According to one East German leader, the indications that the Soviet army would not intervene filled them with "a growing insecurity as to whether to give the order to shoot... Our self-confidence crumbled".[27]

But credit for the non-violent and successful outcome of 9 October

---

26: Hollitzer, 1999, p286.
27: Kuhn, 1992, p32.

belongs above all with the participants themselves, both those who gathered on the day and those who had shown the efficacy of public protest in previous weeks. Two aspects of these events were decisive. Most important was their sheer size; as the head of the *Stasi*, Eric Mielke, reportedly lamented to Honecker, "Eric, we can't beat up hundreds of thousands of people".[28] In addition, the attitude of participants deserves mention, combining as it did determination with a clearly signalled non-violent stance. A clear signal was given: the movement would not retreat nor would it provoke trigger-happy officers into opening fire.

These eight days in Dresden, Plauen and Leipzig revealed the exhaustion of a strategy based upon police methods and weakened its authors, notably Honecker himself. The East German leadership was in a state of siege. A steady drip of reports arrived on their desks warning of vacillation in the security forces, strike threats, and a torrent of criticisms of the leadership's obdurate position and haughty tone. With Gorbachev's tacit approval, members of the Politburo plotted Honecker's removal, which they secured on 17 October.

A short autumn of utopia

The ousting of Honecker did not mark a comprehensive break with the past. The new leader, Egon Krenz, had long been seen as Honecker's crown prince; he had, said one worker, "been fed the same shit; he was, in fact, the same old shit. Nothing, absolutely nothing, was possible with him".[29] Nevertheless, this was a major turning point, coming as it did after 18 years of continuity at the top. And it was utterly unexpected. I was in a cafe on Berlin's Alexanderplatz when the news broke. Looking up, I noticed somebody hurry in and speak to guests near the entrance. The word then passed from table to table. Animated exchanges followed: "Could it really be true?" people asked. "After this miracle, what on earth will happen now?"

The hope of the East German leadership was that the replacement of Honecker, a slight softening of rhetoric and a few reforms would suffice to convince the public that change was under way and to appease the protest movement. In fact, the reforms announced by the new administration only boosted the numbers on the streets. Political questions that had once seemed impossibly abstract now appeared concrete and urgent. Individuals began to test the newly won room for manoeuvre; the public sphere filled with a tumult of demands. "Wall newspapers" were transformed into hives

---

28: Przeworski, 1991, p64; Allen, 1991, p186.
29: Philipsen, 1993, p285.

of information exchange and comment—in one factory they extended to several hundred meters. At my own college I attended one student gathering at which discussion raged and meandered for hours. I noted some 32 demands that were raised, a flavour of which may be given by this selection: for independent student councils, student co-determination in university decisions, the establishment of partner universities and student exchanges, an end to Saturday classes and to obligatory courses in Marxism–Leninism, the abolition of military training in schools and of military service, more pianos, improved heating, and a public investigation into the "blank spots" in official East German historiography.

The autumn drama was played out not only on the streets but in living rooms, bars and workplaces. Curiosity about public affairs blossomed in workplaces and neighbourhoods. I recall looking out of my window to see knots of people on the street in conversation. Among friends and colleagues question piled upon question: should we go to the demonstration? What slogans should we write on placards? Practical deliberations of this sort necessitated and nourished wider ranging discussion. Was the analysis in this newspaper article correct? What is the nature of this or that aspect of society? Should it be so? Can it be changed? If so, how do we get there? Is German unification a possible and desirable goal?

Perhaps the most memorable aspect of the autumn of 1989 was the extraordinary eruption of civic activity. Opportunities were opening up for all manner of projects that had been illegal or indeed still were. Every day two to three applications to register new associations reached the interior ministry. By January some 250 had been granted a licence, including "initiatives, associations, organisations and movements of both local and regional nature. There were civic rights groups, democratic, liberal, liberal-conservative and conservative ones; left-democratic, Marxist, Trotskyist, anarchist and many more".[30] A civic initiative to change the name of Karl-Marx-Stadt back to Chemnitz was established. Committees were formed to launch investigations into brutality by the security forces. Houses were squatted, and art galleries and bars were opened in some. Students and workers established independent unions; women's rights activists set up centres, cafes and libraries.[31]

One by one sealed areas of state control were prised open. As censorship evaporated, outlawed films began to be shown at cinemas, banned books were lined up for publication and former dissidents spoke and sang

---

30: Müller-Mertens, 1997, p52.
31: Schäfer, 1990, p28.

to crowded galleries. In ever-expanding areas of life orders were opened up to challenge and traditional habits scrutinised. As individuals perceived that they could "make a difference", both within their immediate environment and on the national political stage, the new-found democratic space was exploited, and with relish. Attitudes of resignation and deference, rooted in the seeming omnipotence of the ruling class, were cast aside. Injustices hitherto accepted as inevitable were reinterpreted as subject to human intervention. What Paul Foot once called the "balance of class confidence" was shifting: as the strength of power holders melted away the powerless gained heart and old forms of deference and self-censorship evaporated.

Fall of the Berlin Wall

Having failed to stop the movement in its tracks the regime opted to introduce reforms and, in the process, events hitherto considered inconceivable suddenly materialised. "That Honecker could be deposed was unthinkable," one interviewee recalls. "Previously we had harboured vague hopes that he'd go, but that was all." Yet if the East German leader could be overthrown, she now thought, why not his loyal lieutenant Krenz? And if the border to Czechoslovakia could be reopened (as occurred on 27 October), what about that other "iron" one with its dogs and landmines? Why acquiesce to new limits? Like a hill climber reaching successive ridges, each concession wrung from the regime spurred further momentum towards new horizons, new goals.

Hardly had Honecker been ousted than Krenz became the target of anger and derision on the streets. The movement, as a leader of the New Forum, Jens Reich, perceived with apprehension, was developing "aggressive traits". Demands were now for "everything" and "at once".[32] *Stasi* documents record that the content of banners and chants:

> Are now directed with greater strength and aggression against the Party and its leading role, and also increasingly against the activities of the MfS [*Stasi*]. From the comments of participants, demonstrative applause, and the general tolerance shown towards these chants specifically, it is evident that people are increasingly identifying with them.[33]

A growing body of protesters raised slogans that challenged the core institutions of the regime. They called for the entire government to resign,

---

32: Reich, 1991, p171.
33: Mitter and Wolle, 1990, p250.

for the Communist Party to relinquish its power monopoly, for Honecker and his henchmen to be brought to justice, and for the abolition of the *Stasi* and the redeployment of its officers "into the economy" or "into their own prisons!" But of all these demands that were attacking the pillars of state power the one which rang out the loudest was the call for the freedom to travel.

If the new, reforming regime was to retain any credibility, major concessions on the issue of travel rights were unavoidable. In early November a draft travel law was duly published, promising the right to travel for every citizen. It was phrased in a tortuous style, lacked any reference to when it would come into effect and placed bureaucratic burdens and restrictions on those who wanted to take advantage of it.[34] A sceptical public scented duplicity. Such had been the pace of change that a concession inconceivable only a month earlier was met not with gratitude, but with a clamour of indignation which focused in particular on the government's failure to promise adequate provision of the hard currency that visiting the West would require. The reaction of demonstrators was graphic. Banners were painted with slogans such as "Put the *Stasi*'s Hard Currency into the Travel Account!" and "We don't Need Laws—Just get Rid of the Wall!"[35] According to one East German leader:

> We were particularly alarmed that strike threats were...coming from the workplaces. The workers felt discriminated against by the law, because in effect it denied them the material prerequisites for travel in the West. In this situation, strikes were the last thing we needed.[36]

In disarray the government announced the decision that at once symbolised the irrevocability of change and the movement's greatest triumph: the border to the West was to be opened.

Luxury lifestyles, dirty deals

Socio-economic issues came to the fore on protests following the fall of the Wall. One common grievance concerned access to the West German currency—deutschmarks. In the 1980s those who lacked them had become increasingly irritated by the growing income and status gap separating them from deutschmark recipients—the elite and citizens with an "aunt in the

---

34: Hertle, 1996b, p91.
35: Maximytschew and Hertle, 1994, p1145.
36: Schabowski, 1990, p135; 1991, p304.

West". The avarice and corruption of senior functionaries were another target. In its reports on the "mood" of the population the *Stasi* noted the ubiquity of workers' complaints that they bore the brunt of economic problems, of the wish that elite groups should sacrifice their privileges and of criticisms of the abuse of power by officials. A common grumble was that export receipts flowed directly into the pockets of functionaries. Rumours and mutterings of this sort circulated widely. A typical story that I recall was of a neighbour's cousin who worked in a carpet factory: a visit by an East German leader, although intended to boost morale, had precisely the opposite effect when he departed—taking with him one of the factory's finest products.

Tales of functionaries' greed were legion and discussion of distributive injustice was endemic, but in autumn 1989 these grew ever more heated. *Stasi* reports from early October warned that regime loyalists:

> In the workplaces are being confronted, on a large scale, with arguments concerning the existence of a so-called privileged class in East Germany (including functionaries of Party, state and economy) and of a massive increase in profiteering and speculation. The thrust of the argument, which is conducted very aggressively, is that these groups have been the true beneficiaries of socialism.[37]

In November and December questions of social justice and corruption began to take centre stage. The findings of a government committee investigating ruling class corruption began to be publicised by the (now uncensored) media. The luxury lifestyles of the state's leaders, who had tirelessly preached equality and austerity to their subjects, were exposed to public view. Honecker, astonished citizens learned, owned a fleet of 14 cars, including a Mercedes, while presiding over a system in which his subjects were obliged to wait 14 years to buy a Trabant. Each year, it was revealed, millions of deutschmarks were diverted from the hard-pressed economy to buy Western commodities for bureaucrats who, in public, would unashamedly champion the superiority of "their" economy.

A series of scandals inflamed public opinion, and banners on demonstrations reflected the new mood: "Manual Labour for Bureaucrats!" and "Minimum Wage for the Politburo!" The popular outrage was similar in nature to the spring 2009 anger in Britain at the activities of parliamentarians—and even some of the more bizarre of the items that

---

37: Mitter and Wolle, 1990, p205.

East German and British leaders charged the taxpayer, such as mole-killing equipment, were identical. In the East German autumn, however, revelations of the taxpayer-funded lifestyles of the political class were overlayed by a series of other scandals. The country, incredulous citizens learned, had engaged in a secretive trade with apartheid South Africa despite the official government commitment to boycott. It had even, allegedly, arranged the supply of Soviet Bloc weapons and military technology to the US military and to the CIA.[38] Deals had been arranged with Western and Japanese pharmaceutical companies to test drugs on East German citizens (without their consent) and blood, donated by citizens on grounds of humanitarianism and "international solidarity", had been diverted for sale to Western businesses.[39]

In the wake of these revelations protests broke out in new arenas. Prisons erupted in revolt, with inmates demanding an amnesty, reform of the criminal code, improved conditions and participation in prison decision making. The movement began to enter the workplaces too. There had been activity here in previous months but largely of a low-key sort. Now a wave of industrial action occurred, affecting a hundred workplaces and tens of thousands of workers. Demands included the sacking of managers and the dissolution of "factory battalions" and similar organisations. National political issues were also addressed, most commonly in the call for the unconditional dissolution of the *Stasi*. One worker in a Karl-Marx-Stadt vehicles plant reported to the New Forum leadership that, as things stood, his colleagues saw no future with either their firm or the state. "Them at the top drive big Western company cars that are paid for with urgently needed hard currency," was one grievance outlined in his letter, which added, "We passed a resolution stating that this state of affairs should be abolished, with supervision by ourselves".[40]

"Privileged of the world: abdicate!"

The most important and most public arena of protest in 1989 was the street and town square, and it is sometimes said that the revolution passed the workplace by. But look inside the offices and factories and a different story emerges. Already in September and October many workplaces were seething with political discussion. A manual worker told me that in early and mid-October his workplace witnessed:

38: *Die Tageszeitung*, 5 December 1990; Koch, 1992, pp228–261; Przybylski, 1992, p309.
39: Wolle, 1998, p208; *Der Spiegel*, January 1991.
40: Mitter and Wolle, 1990, p205; Klenke, 2006; Krone, 1999, p84.

An incredible and rapid politicisation, an astonishing ferment that was taking place everywhere—on the shop floor, over lunch, in the toilets, or at meetings of the FDGB [the state-run trade union]. At first you'd find one or two others who you could talk to and then, gradually, more and more.[41]

This meant that when the protests began:

Solidarity did not need to be manufactured from scratch. It already existed within small pockets of workers across East Germany, and it provided the building block from which many worker activists launched their efforts for change.[42]

These efforts included building street protests but also the internal politics of the workplace, notably the probing, pushing back and redrawing of the frontiers of managerial control. The successes of the public protests lowered morale among managers and encouraged workers to gather, discuss, formulate demands and take action. Employees demanded the firing of certain managers, or the abolition of the state's workplace organisations. At one Berlin factory a group of skilled workers organised a meeting of the workforce that pushed successfully for the resignation of the general director.[43] In a Karl-Marx-Stadt factory workers resolved to eject state functionaries from their positions. One of those present recounts the story:

The apparatchik would just sit in his office, hiding behind *Neues Deutschland* [a newspaper]. So we said: By the Xth of the month he must be gone! When that day arrived, colleagues pulled the lever, switching off the current. All the machines were now silent and we, the works council, together with the rest of the workforce, walked three laps of the main hall until we could see that he had packed his case and left the factory grounds.[44]

Elsewhere demands were for free speech within the workplace and for the freedom to pin critical statements or oppositional literature on "wall newspapers". In some workplaces a "paper war" took place in which "each would pin a message on the noticeboard, and someone else would take it off again".[45] An engineer from a power station in Saxony recalls:

41: Uwe Rottluf, interview.
42: Fuller, 1999, p140.
43: For this and similar examples, see Gehrke and Hürtgen, 2001.
44: Gerd Sczepansky, in Gehrke and Hürtgen, 2001, p44.
45: Roesler, 2002.

Colleagues in one plant would write little notes that expressed their discontent and pin them to a wooden pillar in the canteen. Every day the plant director would make sure the messages were removed—I won't say trashed, as I'm sure that he and others were keen to discover how the workforce was feeling in these tense times.[46]

Widespread too was the call for firms' accounts (or, less frequently, ecological data) to be opened to scrutiny by the workforce or the public. In Berlin workers in the Narva lightbulb factory demanded that the company accounts be published in order that the workforce could participate in drawing up future business plans.[47] Also in Berlin an engineer at a lift manufacturing company told me:

> Opposition activists in my workplace organised a "workers committee" that held weekly meetings and raised demands for workers' supervision of management, for the publication of data relating to the environment—those sorts of things. It was attended in the main by white-collar employees, but sometimes by significant numbers of blue-collar workers too.

In some workplaces, from out of political discussions small groups of oppositional spirits would crystallise, arranging to meet in order to discuss further activities. One elderly engineer from Görlitz recalls that in September he, together with a group of younger workers (20 to 25 all told), met in a nearby tavern in order to "exchange views as to the general situation and what could be done".[48] The discussion was free-wheeling, but the experience inspired some of those present to organise more substantial activities in subsequent weeks and months, including the establishment of a New Forum factory branch. Or take the case of "Margrid Sch", a socialist (but Communist Party) shop steward in a steelworks north of Berlin. Hearing of the police brutality against demonstrators she decided that "something has to be done". She drafted a protest letter and presented it to her FDGB branch, where it received 90 percent support.[49]

According to Francesca Weil, a Leipzig University sociologist, this sort of experience was quite common: workplaces were the "relay stations" of the protest movement. In some Leipzig workplaces, she reports,

---

46: Roesler, 2002.
47: *Tribüne*, 7 December 1989.
48: Gehrke and Hürtgen, 2001, pp271-272.
49: Gehrke, 2001a, pp229-230.

those who attended the "peace prayers" in the early autumn would return to work the next day and describe the experience to colleagues, sparking political discussions.[50] Conversely, some workplace networks of militants originated not in factory discussions but at peace prayers or civic group meetings. One group, for example, that was later to play a prominent role in the ousting of a senior functionary at the SKET plant in Magdeburg, first crystallised when they met at a peace prayer earlier in the autumn.[51]

Evidence of synergies between workplace militancy, the civic groups and street protests is to be found in FDGB and *Stasi* documents, too. In mid-October an FDGB report warned that "forces linked to New Forum" and other oppositional groups are active in a series of workplaces".[52] A *Stasi* document noted that the New Forum's growth was "especially in the working class", and that "sometimes entire work collectives go to their meetings. There have been cases of worker resistance to the ban on New Forum activity in firms, even a strike of 50 workers to get them permitted".[53] In late October one *Stasi* chief warned that "New Forum is becoming active throughout our republic, and is seizing above all upon problems—and this is where the real danger lies—that are the concerns of workers in particular." A very real threat was facing the regime, it continued: "the enemy", ie the civic groups and other "anti-socialist" forces, could:

> Succeed in gaining a foothold in the working class. It is imperative that we ensure that order reigns in the enterprises and workplaces and that production is not disrupted by go-slows, labour indiscipline or strikes. Provocateurs, ring leaders and those who whip up a negative atmosphere must be recognised in time and rendered harmless.[54]

Protest on the streets and in the workplaces were not separate worlds; the demands in the latter tended to echo those on the streets: "No more bureaucratic impositions!", "Abolish all privileges!", "Communist Party out of the factory". As the movement radicalised, its working class element grew and this influenced the agenda. "Workers were especially attuned to economic and material issues," one worker explained to me. "They would ask, 'What can the country afford?'; 'Should so much money be spent on arms or on aid for the Third World?'; and 'Am I on a fair wage?'" On the

---

50: Weil, 1999, p536.
51: Gehrke, 2001a, p227.
52: FDGB Archive, document dated 17 October 1989.
53: Peterson, 2002, pp180, 191, 216.
54: General Lieutenant Kleine, in Bastian, 1994, p34.

streets questions of economic organisation, exploitation and social justice came to the fore. Some banners called for market reform. Some addressed terms and conditions of work, calling for a 40-hour working week or declaiming "It's outrageous—your prices, our wages!" Other chants and banners broached questions of economic priorities and class relations, such as "Bosses out!" and "Evict the *Stasi* from their quarters—make nice homes for our sons and daughters!" Within this strand a sub-genre parodied party propaganda, with slogans including "Privileged of the world, abdicate!" and "Expropriate the privileged!"

General strike or Round Table?

As the movement radicalised and entered the workplaces the regime reviewed its relationship with the civic groups. No longer were they to be seen as the "enemy". Rather, enlisting their aid seemed the only way of restoring stability and helping it to regain a modicum of credibility. The method chosen was the "Round Table", negotiations on which began with the civic groups in late November. For the civic groups, the Round Table seemed to offer the prospect of influence over the process of democratisation while evading the uncertainties inherent in the alternative course of mobilising for the overthrow of the regime. On the other hand, they feared, it could be a mere talking shop, with negligible influence on policy.

In early December the civic groups were put to the test. A wave of workers' militancy was cresting, with strikes in Gera, Suhl, Klingenthal and Markneukirchen, and a local general strike in Plauen. One impetus behind this turn came from the scandals mentioned above. Another was from a two-hour general strike in neighbouring Czechoslovakia—which "was followed by East Germans, and especially by participants in protests, with great attention and sympathy, and sparked discussions in the workplaces as to the potential for a general strike here too".[55] It was at this moment that the Karl-Marx-Stadt New Forum issued an appeal, for a political general strike. The appeal, one New Forum leader recalls:

> Spread like wildfire throughout the land; everyone was talking about it. There was a widespread readiness to strike, and strikes already began to break out in many places. And we were initially surprised—for who on earth was doing it? These were people that we [New Forum leaders] scarcely knew.[56]

55: Gehrke, 2001b, p256.
56: Klaus Wolfram, interview.

For the New Forum the moment of truth had arrived. On the one hand, its leadership was aware that the opportunity existed for the Communist Party to be swept aside. "Power to New Forum!" was a popular slogan on demonstrations. On the other, inter-elite negotiations at the Round Table depended upon a spirit of compromise with the regime that would be negated by support for confrontational mass action.

On 3 December New Forum leaders, then in emergency session, heard word of a further strike call. "Representatives from all parts of the country were at the meeting," one of those present recalls, and then Jochen Tschiche, a New Forum leader:

Arrived from Magdeburg and said the town square was overflowing. 100,000 people wanted him to tell them what should now happen in East Germany, and the workers from SKET—a heavy engineering factory of 12,000 workers, a gigantic thing—had told him that they were resolved to take strike action and would he suggest some demands? So, Tschiche arrived at the meeting and asked: "What should I tell them, what demands should be proposed?"

This was, one would imagine, a happy scenario for the New Forum. A mobilised public had taken the streets but the institutions remained intact. Now they were beginning to face pressure with the occupations of *Stasi* premises and, it appeared, the regime could be toppled. That was the significance of the strike issue: it would galvanise, mobilising wider layers and testing the movement's capacity to dictate terms to government. A widespread readiness for industrial action was reported by activists—in Saxony it was "overwhelming".[57] The call for a political general strike, New Forum leader Klaus Wolfram has argued:

Would have been the opportunity to force the government to resign, by saying: we oppositionists want to form a government and if not, we'll call upon the country to strike. And that could have begun in Magdeburg— that particular offer [from SKET] could have played a decisive role. And the political situation was such that—I don't think this can possibly be denied— the government would have been forced to yield, and would have been prepared to do so. Shots wouldn't have been fired. The readiness to strike of the largest factories—in Berlin similar enquiries had been coming in since October—would have left the government no choice.

57: According to Jens Reich, in Joppke, 1995, p163.

It was a moment of "alternativity", a potential turning point. By this stage in proceedings, a leader of another civic group, the SDP, told me, "We knew that the [Communist Party] had effectively lost power." In the opposition leadership "many of my colleagues", Wolfram continues:

> Were aware of the opportunities at an early stage, yet these did not appeal. "Yes yes, power lies on the streets," they would say. "And so? Well, let's carry on talking. We'll sound out the membership—for everything is decided at the grassroots." When Karl-Marx-Stadt New Forum then issued its general strike call, they took fright, and the New Forum leadership met and we hurriedly repudiated the call and said "it won't happen!" and "we're all opposed" and "impossible!" and "what on earth are they up to?" and "why general strike?" That was the stance of most of those in leadership positions.

The Karl-Marx-Stadt New Forum was leaned on to overturn its earlier decision. In justifying their negative response, New Forum spokes-people argued that strike action is a "last resort" in political conflicts and should be exercised "with great caution". Moreover, a successful strike, in the current economic climate, threatened to "bring about economic and political collapse, as well as the danger of an uncontrolled and accelerating strike dynamic".[58] In the current situation "political" (by which they meant "institutional") means must be fully utilised, by which they meant the Round Table talks; and their success required rescinding the strike call.[59] It was a decision that the state-controlled media summarised, not inaccurately, as "New Forum demands Round Table instead of general strike".[60]

An extraordinary reversal had taken place. Before the 1989 uprising dissidents had bravely engaged in protest and tended to be dismissive of "the masses", who were perceived as having accommodated to "the system". Now, precisely with ever larger swathes of the population turning against the regime, many of those same dissidents, now leaders of the civic groups, were pleading for rapprochement. The culmination of this process occurred in January 1990 when they accepted an invitation to join a Communist-led national government.

58: From New Forum leadership discussion papers, Robert Havemann Archiv. See also Schulz, 1991, p28.
59: Schulz, 1991, p28.
60: *Tribüne*, 13 December 1989.

German unification and market reform

The gap between the opposition groups and the crowds on the streets reflected divergent attitudes to the regime, to the Communist Party, but also to East Germany's independence. The oppositionists, for the most part, focused their hopes on reforming the existing state. Those whose views had evolved within the opposition of the 1980s in particular showed a stubborn respect for East Germany's borders. It was a view that reflected the "system immanent" character of much of the opposition, its acceptance of the East German state's legitimacy, and its desire to achieve change by legal routes, notably through negotiation with the regime. It also expressed a critical stance towards Western capitalism and, for some, the perception that the pressure exerted by West German business circles and political elites to extend their power eastwards was in essence imperialistic.

As regards the rest of the population, a large section had little or no commitment to East Germany. By late November calls for unification were beginning to take centre stage on the street protests, and before long the demonstrations were awash with the black-red-gold of the Federal Republic. The movement's turn towards unification did not directly contradict the radicalisation process referred to above. In fact, the issue vaulted to prominence in late November and early December, precisely when public opinion was inflamed by the revelations of privileges and corruption. In a sense, unification was a pragmatic, nationalist formulation of a revolutionary demand, to overthrow the Communist-*Stasi* state. Regarding "pull factors", unification bore the promise of economic prosperity, of hard currency to reward hard work, of institutionalised political freedoms and of strong, independent trade unions. The "push factors" were East Germany's continuing economic crisis, exodus and political collapse. The feeling grew that the situation was becoming so catastrophic that only assistance from the West would provide a remedy. "The growing helplessness of the Modrow government is fuelling people's flight into the national question," wrote an adviser to West German chancellor Helmut Kohl in early 1990.[61]

If the major forces that pushed for German unification were the East German streets and the West German ruling class, the way had already been prepared by the embrace of market reform by the East German ruling class and the civic groups. Ever since the late 1970s when the Soviet Bloc entered crisis, ideas of market reform had gained ground throughout the region. As a result, as Harman argued in this journal, it did not require a great deal of:

61: Teltschik, 1991, p111.

Pressure for the edifice of East European "communism" to collapse. The old people at the top...raved about betrayal and even on occasions fantasised about telling their police to open fire. But key structures below them were already run by people who, at least privately, accepted the new multinational capitalist common sense.[62]

In East Germany these processes were complicated by the claims upon its territory by West Germany. Increasingly it was kept afloat economically by West German loans—a fact that, paradoxically, enabled a false sense of security to reign among the majority of leaders and officials, and which was a contributing factor to the absence of an organised reformist current in the Communist Party. When the conditions underpinning the stability of its rule began to crumble in 1989—with the ending of the iron curtain, the exodus and the growth of protests—many functionaries "discovered", more or less rapidly, their long-harboured belief in market reform, trade and currency liberalisation and parliamentary democracy. A consensus developed to the effect that the bulk of economic decision making should be handed to the market, labour relations be made more "flexible" and social spending be slashed. There was also wide agreement that opportunities for attracting foreign capital and know-how, and for marketing abroad had to be widened: in several industries a skilled low-wage workforce already functioned as an "extended workbench" for West German firms, and East German political and business leaders were well aware that major Western firms such as Siemens and Volkswagen were actively considering expanding their operations there.[63]

Initially, unification with the West did not come into the question. Communist leaders, as Harman put it, were determined to "preserve their own position as the political mediators" between East German capital and the world economy.[64] However, the new economic strategy depended upon two conditions. One was that the border would remain reasonably tightly controlled, in order that a large wage gap with West Germany and a protected domestic market could be maintained. This condition fell along with the Berlin Wall. The other was that workers accept the imposition of "flexibility" (insecurity), low wages, unemployment and reduced welfare. Given the expanding movement on the streets and the growing indications that revolution was entering the workplaces—most dramatically in a

---

62: Harman, 1990, p66.
63: Nakath and Stephan, 1996, p219.
64: Harman, 1990, p23.

renewed strike wave in January 1990—the difficulties that implementing the reform package would face were unmistakable. Krenz summarised them concisely in his warning that "a repeat of the situation that developed in Poland with Solidarność must be prevented".[65]

From this position some sort of economic unification between the two Germanies was seen as a necessity if transition was to proceed under the control of at least core sections of the existing elite and with even a semblance of "order". Then, in January 1990, the Kremlin gave the green light for political unification—in exchange for promises (soon to be broken) by West Germany, the USA, Britain and France that Nato would not take the opportunity to expand eastwards.[66]

Elections and protest demobilisation

By February 1990 the street demonstrations were winding down and giving way to party political rallies as East Germany's first unrigged general election approached. The results of the election, held in March, defied all predictions. Helmut Kohl's conservative Christian Democrat-led "Alliance for Germany" won a landslide, with the social democrats trailing far behind, followed by the reformed Communist Party (now renamed the Party of Democratic Socialism). The civic groups, including the Green Party, brought up the rear with a disappointing 5 percent. The Christian Democrat vote was atypical for a conservative party: it was strongest among manual workers, and expressed a desire for rapid change, as against the gradual, less ideological and more pragmatic approach of the social democrats. But if the desire for fundamental change drew upon the radical mood that had developed in November and December, it also reflected a lack of confidence in collective action. Fierce opposition to the Communists melded with a consciousness of workers' own abject positions to produce an attitude that, at the extreme, found expression as supplication. One placard at a Christian Democrat election rally in Leipzig provided a graphic illustration: "Helmut, take us by the hand, show us the way to economic miracle land!"[67]

Aside from the success of the right, the other surprise in the March 1990 election was the poor performance of the civic groups. Why they fared so dismally has been the subject of some debate. Was it their lack of experience, shortage of time or the divisions in their ranks? Were they

---

65: Krenz in conversation with Gorbachev, in Hertle, 1996a, p477.
66: Stent, 1998, p225; Zelikow and Rice, 1995, pp180-184; Adomeit, 1998, p501.
67: Pritchard, 1996, p167.

marginalised by the "steamroller of West German parties"?[68] There is doubtless some truth in these suggestions. But another factor was the disconnect between the civic groups and the bulk of the street movement. It was not only that they lacked popular roots, and that they cultivated a "lifestyle politics" and other traits that confirmed their distance from the mass of the population. It was also that they chose to cooperate as a junior partner with the regime, rather than mobilise against it. They neglected the goals and values of ordinary working people, declined to rally the movement to topple the regime and so allowed a vacuum of leadership to develop which the Western parties were quick to exploit. In their disavowal of power, the journalist Klaus Hartung has suggested, they were partly responsible for the rapid incursion and easy triumph of political parties from the Federal Republic. "The politics of the opposition", he writes, "meant that, as the scissors between mass movement and government widened, a power vacuum resulted which drew in the West German parties".[69]

Nomenklatura privatisation

The story of Eastern Europe's transition is one of a learning process, in which members of the *nomenklatura*—the ruling class—came to see that although democratisation would spell the collapse of the system of one-party rule it need not spell the demise of their class's power. "Communism" itself was dispensable since functionaries had paid obeisance to Marxism not as a guide to, but as sanctification of, their practice. For company managers, state officials and a range of other elite groups, their allegiance to the Party was a particular form of organising their loyalty to, and identification with, the national ruling class. Industrialists, for example:

> Did not care too much about ideology, providing they could run their enterprises successfully, accumulating capital to protect their very substantial privileges. They would hold party cards because party membership helped them to succeed—and because the party helped stamp out dissent among the workforce. But they did not take the party's avowed beliefs seriously.[70]

This style of "pragmatic" Communism was also pervasive in the state apparatuses, and even among party cadre. Soviet-type institutions were given support in so far as they provided a viable framework for the

---

68: Batt, 1991, p386.
69: Hartung, 1990, p60.
70: Harman, 1990.

achievement of economic growth and social control, but could be discarded without undue fuss when these conditions no longer obtained.

As Chris Harman pointed out, in the course of a comparison between the transitions in Eastern Europe and regime changes of earlier times, a ruling party and a ruling class are never quite the same thing. The former *represents* the latter:

> Binding its members together in a common discipline which helps them achieve their common goals against the rest of society. But the class can preserve the real source of its power and privileges, its control over the means of production, even when the party falls apart. This was shown in Germany, Italy, Portugal and Spain after the fall of their fascisms.[71]

In the post-fascist cases the single party that bound industrialists, landowners, police chiefs, army officers and government ministers into a tight network disintegrated but, a measure of elite replacement and reforms to corporate ownership notwithstanding, was replaced in each instance by a pluralist political system that preserved the class divisions upon which capitalist order rests. In Eastern Europe, Harman elaborates, changes to ownership structures were greater but here too "the enterprise heads, the ministry officials, the generals, even most of the police chiefs, remain[ed] in place". They did not abdicate but sought positions in new or reformed institutions, establishing new political parties and creating new structures of accumulation.

Harman's study, published in 1990, was prescient. As the years have passed, evidence has accumulated that shows high rates of elite continuity in Eastern Europe. One summary, from 1996, concluded that:

> During and after the transitions of 1989-91, Communist leaders scrambled to protect their power bases or to create new ones. Their manoeuvres were varied. Some negotiated places for themselves in post-Communist regimes through the famous "Roundtable talks". Many cashed in the credits they had accumulated through patron-client networks and appropriated large parts of state-industrial enterprises ("*nomenklatura* privatisation"); still others colluded in "mafia" activities to profit from weakened state oversight and regulation.[72]

71: Harman, 1990, p66.
72: Higley, Kullberg and Pakulski, 1996, p137.

Democracy, the same study observed, did not constitute a major threat to established elites in the region:

> Instead of having to fight tooth and nail to defend their power and status, most elites associated with the old order have adapted to democratisation without major loss...nothing approaching a "revolutionary" circulation of elites occurred; in this key respect there were no Central and East European revolutions in 1989-91.[73]

In a similar study the German political scientist Klaus von Beyme concluded that "there was no fundamental turnover of elites". Although Communist parties sometimes excluded the most dogmatic members from the party, the goal was to "open better chances for the younger generation within the party", the overall effect of which was to produce an "accelerated *turnover of generations*".[74]

In East Germany the alchemy that saw "old" bureaucratic power transmuted into investments in the embryonic new Germany was an important aspect of the transition period. The process began towards the end of 1989 and continued apace in 1990 under Communist and Christian Democrat governments alike. Under the reforming Communist administration of early 1990 the liberalisation of land and property markets enabled thousands of functionaries to exploit the resultant opportunities, buying up land and scooping luxury properties at bargain basement prices. Those in positions of economic authority, and with appropriate connections and knowledge, were able to siphon "people's own" funds into their own newly established firms or bank accounts, transferring vast sums with a few strokes of the pen. Loopholes in the State Treaty (which unified the currencies of the two Germanies) enabled functionaries to convert colossal sums of East German marks and "transfer roubles" into deutschmarks at parity, by illicit methods—for example, through the "export" to the Soviet Union of goods that existed only in accounting books.

As the "Communist" elites filed across their hastily constructed bridge to capitalist democracy the readiness with which most of them shed the ideological commitments and trappings of their previous calling was striking. Senior army officers, to give an example that stands for many, would cheerfully exchange the title *Genosse* (comrade) for Herr.[75] Managers resigned

---

73: Higley, Kullberg and Pakulski, 1996, pp138-139.
74: Von Beyme, 1996, pp67-68, 74, 165.
75: Peter Chemnitz, in Golombek and Ratzke, 1991, p125.

their party membership in droves and actively sought partnership with the Western "enemy". In the long run, of course, German unification led to far greater elite replacement in the former East Germany than elsewhere in Eastern Europe. Indeed, the threat of unification had haunted Communist leaders throughout the transition period—for them, it greatly exacerbated the dilemmas of liberalisation. According to his memoirs, Egon Krenz was interested in the developing situation in Poland in which a "shared position with regard to the interests of state" was emerging between Communist Party and Solidarność leaders, but the question of "what are the interests of state?" nagged at him. "However much is reformed in Poland, the state remains Poland. But what if the Communist Party loses? Without it East Germany would not exist... There would be no *raison d'être* for two capitalist German states. East Germany's existence as a German state depends upon its socialist nature".[76]

Conclusion

What, then, have the events of 1989 given us to celebrate? To the extent that they embodied a recalibration of structures of exploitation and political power, nothing whatsoever. One imperialist alliance crumbled but the vacuum left by its collapse was rapidly filled by another. Bureaucratic state capitalism was replaced by neoliberal market capitalism. But there was nonetheless a great deal to cheer. One less tangible but momentous gain was the consigning of Stalinism to its grave. For more than half a century it had dominated the world's left, perfecting its characteristic technique of signalling left while turning right. The task of reclaiming Marxism as a theory of working class self-emancipation became somewhat more straightforward. More visibly, the institutionalisation of civic freedoms—including the rights to assembly and to trade union organisation—across Eastern Europe represented a historic victory for the millions who had taken to the streets. In East Germany a period of 40 years in which collective action was systematically suppressed was thunderously brought to an end, as the country was rocked by some 2,600 public demonstrations, over 300 rallies, over 200 strikes, a dozen factory occupations and army mutinies. From a total population of 17 million at least several million (and perhaps as many as five million) people took part, giving a glimpse of the potential that arises when established order breaks down in the face of collective protest.

76: Krenz, 1999, p207.

References

Adomeit, Hannes, 1998, *Imperial Overstretch: Germany in Soviet Policy from Stalin to Gorbachev* (Nomos Verlagsgesellschaft).

Allen, Bruce, 1991, *Germany East* (Black Rose).

Bahr, Eckhard, 1990, *Sieben Tage im Oktober* (Forum).

Barker, Colin, 1986, *Festival of the Oppressed: Solidarity, Reform and Revolution in Poland* (Bookmarks).

Bastian, Uwe, 1994, "'Auf zum Letzten Gefecht...', Dokumentation über die Vorbereitungen des MfS auf den Zusammenbruch der DDR Wirtschaft", Arbeitspapiere des Forschungsverbundes SED-Staat, No 9, Berlin, Freie Universität.

Batt, Judy, 1991, "The End of Communist Rule in East-Central Europe", *Government and Opposition*, volume 26, number 3.

Beyme, Klaus von, 1996, *Transition to Democracy in Eastern Europe* (Macmillan).

Bukharin, Nikolai, 1982 [1916], "Toward a Theory of the Imperialist State", in *Selected Writings on the State and the Transition to Socialism* (Spokesman), www.marx.org/archive/bukharin/works/1915/state.htm

Callinicos, Alex, 1991, *The Revenge of History* (Polity).

Cliff, Tony, 1964, *Russia: A Marxist Analysis* (International Socialism), www.marxists.org/archive/cliff/works/1964/russia/

Friedheim, Daniel, 1993, "Regime Collapse and the Role of Middle-level Officials", *German Politics*, volume 2, number 1.

Fuller, Linda, 1999, *Where Was the Working Class? Revolution in Eastern Germany* (University of Illinois).

Gehrke, Bernd, 2001a, "Demokratiebewegung und Betriebe in der 'Wende' 1989. Plädoyer für einen längst fälligen Perspektivwechsel?", in Bernd Gehrke and Renate Hürtgen, 2001.

Gehrke, Bernd, 2001b, "Die 'Wende'-Streiks. Eine erste Skizze", in Bernd Gehrke and Renate Hürtgen, 2001.

Gehrke, Bernd, and Renate Hürtgen (eds), 2001, *Der betriebliche Aufbruch im Herbst 1989: Die unbekannte Seite der DDR Revolution* (Bildungswerk).

Goodwyn, Lawrence, 1991, *Breaking the Barrier* (Oxford University).

Golombek, Dieter, and Dietrich Ratzke, 1991, *Facetten der Wende* (IMK).

Harman, Chris, 1976, "Poland: Crisis of State Capitalism", *International Socialism* 93 and 94, first series (November 1976 and January 1977), www.marxists.org/history/etol/writers/harman/1976/11/poland.htm and www.marxists.org/history/etol/writers/harman/1977/01/poland2.htm

Harman, Chris, 1990, "The Storm Breaks", *International Socialism* 46 (spring 1990).

Harris, Nigel, 1983, *Of Bread and Guns* (Penguin).

Hartung, Klaus, 1990, *Neunzehnhundertneunundachtzig* (Luchterhand).

Hertle, Hans-Hermann, 1996a, *Der Fall der Mauer* (Westdeutscher Verlag).

Hertle, Hans-Hermann, 1996b, *Chronik des Mauerfalls* (Links).

Higley, John, Judith Kullberg and Jan Pakulski, 1996, "The Persistence of Communist Elites", *Journal of Democracy*, volume 7, number 2.

Hollitzer, Tobias, 1999, "Der Friedliche Verlauf des 9 Oktober 1989 in Leipzig—Kapitulation oder Reformbereitschaft? Vorgeschichte, Verlauf und Nachwirkung", in Günther Heydemann and others (eds), *Revolution und Transformation in der DDR* (Duncker and Humblot).

Joppke, Christian, 1995, *East German Dissidents and the Revolution of 1989* (Macmillan).

Klenke, Olaf, 2006, *Zwischen Rationalisierung und sozialem Konflikt. Das Mikroelektronik-Programm in der DDR (1977-1989)* (Links).

Koch, Egmont, 1992, *Das geheime Kartell* (Hoffmann & Campe).

Krenz, Egon, 1999, *Herbst '89* (Neues Leben).

Krone, Martina (ed), 1999, *"Sie haben so lange das Sagen, wie wir es dulden": Briefe an das Neue Forum September 1989-März 1990* (Robert-Havemann-Gesellschaft).

Kuhn, Ekkehard, 1992, *Der Tag der Entscheidung* (Ullstein).

Lange, Oskar, 1969, "The role of Planning in Socialist Economy", in Morris Bornstein (ed), *Comparative Economic Systems* (Richard Irwin).

Lenin, Vladimir, 1980, *Werke*, volume 21 (Dietz).

Maximytschew, Igor, and Hans-Hermann Hertle, 1994, "Die Maueröffnung", *Deutschland Archiv*, volume 27.

Mitter, Armin, and Stefan Wolle, 1990, *"Ich Liebe Euch doch Alle..."* (BasisDruck).

Müller-Mertens, Eckhard, 1997, *Politische Wende und deutsche Einheit* (FIDES).

Nakath, Detlef, and Gert-Rüdiger Stephan (eds), 1996, *Countdown zur Deutschen Einheit* (Dietz).

Ost, David, 1990, *Solidarity and the Politics of Anti-Politics* (Temple University).

Peterson, Edward, 2002, *The Secret Police and the Revolution: The Fall of the German Democratic Republic* (Praeger).

Philipsen, Dirk, 1993, *"We Were The People"* (Duke University).

Pritchard, Gareth, 1996, "National Identity in a United and Divided Germany", in Robert Bideleux and Richard Taylor (eds), *European Integration and Disintegration* (Routledge).

Przeworski, Adam, 1991, *Democracy and the Market* (Cambridge University).

Przybylski, Peter, 1992, *Tatort Politbüro*, volume two (Rowohlt).

Reich, Jens, 1991, *Rückkehr nach Europa* (Carl Hanser).

Roesler, Jörg, 2002, "Die VEB in der Herbstrevolution 1989/90", manuscript in possession of the author.

Schabowski, Günter, 1990, *Das Politbüro* (Rowohlt).

Schäfer, Eva, 1990, "Die Fröhliche Revolution der Frauen", in Gislinde Schwarz and Christine Zenner (eds), *Wir wollen mehr als ein "Vaterland": DDR-Frauen im Aufbruch* (Rowohlt).

Schulz, Marianne, 1991, "Neues Forum", in Helmut Müller Enbergs and others (eds), *Von der Illegalität ins Parlament* (Links).

Stent, Angela, 1998, *Russia and Germany Reborn* (Princeton University).

Teltschik, Horst, 1991, *329 Tage* (Siedler Verlag).

Weil, Francesca, 1999, "Wirtschaftliche, Politische und Soziale Veränderungen in einem Leipziger Betrieb 1989/90", in Günther Heydemann and others (eds), *Revolution und Transformation in der DDR* (Duncker and Humblot).

Wolle, Stefan, 1998, *Die heile Welt der Diktatur* (Links).

Yoder, Jennifer, 1999, *From East Germans to Germans?* (Duke University).

Zebrowski, Andy, 1988, "Turning the Tables", *Socialist Worker Review 113* (October), www.marxisme.dk/arkiv/zebrowskia/1988/10/poland.htm

Zelikow, Philip, and Condoleezza Rice, 1995, *Germany Unified and Europe Transformed*, (Harvard University).

Zirakzadeh, Cyrus, 1997, *Social Movements in Politics* (Longman).

End of the liberal dream: Hungary since 1989

Adam Fabry

This year marks the twentieth anniversary of the political revolutions that shook Central and Eastern Europe.[1] The authoritarian one-party regimes that had dominated societies in Bulgaria, Czechoslovakia, East Germany, Hungary, Poland and Romania since the late 1940s disintegrated almost overnight, and with remarkably little resistance, under the pressure of economic crisis and public discontent.[2]

With the Berlin Wall in rubble, many commentators drew the conclusion that liberal democracy and capitalism represented the only viable future in Central and Eastern Europe. According to this view, which quickly became hegemonic in East and West alike, the downfall of Stalinism symbolised "the failure of an entire system";[3] the ultimate proof of the market's superiority over central planning as an organisation of society.[4] This idea was most famously summed up in a highly influential article by the neoconservative American philosopher and political economist Francis

---

1:   I am grateful to Gareth Dale for comments on earlier drafts of this paper.
2:   With the exception of Romania, the absence of large-scale social conflict and violence was a remarkable feature of the East European revolutions. In fact, as Tony Cliff noted, "there were fewer violent clashes in East Germany, Czechoslovakia and Hungary during the fall of these regimes than there were between the police and striking miners in Thatcher's Britain of the mid 1980s"—Cliff, 1996, p ix.
3:   Jeffries, 1993, p1.
4:   Åslund, 2002; Kornai, 2006.

Fukuyama which argued that the demise of Stalinism represented the "unabashed victory of economic and political liberalism", marking not only the "triumph of West", but also "the end of history as such…the end point of mankind's ideological evolution and the universalisation of Western liberal democracy as the final form of human government".[5] In many ways Fukuyama's article summed up the spirit of the time.[6] The political and economic conclusions of his argument were simple enough. Accordingly, socialism, as a political philosophy as well as a project of human development, was now only a memory from the past.[7]

Such arguments came to provide the ideological basis for the neoliberal reforms in Central and Eastern Europe after the toppling of the Stalinist regimes. At the heart of these reforms was the idea that the combination of political reforms and a rapid liberalisation of the economy would bring not only greater individual freedom, but also economic success and higher living standards to the crisis-ridden economies of the region.[8] Hungary, with its history as a front-runner of market reforms within the Soviet Bloc, was generally considered to be a future model for successful transformation in the region.[9]

However, two decades on, the outcome of transition-associated adjustments in Hungary has been far from satisfactory. The effects of neoliberal restructuring on Hungarian society have been at best highly uneven and more often devastating. The country has seen a significant decline in economic output, a sharp rise in unemployment (a factor that remained unknown prior to 1989 as a result of the enforced nature of labour under the authoritarian regimes), declining standards of living for the majority of the population, growing social inequality and the development of poverty as an emblematic feature of Hungarian society.[10] Trends elsewhere in the region point in the same direction.[11]

As if this were not enough, the current world economic crisis has placed further strains on the already beleaguered economies of the region. The Hungarian economy has been particularly badly hit by the downturn

---

5: Fukuyama, 1989, pp3-4. Interestingly, Fukuyama's article actually preceded the political upheavals of 1989, written as it was in the summer of that year.
6: For a wider discussion on Fukuyama's article, see Callinicos, 1991.
7: Callinicos, 1991, p10.
8: Åslund, 2002; Kornai, 2006; Marangos, 2004; Sachs, 1990; Williamson, 1992.
9: Jeffries, 1993.
10: Eurequal, 2006; UNDP, 2003; World Bank, 2002.
11: The works of Dale, 2004, and Hardy, 2009, point to similar trends in former East Germany and Poland.

and the government was forced to ask for a $25 billion bailout from international lenders when faced with a mounting debt crisis and a potential risk of a "run on the banks" in late 2008.[12] Adding to Hungary's woes, its economic crisis is rapidly turning into a political crisis: the ruling socialist-liberal coalition is in complete disarray, and the recent European Parliament elections confirmed the rise of the extreme right, with the fascist Jobbik Party coming third in the elections with around one sixth of the overall vote. But Hungary's problems are nowadays not only a cause for concern among its own politicians. Increasingly its fate is being watched with interest and alarm in Washington and Brussels as well.[13]

Between state capitalism and the market

Arguably, the question of why the liberal dream of 1989 turned out so badly in Hungary cannot be understood through the lenses of a nation-state perspective but must instead be understood in relation to recent changes in global capitalism.

For the region as a whole, dark clouds began to gather more than two decades before the fall of the Berlin Wall with the structural crisis of global capitalism in the early 1970s and the end of the long period of post-war economic boom.[14] Leaders across the world were faced with lower returns on investment and the reappearance of mass unemployment. However, the response taken to the crisis differed markedly between the two sides of the Berlin Wall.

In the West leaders chose to abandon Keynesian policies of state-led economic development, which had been accepted as "self-evident" within economic policymaking since the late 1940s, instead opting for "the discipline of the world market".[15] In order to restore profit levels to their pre-crisis levels, governments in the West allowed capital to break free from the fetters of national regulation. First evidenced in Washington and London, this shift in policymaking accentuated what has sometimes been

---

12: The fear of a bank run was, as Gideon Rachman recently revealed in the *Financial Times*, a very real one. Those with a weak heart for conspiracy theories or superstitions might even read something into the actual date when this fear was supposed to have reached its climax: Friday 13 March 2009—*Financial Times*, 11 May 2009.

13: For example, referring in particular to the economic woes of Hungary and Ukraine, US president Barack Obama was warning Americans in a speech in March about the dangers of "these enormous ripple effects...wash[ing] back on to our shores".

14: Aldcroft and Morewood, 1995. See also Brenner, 2006.

15: Maier, 1997, p91, in Dale, 2006, p208.

described as "the logics of competitive deregulation",[16] with other governments compelled to follow similar policies in order to maintain their competitive position within the world system. While these changes contributed to a spectacular growth and centralisation of international finance, and the rise of transnational corporations, they placed increasing difficulties on the economic policymaking of nation states.[17] The age of the Keynesian "regulatory state" was rapidly giving way to what Phil Cerny has described as "the competition state", whose primary objective was to adapt the domestic economy to the exigencies of the global market.[18]

The initial reaction in the East was to resist the pressures of the world market. However, as it turned out, this policy only came to reveal the shortcomings of the state capitalist economies. Internally, the structure of the command economies remained heavily in favour of industrial production over specialisation in goods and services.[19] As Mike Haynes has pointed out, the Soviet Bloc economies "developed over-large industrial sectors which gave them the base for military and great power competition, but which made little sense from the view of the world market as a whole".[20] Externally, pressures to comply with Soviet interests meant not only that the integration of the East European economies into the world market remained limited, but also that the mode of integration was fundamentally flawed. And by the late 1970s the effects of the slump in the world economy became increasingly evident. Faced with the fear of growing public discontent, the leaders of the one-party regimes began to seek alternative approaches, eventually looking to seek greater integration with the world economy.[21] This was to be achieved through a policy importing technologically advanced goods from the West in return for exports of industrial and agricultural products. As often before, Hungary proved to be a regional forerunner, with its Western imports growing at a faster rate than those from other Soviet Bloc states.[22] But the question that remained was how this increasing trade was to be paid for.

East European governments sought to overcome the problem by

16: Dale, 2004, p193.
17: Harman, 1984, p116.
18: Cerny, 1990, in Dale, 2004, p14.
19: Aldcroft and Morewood, 1995, p126.
20: Haynes, 1994, p129.
21: As argued by Dale elsewhere in this journal, this decision, while raising the vulnerability of the Soviet Bloc economies to the fluctuations of the world market, was not a completely irrational one.
22: Köves, 1985, p101.

seeking loans in convertible currencies from Western countries, banks and international organisations.[23] As a result, their debt burden rose significantly from the 1970s and onwards. Once again Hungary proved to be a model, this time in a negative sense: its convertible currency trade deficit amounted to more than $3 billion by 1978.[24] For the region as a whole, the negative trends showed no signs of lessening in the 1980s (see table 1).

Table 1: The growing debt burden of the Eastern Bloc ($ billions)
Source: OECD

	1985	1986	1987	1988	1989	1990
Bulgaria	1.6	3.6	5.1	6.1	8.0	9.8
Czechoslovakia	3.6	4.3	5.1	5.6	5.7	6.3
Hungary	11.5	14.7	18.1	18.2	19.4	20.3
Poland	28.2	31.9	35.8	34.1	37.5	41.8
Romania	6.5	6.3	5.1	2.0	-1.3	1.3
USSR	15.8	16.6	25.1	27.7	39.3	43.4
Total	67.3	77.5	94.3	93.8	108.9	122.9

Leaders of the one-party regimes were now increasingly caught in a bind as external pressures from the world economy came together with growing demands for reforms—from within the ruling bureaucracy as well as by opposition groups.[25] The election of the reform-minded Mikhail Gorbachev in March 1985 as the general secretary of the Communist Party of the Soviet Union initially seemed to ease this pressure. Gorbachev's policies of *glasnost* (openness) and *perestroika* (restructuring) sought to undertake fundamental reforms of the command economies.[26] The idea was to allow greater political freedom, while at the same time seeking to remove corruption by introducing market incentives in the economy.[27] But Gorbachev's

23: Aldcroft and Morewood, 1995, p157.
24: Swain, 1992, p131.
25: The most visible example of the growing unrest were the ship workers' strikes that shook Poland in 1980-1, which gave birth to the opposition Solidarity movement.
26: Aldcroft and Morewood, 1995, p177.
27: Aldcroft and Morewood, 1995, p178.

reforms opened a Pandora's box among the ruling layers of the bureaucracies within the Soviet Bloc.

Once more developments in Hungary were to be an indication of things to come throughout the region. Its ruling class started to show increasing signs of insecurity and desperation in the face of the country's mounting debt problems. In what was somewhat of a last-ditch effort to save its rule through methods of social engineering from above, the ruling party (MSZMP) introduced economic reforms in 1985 and 1986 which enabled managers of state enterprises greater freedom in hiring and firing workers, while also introducing a bankruptcy law and unemployment benefits.[28] However, as these efforts failed, voices for change were raised, not only in society in general,[29] but also within sections of the MSZMP. Reform-minded *nomenklatura*[30] members started to raise demands for the removal of the ageing party leader, János Kádár, and he was replaced as general secretary by the reformist Károly Grósz in May 1988. There then followed a period of fierce power struggle within the MSZMP as "hardliners" and "reformers" fought for the control of the party.[31] However, rather than strengthening its position, these internal struggles made it increasingly difficult for the ruling party to uphold its hegemonic role in society—instead allowing opposition forces to grow increasingly assertive.[32] The ruling party was increasingly squeezed from two sides, and within a year the bureaucracy had decided to "jump before it was pushed".[33] It initiated discussions with a combination of opposition forces from June to September 1989 over the dismantling of the one-party regime and the passage to a multi-party system.[34] In the autumn of 1989 the parliament accepted a law transforming Hungary into a parliamentary democracy and from 23 October the country was no longer a "socialist people's republic". The door was now open for Hungary to step into the wonderland of liberal democracy and free-market capitalism.

28: Aldcroft and Morewood, 1995, p188.

29: The Hungarian opposition became increasingly organised following the creation of the first opposition party, the Hungarian Democratic Forum, in 1987.

30: This term is used here to refer to the lists of senior positions in the party, state and economy—Dale, 2006, p10.

31: This struggle is explained in detail by Ripp, 2006.

32: By 1988 the signs of the MSZMP's moral crisis were evident: membership diminished by 7 percent in the first half of the year, while among those members who remained there was a growing tendency to push individual interests, instead of those of the party as a whole, resulting in growing corruption within the party—Ripp, 2006, pp242-249.

33: Aldcroft and Morewood, 1995, p195.

34: These discussions became known as the "Round Table Discussions".

The logic of economic reform

During the first couple of years following the end of the one-party regime the mood in Hungary was generally optimistic. People believed it was possible to enjoy the same freedom and living standards as their neighbours in the West.[35] Some of the country's newly elected leaders made overblown claims about the possibility of "convergence" with Western Europe in the not too distant future.[36] The hopes of the time were summarised well by the author and politician Miklós Vásárhelyi. In 1989 he told the *New York Times*:

> First of all there will really be a Europe again. The countries of Central and Eastern Europe will finally get an opportunity to unite with the West. We will begin to live under the same conditions. It will take time, but socially, politically and economically we will achieve what the Western countries have already achieved. The door is now open.[37]

The answer to how to achieve this was provided by mainstream economists, policymakers and international financial organisations, such as the IMF and the World Bank. Building on a combination of conservative and liberal political economic theory, derived from the likes of Friedrich Hayek and Milton Friedman, they argued that "catching up" with the West would be achieved through a quick and radical overhaul of the economy. What the Austrian economist Joseph Schumpeter had called "creative destruction" would cause previously unproductive sectors of the state capitalist economies to disappear, making room for new innovative capitalists that would provide the basis for a period of sustained long-term economic growth.[38] To this end, emphasis was placed on the rapid removal of controls on the economy, marketisation and privatisation. Governments were encouraged to pursue what became known as "shock therapy" reforms, which encouraged them to move away from their state capitalist habits of active state intervention towards pursuing restrictive fiscal and monetary policies. However, while this model provided a rather different view of the role of the state within the economy than the "regulatory state" envisioned by Keynesianism, it is

---

35: GM Tamás has described the years between 1988 and 1992 as being "a period of social imagination out of which nothing much came but it was a moment of perceived and hoped-for freedom"—Tamás, 2009, p28.
36: While only in my early teens at the time, I still remember Hungarian politicians seriously arguing in the early 1990s for the possibility of "catching up" with the West within a decade. Towards the end of the decade the time frame of this "promise" was changed to two decades.
37: Quoted in Gwertzman and Kaufman, 1990, pp225-226.
38: Schumpeter, 1975.

important to underline that it did not argue for a complete abandonment of the state's capacities. On the contrary, adherents of the neoliberal paradigm have continuously stressed, in theory as well as in practice, the need for a "strong state" in order to provide for a suitable environment in which "growth-promoting mechanisms" could work properly.[39]

To its supporters, the success of neoliberal transformation was virtually a certainty. As the liberal Hungarian economist László Csaba put it, this "market-based approach to development"[40] would allow for a fast integration with the global economy, which in turn would bring economic success and higher living standards to the peoples of Eastern Europe.[41] On the basis of these claims, policymakers throughout the former state capitalist economies fell for the lure of the market.

As the front runner of market reforms, Hungary was generally predicted by experts in the West to develop into a future model for successful political and economic transformation in the region.[42] The dominant political forces in the country believed neoliberal reforms were going to spur the arrival of foreign direct investment, and thereby transform Hungary into the financial hub of Central Europe.[43] Reality, however, has proved to be radically different from the neoliberal dream.

"Creative destruction" without creativity

With two decades of hindsight, the results of these transition-associated adjustments opening up the former state capitalist economies to the circuits

---

39: Csaba, 2007, p101. Since the early 1970s, when neoliberal theories came into prevalence within policy debates, the emphasis on the need for a "strong state" has resulted in private interests and many governments in the West directly supporting non-democratic regimes. The most obvious case in point would be the case of Pinochet's dictatorship in Chile, which was viewed as the laboratory of monetarism in the 1970s. In Hungary violent demonstrations in 2006 were used as a pretext to strengthen the repressive arm of the state and crush resistance to the government's neoliberal policies.

40: Csaba defines the central feature of this approach as resting on the view of the market as "the fundamental coordination mechanism through which the vicious cycle of poverty can be overcome"—Csaba, 2007, p101.

41: Åslund, 2002; Marangos, 2004; Sachs, 1990; Williamson, 1992. In their sober critique of neoliberal reforms in Eastern Europe, radical political economists László Andor and Martin Summers have described the architects of these policies as "Market Maoists", whose blind fate in the blessings of the market could be likened to the utopianism that characterised the economic programme of China's Cultural Revolution of the 1960s and 1970s—with the only difference that, this time around, the "great leap forward" was to be into capitalism and not Communism—Andor and Summers, 1998.

42: Jeffries, 1993.

43: Tamás, 2009, p36.

of global capital have been far from impressive. For the region as a whole economic restructuring in the 1990s contributed to an unprecedented collapse in output.[44] The results of the first decade of economic transformation were so bad that even the World Bank, which throughout the period remained one of the staunchest advocates of free-market capitalism in the region, had to admit, "The magnitude and duration of the transition recession was, for all countries, comparable to that for developed countries during the Great Depression, and for most of them it was much worse".[45]

The 1990s became something of a "lost decade" for the Hungarian economy. There were prolonged crisis and economic stagnation, with output only returning to its 1989 level by 1999.[46] The economy finally started to recover after 2000, growing by a rate of 4 percent annually until 2006. Then it hit new problems with the introduction of further austerity measures, instituted in the name of "global competition" as well as to curb the country's growing budget deficit, which reduced annual growth to less than 3 percent.[47] The current economic downturn has brought an end even to this meagre growth. In 2009 the economy might contract by as much as 10 percent and experts see few, if any, signs of recovery ahead.[48]

As a result of the sharp drop in production, chronic unemployment developed into an emblematic aspect of the Hungarian economy.[49] The foreign capital and new technologies attracted by the abundance of cheap and well qualified labour did not in any way prove to be enough to counterbalance the jobs being shed. Between 1989 and 1997 the Hungarian labour force decreased by 1.5 million, from 5 million to 3.5 million, and the official unemployment rate is currently 9.6 percent.[50]

Economic restructuring also contributed to a major decline in living standards and general welfare until 1995, with little recovery afterwards.[51] Real wages only reached their 1980s level by 2003, and according to a study conducted by the United Nations Development Programme in 2003, the number of poor people was as high as one third of the Hungarian population

---

44: Kolodko, 2000, p109.
45: World Bank, 2002, p3.
46: Eurequal, 2006, p2.
47: Eurequal, 2006, p2.
48: Latest in line to express his doubts about the Hungarian economy was the former chairman of the National Bank, Péter Á Bod, who in a recent interview claimed that the economy would only reach its 2008 level in 2013—*Népszabadság*, 23 August 2009.
49: UNDP, 2003, p. 19.
50: Adam, 1999, p92. More recent studies have confirmed this trend—Eurequal, 2006; Tárki, 2004. For most recent unemployment figures, see the *Economist*, 15 August 2009.
51: Eurequal, 2006, p3.

(nearly three million people).[52] As a telling indication of the widespread malaise characterising Hungarian society today, meat consumption still lags behind its 1980 level (which is even more telling considering that Hungary is a country renowned for its preference for meat).[53]

To make things worse, welfare provisions have been strenuously cut by both social-liberal and right wing governments since the transition to the free market. Fees have been introduced in public hospitals and unemployment benefits reduced to six months only, and now the current global crisis is further raising unemployment and reducing real wages, while the government is promising to carry out further cuts in social spending.

Adding to Hungary's woes, its post-transition depression has increased class, ethnic and regional inequalities. Recent figures on class inequality levels show that the ratio between the highest and lowest 10 percent of per capita household income has increased from 7.5 in 1992 to 8.4 in 2003.[54] The major beneficiaries of the economic transformation have been a small minority of the population (10 to 12 percent), which has clearly improved its status in the new system.[55] Comprising a combination of former *nomenklatura* members benefiting from privatisation schemes and those who have gained from the arrival of foreign multinationals, the members of this group today live similarly lavish lives to their counterparts in other parts of the world. In addition to this group there is the middle class (constituting about 30 percent of the population) for whom the transformation has been something of a mixed blessing.

Apart from these two groups there are the working class and the "deprived". Comprising around 40 percent of society, the working class has been severely hit by the effects of the economic crisis and the narrowing labour market in the 1990s.[56] The situation has hardly been better for those workers who managed to survive the initial transition depression. Since 1989 these workers have experienced a significant rise in exploitation, as evidenced by an increase in working hours while real wages have fallen. At the bottom end of the scale are the remaining 20 percent in society—the "deprived". Mainly comprised of peasants, unskilled manual workers, the

52: Eurequal, 2006, p2; UNDP, 2003, p56. On the basis of this it is difficult to understand how the *Economist* could claim in 2005 that Hungary "has almost no people living in poverty"—the *Economist*, 26 November 2005. (It should be noted that the UNDP's figures were calculated on the minimum subsistence level, while the *Economist* based its claims on the World Bank's standards, which amount to a crude economic definition of poverty of $2.15 per person per day.)

53: Eurequal, 2006, p3.

54: Tárki, 2004, p51.

55: Tárki, 2004, p69.

56: Tárki, 2004, p69.

unemployed and homeless people, they have fared worst as a result of transformation and face little, if any, hope of improvement in the future.[57]

Poverty also has an ethnic dimension in Hungary.[58] The economic transformation had catastrophic consequences for the Roma population. The employment rate of the Roma dropped by more than half, falling from 75 to 30 percent in the period between the mid-1980s and mid-1990s.[59] The incidence of poverty is almost seven times as high for households with a Roma head of the family as for others.[60] Today the Roma are not only exposed to the dangers of unemployment and poverty, but also face widespread discrimination and segregation, as well as increasingly serious threats to their lives.

Finally, regional differences tend to further accentuate inequalities within Hungary. While Budapest and the western parts of the country bordering Western Europe have received the bulk of investment flowing into the country since 1989, other parts of the country have seen little of this. Particularly badly hit have been the industrial areas in the north and the east, which suffered heavily from "the collapse of heavy industrial production and mining soon after 1989".[61] In a striking parallel with the areas of Britain that have seen the greatest job losses in manufacturing and the mining industry, these are today the areas of Hungary that exhibit the highest levels of unemployment, poverty and related social problems.

Conclusions

The contradictions involved in Hungary's post-1989 development need to be viewed in the light of recent changes in global capitalism, a process that has involved a "shift from national capitalism to multinational capitalism".[62] This change, which came about as an attempt by nation-states to restore profits to the levels enjoyed prior to the prolonged economic crisis of the 1970s, contributed to the growth of global trade and financial markets, as well as the rise of transnational corporations. At the same time "the logics of competitive deregulation"[63] heightened the contradictions of capitalism. These contradictions of capitalist expansion, between a tendency for "unification" and a counteracting tendency to "divergence", were brilliantly captured by Leon Trotsky:

57: Adam, 1999, p120; Tárki, 2004, p69.
58: Adam, 1999, p161.
59: UNDP, 2003, p21.
60: Tárki, 2004, p103.
61: Eurequal, 2006, pp21-22.
62: Harman, 1990.
63: Dale, 2004, p193.

By drawing the countries economically closer to one another and levelling out their stages of development, capitalism...operates by methods of its own...by anarchistic methods which constantly undermine its own work, set one country against another, and one branch of industry against another, developing some parts of world economy, while hampering and throwing back the development of others. Only the correlation of these two fundamental tendencies—both of which arise from the nature of capitalism—explains to us the living texture of the historical process.[64]

In the light of this, it becomes clear that Hungary's thorny road since 1989 has not been the result of "bad policies" (in the shape of neoliberal reforms) or "corrupt governments" (though these factors have certainly added to Hungary's woes), but of the general contradictions inherent in capitalism. To make things worse for small countries such as Hungary, recent shifts within capitalism, together with its corollary feature of imperialist rivalry, "itself...the outgrowth of the workings of capitalism's inner tendencies to expansion and centralisation",[65] have tended to accentuate the burdens of "backwardness".

This fact has been brutally reinforced by the current crisis, which has left the small and fragile economies of Central and Eastern Europe as "the weakest link in the capitalist chain". In Hungary "the whip of external necessity" has led the government to vehemently pursue its policies of downsizing, privatisation and economic liberalisation in the desperate hope that these would sooner or later help to turn the economy round. But such policies only worsen the situation. The economy is in virtual freefall; living standards are falling; and social inequalities are rising. Public discontent with the current state of affairs is near total. The extreme right has been able to mobilise parts of the middle class, blaming "conspiring Jews" for causing the crisis, and "benefit scroungers" (and the Roma in particular) for supposedly stealing the little money still left in the state's treasury. At the same time the working class is left without any political representation, making it particularly vulnerable to attacks from the ruling class.

To offer a progressive alternative to the forces of reaction, a return to classical Marxism seems to be particularly pertinent. Building on the works of Karl Marx, Trotsky and others within this tradition, we can not only develop a stronger understanding of the reasons behind Hungary's

---

64: Cited by Barker, 2006, p82.
65: Barker, 2006, p82.

uneven development since 1989 but also awaken the working class, which still remains, in Trotsky's words, "the initiator of the liquidation of world capitalism".[66]

References

Adam, Jan, 1999, *Social Costs of Transformation to a Market Economy in Post-Socialist Countries: The Cases of Poland, the Czech Republic and Hungary* (Palgrave Macmillan).

Aldcroft, Derek, and Steven Morewood, 1995, *Economic Change in Eastern Europe Since 1918* (Edward Edgar).

Andor, László, and Martin Summers, 1998, *Market Failure: A Guide to the East European "Economic Miracle"* (Pluto).

Åslund, Anders, 2002, *Building Capitalism: the Transformation of the Former Soviet Bloc* (Cambridge University).

Barker, Colin, 2006, "Beyond Trotsky: Extending Combined and Uneven Development", in Bill Dunn and Hugo Radice, *100 Years of Permanent Revolution: Results and Prospects* (Pluto).

Brenner, Robert, 2006, *The Economics of Global Turbulence: the Advanced Capitalist Economies from Long Boom to Long Downturn, 1945-2005* (Verso).

Callinicos, Alex, 1991, *The Revenge of History: Marxism and the East European Revolutions* (Polity).

Cerny, Phil, 1990, *The Changing Architecture of Politics: Structure, Agency and the Future of the State* (Sage).

Cliff, Tony, 1996, *State Capitalism in Russia* (Bookmarks), www.marxists.org/archive/cliff/works/1955/statecap/

Csaba, László, 2007, *The New Political Economy of Emerging Europe* (Akadémiai Kiadó).

Dale, Gareth, 2004, *Between State Capitalism and Globalisation: The Collapse of the East German Economy* (Peter Lang).

Dale, Gareth, 2006, "'A Very Orderly Retreat': Democratic Transition in East Germany, 1989-90", *Debatte: Journal of Contemporary Central and Eastern Europe*, volume 14, number 1.

Eurequal, 2006, *The State of Inequality in Central and Eastern Europe: Desk Research on Hungary*, available at http://eurequal.politics.ox.ac.uk/papers/desk_research.asp.

Fukuyama, Francis, 1989, "The End of History?", *The National Interest* (summer 1989), www.wesjones.com/eoh.htm

Gwertzman, Bernard, and Michael Kaufman, 1990, *The Collapse of Communism* (Random House).

Hardy, Jane, 2009, *Poland's New Capitalism* (Pluto).

Harman, Chris, 1984, *Explaining the Crisis: a Marxist Re-Appraisal* (Bookmarks).

Harman, Chris, 1990, "The Storm Breaks", *International Socialism* 46 (spring 1990).

Haynes, Michael, 1994, "Class and Crisis in Eastern Europe", in Alex Callinicos, John Rees, Michael Haynes and Chris Harman, *Marxism and the New Imperialism 1994* (Bookmarks).

Jeffries, Ian, 1993, *Socialist Economies and the Transition to the Market: A Guide* (Routledge).

Kolodko, Grzegorz W, 2000, *From Shock to Therapy—The Political Economy of Postsocialist Transformation* (Oxford University).

Kornai, János, 2006, "The Great Transformation of Central Eastern Europe: Success and Disappointment", *Economics of Transition*, volume 14, number 2.

66: Trotsky, 1969, p. 108.

Köves, András, 1985, *The CMEA Countries in the World Economy: Turning Inwards or Turning Outwards* (Akadémiai Kiadó).

Maier, Charles, 1997, *Dissolution: The Crisis of Communism and the End of East Germany* (Princeton University).

Marangos, John, 2004, *Alternative Economic Models of Transition* (Ashgate).

Ripp, Zoltán, 2006, *Rendszerváltás Magyarországon 1987-1990* (Napvilág Kiadó).

Sachs, Jeffrey, 1990, "What is to be done?", *Economist*, 13 January 1990.

Schumpeter, Joseph, 1975 [1942], *Capitalism, Socialism and Democracy* (Unwin University).

Swain, Nigel, 1992, *Hungary: the Rise and Fall of Feasible Socialism* (Verso).

Tamás, Gáspár Miklós, 2009, "Interview—Hungary: 'Where We Went Wrong'", *International Socialism 123* (summer 2009), www.isj.org.uk/?id=555

Tárki, 2004, *Hungary: Social Report 2004*, www.tarki.hu/en/publications/SR/2004/

Trotsky, Leon, 1969 [1930/1906], *The Permanent Revolution and Results and Prospects* (Merit).

UNDP, 2003, "Towards Alleviating Human Poverty 2000-2002, Human Development Report: Hungary, 2000-2002", available from http://tinyurl.com/UNDP-hungary

Williamson, John, 1992, *The Eastern Transition to a Market Economy: A Global Perspective* (Centre for Economic Performance).

World Bank, 2002, *Transition—The First Ten Years. Analysis and Lessons for Eastern Europe and the Former Soviet Union*, available from http://tinyurl.com/WB-1989

Pinning the blame on the system
Andrew Kliman

This is the first in a series of responses to Chris Harman's latest book, **Zombie Capitalism: Global Crisis and the Relevance of Marx**.

When Chris Harman began work on *Zombie Capitalism* in late 2006 his goal was to criticise what he calls "the great delusion", the belief that "capitalism had found a new way of expanding without crisis".[1] At the time the task of persuading readers that this belief was delusional was formidable. "Even some Marxists spoke of a 'new long upturn'".[2] Others, in more guarded fashion, told us that capitalism "maintains a certain coherence over time. The homeostatic aspects must be balanced against the transformative, crisis-provoking ones. The term 'equilibrium'…has different meanings… and some of them are crucial to the Marxist enterprise".[3]

   Of course, the economic crisis that erupted shortly thereafter made it unnecessary for Harman to persuade anyone of what had been his main thesis. Those who had proclaimed that "capitalism had found a new long-term stability [or had entered] a 'new long upturn'…were soon to look as foolish as those who forecast endless peace in the early summer of 1914".[4] And talk of capitalism's coherence, homeostatic aspects and equilibrium was replaced by the thunderous proclamation that "*the Marxist understanding of the inherent instability and progressive unworkability of capitalism has been vindicated!*"[5]

1:   Harman, 2009, pp15-16.
2:   Harman, 2009, p253.
3:   Laibman, 2004.
4:   Harman, 2009, p253.
5:   Laibman, 2009, emphasis in the original.

The focus of *Zombie Capitalism* thus shifted from prognostication to explanation. Why had the economic crisis erupted? Why was it inevitable? And most importantly, why will capitalism's crisis tendencies continue into the future? (If it recovers from the current crisis, which is not yet a sure thing in my view.) The downside was that Harman had to scrap about a third of what he had drafted and significantly recast the rest. The upside was that it is more pleasant to explain after the fact why one was right than to try to convince people before the fact that one will be proven right.

But having the opportunity to explain is one thing; having the explanations taken seriously by those whose perspectives have been disproved by events is another. To be sure, key proponents of free-market capitalism such as Alan Greenspan have admitted that their models and worldviews were wrong. Richard Posner, a chief architect of the conservative, market-oriented "law and economics" movement, has come out with a book on the crisis entitled *A Failure of Capitalism*. Yet as Harman recognises, such rethinking is ephemeral: "A few months when banks are not collapsing and profits are not falling through the floor and the apologists will [again] talk about the wonders of capitalism and the impossibility of any alternative—until crisis hits again".[6] Indeed, such talk is already well under way as I write this, even though no one knows yet whether the current economic slump has really ended or whether it will resume once the temporary government "stimulus" stops.

On the left there has been even less rethinking than on the right. This is because the crisis has the "form of appearance"—to use an apt Hegelian-Marxian expression—of being a crisis of free-market, deregulated capitalism and specifically a crisis emanating from the financial sector. In other words, it appears to be a crisis of things the left never celebrated (though those who spoke of a new long upturn tended to regard them as successful), and thus an ideological predicament only for the other guys.

The basic problem is that those who have not broken completely with capitalist ideology must always try, as Harman puts it, "to pin the blame on something other than capitalism as such".[7] They have only two alternatives to choose from—the free market and state intervention—and they veer wildly from one to the other. The Great Depression appeared to be a crisis of the free market, so they embraced various forms of statism. The global crisis of the 1970s appeared to be a crisis of the interventionist state, so they veered back to the free market and veered further when the collapse of the USSR and its satellites appeared to be the collapse of

6:    Harman, 2009, pp8-9.
7:    Harman, 2009, p292.

capitalism's "other" rather than of capitalism in one of its forms. And now they're veering back to various forms of statism.

The greatest virtue of *Zombie Capitalism* is that Harman will have none of this. He pins the blame on "capitalism as such". What makes this difference more than a rhetorical one is that his conclusions flow out of an analysis of "capitalism as such". When he discusses the trajectory and vicissitudes of the world economy during the past 90 years his primary object of analysis is the capitalist system itself, not only a variety of particular institutional arrangements and property forms.

In other words, in Harman's view (which I share), the system is not reducible to particular institutions and legal forms. They come and go, and differ from place to place, but amid this flux and variety there persist specifically capitalistic goals and processes: the drive to accumulate value; the operation of systemic laws, above all what Marx called "the law of value" or "determination of value by labour-time"; and competition for markets as well as "military competition"[8] between capitalist states, which compels individual units of capital either to accumulate and obey the system's economic laws or to perish. And, as a result of all this, there is a drive to reduce costs and prices by adopting labour-saving technical innovations, a tendency for the rate of profit to fall, and recurrent economic crises and slumps.

The title *Zombie Capitalism* reflects Harman's focus on capitalism itself. Taking seriously Marx's theory of the "fetishism of the commodity", he characterises the system as a zombie, an undead creature. It is a system of things that have escaped the control of the workers who produced them and have come to dominate them. "Capital is labour that is transformed into a monstrous product whose only aim is to expand itself".[9]

The word "itself" is crucial. The notion that capital's only aim is "to expand itself" differs from the notion that its only aim is "to enrich the capitalists who own it". The latter are "themselves…subject to a system which pursues its relentless course whatever the feelings of individual human beings".[10] The "law of value" prohibits them from exploiting their workers significantly less, since doing so raises their costs, making them uncompetitive and unprofitable. Moreover, the dynamic of capitalism itself "hurl[s] the world in a direction that few people in their right mind would want".[11] One example of this phenomenon is climate change; another is the

---

8: Harman, 2009, p200.
9: Harman, 2009, p84.
10: Harman, 2009, p37.
11: Harman, 2009, p11.

current crisis, which has "hurt big capitals and not just those who [labour] for them".[12]

Some of the losses and bankruptcies being suffered by capitalists are even results of conscious governmental decisions. As I argued in this journal a year ago, after the US government prevented Bear Stearns, Fannie Mae, and Freddie Mac from collapsing but caused their shareholders to be wiped out, these events:

> Show [that] the government is not even intervening on behalf of private interests: it is intervening on behalf of the system itself. Such total alienation of an economic system from human interests of any sort is a clear sign that it needs to perish and make way for a higher social order.[13]

But this is clear only if one distinguishes between capitalists and capitalism itself. There has been much bemusement and anger in the US over the fact that the government has been quick and generous when bailing out financial institutions, but slow and stingy when confronted with the imminent bankruptcy of auto firms. These different responses can easily be explained without resorting to conspiracy theory: the US government's goal is to maintain the capitalist system itself, which would be severely threatened by a collapse of the financial sector but not by the collapse of US auto makers. Yet if the concept of "capital itself" is absent, the government is suspected of engaging in conspiracy, or at least of favouring "financial capital" over "productive capital". This makes people more receptive to proposed responses to the crisis that include allying with non-financial capitalists in a multi-class struggle against "financial capitalism" or nationalising finance,[14] and more receptive to the ubiquitous assurances that a future large-scale crisis can be prevented by increased regulation of the financial sector.

Just as Harman was convinced, before the crisis erupted, that another capitalist crisis was inevitable, he is now convinced that "new bubbles and periods of rapid growth in one part of the world or another…will only prepare the way for more burst bubbles and more crises".[15] The source of these convictions is his overall theory of the system's goals and processes—the drive to accumulate, the "law of value", competition, etc—that I discussed

---

12: Harman, 2009, p300.
13: Kliman, 2008, p75.
14: I heard Pratnab Patnaik, an Indian Marxist economist, propose such an alliance in a 13 July 2009 colloquium at Kingston University. Fred Moseley, a US Marxist economist, called for nationalisation of finance in section seven of Moseley, 2009.
15: Harman, 2009, p304.

above. To put it in a nutshell, the value of existing capital (including financial claims) must again and again be destroyed so that value can then temporarily "self-expand" at a faster rate.

I read *Zombie Capitalism* as above all an effort to substantiate the view that capitalist crises are inevitable by explaining and defending this theory. In other words, Harman justifies his view not by pointing to the fact that he predicted the current crisis but by endeavouring to account for the crisis—and more importantly, to account for the major economic events and trends of the past 90 years, booms as well as busts, country-specific phenomena as well as global ones—in terms of the overall theory. How well the book succeeds is thus a matter of how much of this history the theory explains and how plausibly, without "ad-hockery", it does so.

In my view it succeeds admirably. I should caution, however, that I am biased and that economic history is not my particular area of specialisation.

I do have some differences with the book's account of recent economic history. I regard them as minor ones, since I think the book's principal conclusions hold up *better* on the basis of my reading of events. That is because my differences have to do with anomalies, facts that seem incompatible with the theory and that have to be "explained away". On my reading of the facts, little "explaining away" is needed; the fit between facts and theory is more obvious.

The main differences have to do with the boom that began with Second World War and persisted into the early 1970s, and the apparent long-term recovery of profitability since the early 1980s. With respect to the former, Harman and I agree that there was a "long boom" through to the early 1970s. We also agree that the boom can be explained on the basis of the theory by noting two of the theory's implications: the destruction of capital value during crises also sets the stage for the subsequent boom; and the diversion of profit from productive investment to other uses—in this case, persistent military build-up—slows down a falling trend in the rate of profit. But Harman also believes, while I do not, that this period was almost free of slumps and that it lacked a persistent falling rate of profit trend.

He writes that, between 1939 and 1974, the US only experienced one brief recession (in 1948–9) "in which economic output fell";[16] "there was only one brief spell of falling output in the US (in 1949)".[17] However, according to the National Bureau of Economic Research, whose rulings the US government accepts as official, there were six recessions during this

---

16: Harman, 2009, p68.
17: Harman, 2009, p166.

period. According to the Federal Reserve, industrial production fell in each of these recessions. And according to the US Bureau of Economic Analysis, real gross domestic product fell throughout the 1945-7 period and in 18 of the 104 quarters between 1948 and 1973. In 1949, 1953-4, 1957-8 and 1969-70 it declined for at least two quarters in a row. Perhaps there are definitions according to which economic output fell only once during this period but in any case this was not a slump-free era, at least not in the US.

My main remaining empirical differences concern trends in the rate of profit in the US. Harman says that "profit rates did not resume their downward slope" during the long boom,[18] and that there has been a partial recovery of rates of profit since the early 1980s. Bureau of Economic Analysis data I have recently analysed lead me to conclude, to the contrary, that there has been a persistent fall in the rate of profit—at least in the US corporate sector—throughout the whole post Second World War period (except that the nominal rate of profit did not fall, but temporarily levelled off during the 1960s and 1970s, because of that period's accelerating inflation).

To be precise: when fixed assets and depreciation are computed at historical cost, profit (or surplus value) is measured by subtracting employee compensation from value added (net of depreciation), and the rate of profit is measured by dividing profits by the cost of fixed assets, the rate of profit has had the following trajectory. Between the troughs of 1949 and 1961 it fell from 39.3 percent to 31.5 percent. It then fluctuated without trending upwards or downwards for two decades. In the trough year of 1982 it stood at 31.8 percent. In 1992, another trough year, it was 27.1 percent, and the trough after that was 2001, when the rate of profit was 23.3 percent. Thus half of the total fall occurred during the long boom and the other half occurred during the period in which profitability supposedly rebounded![19]

The differences between my profitability estimates and those of the Marxist economists and historians whose data Harman cites grow out of profound theoretical differences. I will address this issue presently, but I first wish to note how my estimates, and the data on US recessions cited above, affect the historical account he offers.

First, Harman's account places a heavy burden on the theory that a diversion of profit from productive investment to military uses causes the rate of profit to fall more slowly. This theory must explain why the rate of profit did not fall, and why the economy remained almost free of slumps, for a full quarter century after post-war reconversion. I agree with him that

18: Harman, 2009, p166,
19: Kliman, 2009.

the theory is "impeccable",[20] but I am not convinced that the slowdown in productive investment had the massive counteracting effect that his account requires of it. The problem is partly empirical but also partly theoretical: a slowdown in productive investment can only cause a slowdown in, not a reversal of, whatever trend the rate of profit has, and it can halt the trend only if productive investment comes to a halt. But on my reading of the data, the anomalous facts that the theory needs to explain disappear, at least in the US case. (The lag between falling profitability and the crisis of the 1970s can be explained by noting that the rate of profit, though falling, remained relatively high, and that the credit system makes the relationship between falling profitability and crisis a very indirect one.)

Second, Harman argues against the notion that the financial and productive sectors of the economy have become uncoupled, and my rate of profit computations significantly strengthen his argument. The issue is a politically important one. Several prominent radical economists have attributed the current economic crisis to financial sector excesses that they portray as largely *unrelated to and separable from* profitability trends and other productive sector phenomena. Their key evidence is the supposed recovery of the US rate of profit since the early 1980s. Moseley, as well as Gérard Duménil and Dominique Lévy, claims that the recovery is now almost complete. In what I regard as characteristically British understatement Harman writes that this uncoupled economy thesis "risk[s] opening the door"[21] to the apologetic claim that the causes of the crisis are nothing deeper than financial sector irresponsibility and deregulation. If the uncoupled economy thesis were right, then, as he says, greater state control over the financial sector would be sufficient to prevent the recurrence of similar crises in the future. But my rate of profit computations, if accepted, would essentially put paid to the uncoupled economy thesis and the political consequences that flow from it.

So the question is: Are my computations acceptable? I don't think Harman will have trouble accepting them. In order to explain why not, and why my profitability estimates differ so markedly from those put forward by proponents of the uncoupled economy thesis, a detour into the theoretical part of *Zombie Capitalism* is necessary.

Harman and I subscribe to what has become known as the temporal single system interpretation of Marx's value theory. A key component of this interpretation is that inputs and outputs are valued temporally, not simultaneously, in Marx's theory. Thus, for instance, the value or price of

---

20: Harman, 2009, p130.
21: Harman, 2009, p299.

corn planted as seed at the start of the year can differ from the value or price of the same kind of corn harvested at year's end.

This is painfully obvious—or should be. But the models of orthodox economists typically assume that valuation is simultaneous, ie that the per-unit prices of inputs and outputs are the same. Since "the simultaneity of the theory is a myth", the conclusions they deduce from these models "bear little relation to really existing capitalism".[22] But slight variations on these models eventually became standard academic "Marxian economics" and, not surprisingly, they turned Marx's value theory and the falling rate of profit theory that results from it into nonsense—garbage in, garbage out. As a result it was almost universally accepted, even among Marxist academics, that his theories were logically inconsistent and therefore false, and that this had been proved definitively. More recently, however, proponents of the temporal single system interpretation "have been able completely to rescue Marx's position by challenging...the reliance on simultaneity".[23]

In the case of the falling rate of profit theory, simultaneous valuation does its damage in the following way. When labour saving techniques are introduced that raise physical productivity, commodities' values and prices tend to fall, and this tends to reduce the rate of profit. But if one values inputs and outputs simultaneously, one takes the decline in the prices of *outputs* that has occurred and retroactively lowers the prices of *inputs* (purchased at earlier dates) to the same degree. This procedure artificially lowers costs of production and the value of the invested capital, and it therefore boosts the rate of profit artificially. The upshot is that, contrary to what Marx argued, "viable" labour saving technical change does not and cannot cause "the rate of profit" to fall.

But this simultaneously determined "rate of profit" is not a rate of profit in any real sense. As Harman notes:

> Investment...takes place at one point in time. The cheapening of further investment as a result of improved production techniques occurs at a later point in time. The two things are *not* simultaneous... When capitalists measure their rates of profit they are comparing the surplus value they get from running plant and machinery with what they spent on acquiring it at some point in the past—not what it would cost to replace it today... [The rate of profit] necessarily implies a comparison of *current* surplus value with

22: Harman, 2009, p42.
23: Harman, 2009, p49.

the *prior* capitalist investment from which it flows. The very notion of "self-expanding values" is incoherent without it.[24]

Quite so.

But proponents of the uncoupled economy thesis, and simultaneist Marxist economists generally, do exactly what should not be done. The "rates of profit" they compute and put forward as evidence are nothing other than ratios of current surplus value to what it would cost to replace plant and machinery today—figments of the simultaneist imagination. (Although government agencies supply the data, they nowhere sanction taking one figure, dividing it by the other, and christening the result "the rate of profit".) My rate of profit figures, on the other hand, are ratios of current surplus value to what was actually spent to acquire the plant and machinery in the past (net of depreciation). This is why our empirical results are so different and why I think that, although Harman had to utilise their figures for want of an alternative, he is likely to accept the temporally determined figures and the conclusion that the rate of profit has not recovered at all since the early 1980s.

The issue of temporal versus simultaneous valuation bears upon an additional facet of *Zombie Capitalism* that I found very intriguing. Although the theory that the rate of profit will fall more slowly when profit is diverted from productive investment to military uses is impeccable, Harman writes that its logic "has escaped many Marxist economists".[25] It escapes them, he suggests, because they are "so bemused by the irrationality of what capitalists are doing as to try to deny that this is how the system works".[26]

I strongly suspect that simultaneous valuation models have also contributed greatly to their rejection of the theory, because the two things are incompatible. Thus proponents of simultaneous valuation cannot make sense of the theory. Here's why. When inputs and outputs are valued simultaneously, "the rate of profit" becomes a purely *physical* measure, basically the ratio of physical surplus to the physical capital invested.[27] A slower rate of productive investment does not alter this ratio, all else being equal. The physical capital grows more slowly, but this causes the growth of the physical surplus to slow down by the same percentage, so the simultaneously valued "rate of profit" remains unchanged.

In addition, the slowdown in productive investment is a

24: Harman, 2009, pp74-75, first emphasis in the original.
25: Harman, 2009, p131.
26: Harman, 2009, p132.
27: See Kliman, 2007, chapters five and seven.

non-equilibrium phenomenon. It has no effect in the imaginary "long run" of economists' static-equilbrium models. If, for example, the other factors that affect profitability are causing the rate of profit to fall from 40 percent to a long-run static equilibrium level of 20 percent, then (given enough time, and in the absence of any changes in these other factors) the rate of profit will ultimately fall to 20 percent whatever the rate of productive investment may be. It just falls toward 20 percent more *slowly* when the rate of investment is low than when it is high.[28] But when one assumes that inputs and outputs have the same per-unit prices, one in effect assumes that the long-run static equilibrium state has already been reached. (Prices are not changing and, since a change in anything else will cause prices to change, nothing else is changing either.) So simultaneous valuation models prevent their proponents from recognising the effects of a slowdown in productive investment because the effects "only" take place in real time, which does not exist for them.

The present moment of crisis calls for some serious rethinking, not only on the right, but also on the left. I do not expect many intellectuals of my generation to engage in such rethinking but I have hopes that younger people and working people, less weighed down by tradition, will do so. Because *Zombie Capitalism* is comprehensive, has a direct style, and constantly brings fact and theory into contact with one another, reading this book is an excellent way for them to begin.

References

Harman, Chris, 2009, *Zombie Capitalism: Global Crisis and the Relevance of Marx* (Bookmarks).

Kliman, Andrew, 2007, *Reclaiming Marx's "Capital": A Refutation of the Myth of Inconsistency* (Lexington).

Kliman, Andrew, 2008, "A Crisis for the Centre of the System", *International Socialism 120* (autumn 2008), www.isj.org.uk/?id=482

Kliman, Andrew, 2009, "The Persistent Fall in Profitability Underlying the Current Crisis: New Temporalist Evidence", http://akliman.squarespace.com/persistent-fall

Laibman, David, 2004, "Rhetoric and Substance in Value Theory: An Appraisal of the New Orthodox Marxism", in Alan Freeman, Andrew Kliman and Julian Wells (eds), *The New Value Controversy and the Foundations of Economics* (Edward Elgar).

Laibman, David, 2009, "The Onset of Great Depression II: Conceptualising the Crisis", emphasis in original. Available at http://tinyurl.com/laibman2009

Moseley, Fred, 2009, "The US Economic Crisis: Causes and Solutions", *International Socialist Review 64* (March–April 2009), www.isreview.org/issues/64/feat-moseley.shtml

---

28: Actually, an increase in unproductive capital expenditures makes the rate of profit fall more quickly, since they increase the invested capital without also causing surplus value to increase. From the vantage point of the national capital as a whole, state military spending does not differ in this respect from private unproductive capital expenditures on security personnel, but since the former is not part of the unproductive capital of the private sector, *its* rate of profit falls more slowly.

Rupture and revolt in Iran
Peyman Jafari

The fallout from the presidential election on 12 June 2009 precipitated the biggest political crisis in Iran since the 1979 Revolution. The official results gave the incumbent president, Mahmoud Ahmadinejad, 63 percent of votes, compared to 34 percent for his main rival, the reformist Mir Hossein Mousavi. As these results were contested by Mousavi, people's power shook the political establishment. Thousands poured onto the streets of Iran's major cities to demand the annulment of the election result and the extension of democratic rights.

The protests and the government crackdown have prompted an animated debate on the international radical left. Faulty analyses, interpreting events in Iran as merely a conflict between two factions of the ruling class and regarding the protests as an imperialist conspiracy, have led some on the left to line up with those who were crushing the protest movement.

There were, of course, good reasons to be critical of the West's hypocritical call for democracy and human rights in Iran: their support for dictatorships in the region and their occupations of Iraq and Afghanistan, for instance. And, given the US's record of encouraging "colour revolutions" in countries such as Ukraine and Georgia, it is not surprising that the Iranian demonstrations met with a sceptical response, especially in the Middle East and Latin America. However, this position was utterly mistaken.

Fortunately, the vast majority of the radical left reacted differently, with excitement and hope, maintaining opposition to imperialism while offering solidarity and support to the political forces that wanted to take

Ahmadinejad, Mahmoud (1956–) president of Iran 2005-9 and officially declared winner of June 2009 election. Previously mayor of Tehran.

American Embassy Centre of US spying operations across Middle East and central Asia. In November 1979 it was occupied by student supporters of Khomeini who held officials hostage for 14 months.

Assembly of Experts Body of 86 Islamic scholars that chooses Supreme Leader and vetoes candidates for election. Elected by popular vote from government-screened list of candidates every eight years.

Bani Sadr, Abolhassan (1933–) Liberal Muslim non-cleric. Elected as president in January 1980. Impeached by parliament and removed from office at Khomeini's instigation in June 1981 as Pasdaran seized the presidential building. Went into hiding and then exile as his close supporters were executed.

Bazaaris Merchants who constitute core of old middle class, merging into bourgeoisie. Traditionally exercised strong influence over religious institutions and clergy.

Bazargan, Mehdi (1907-95) Former follower of Mossadeq who became first prime minister after revolution in February 1979. Resigned after occupation of US embassy in December.

Fedayeen Secular revolutionary guerrilla group. Waged armed struggle against Shah and supported Khomeini in early stages of revolution, then split.

Guardian Council Composed of 12 jurists, six appointed by the Supreme Leader, six elected by parliament. Supervises elections and has veto over candidates.

Hajjarian, Saeed (1954–) prominent journalist and pro-democracy activist. Adviser to President Khatami.

Hezbollahi Groups of Khomeini supporters who attacked the left after the revolution of 1979.

Hostage crisis See American Embassy.

Iran-Iraq War (1980-8) Began with invasion of Iran in September 1980 by Saddam Hussein's Iraq. Clear US blessing at time of the US hostage crisis. Khomeini continued war to punish Iraq even after the invasion was beaten back. It ended after US warships in the Gulf intervened on Iraq's side.

Islamic Left Name given in 1980s and 1990s to the faction in the regime most favourable to state intervention and welfare provision.

Islamic Republic of Iran Name given to regime from 1980.

Islamic Republican Party Party of Khomeini's followers formed by Rafsanjani and others during the revolution and after. Dissolved as factional infighting developed in 1987.

Khamenei, Ali (1939–) President of Iran 1981-9 and Supreme Leader since the death of Khomeini in 1989.

Khatami, Mohammad (1943–) President 1997-2005. Educated as a religious scholar, served as minister of culture. Advocated limited liberal reforms but retreated from enacting them.

Khomeini, Ruhollah (1902-89) Grand Ayatollah, Shia religious dignitary, arrested and then exiled by the Shah in 1964. He returned in February 1979, two weeks after the Shah fled, and became effective leader of revolution. First Supreme Leader of Iran.

Mosaddeq, Mohammad (1882-1967) Nationalist prime minister 1951-2. Nationalised Iranian Oil (then owned by Anglo-Iranian Oil Company, now known as BP). Removed by coup organised by CIA and MI6.

Mousavi, Mir Hossein (1941–) Presidential candidate in June 2009. Imprisoned under the Shah. Helped found Islamic Republican Party after revolution. Vocal critic of Bani Sadr in 1981. Prime minister with Khomeini's backing 1981-9; opponent of dissent during this period. Withdrew from politics after Khomeini's death but remained member of Expediency Council.

Mujahedeen Left Islamist guerrilla group fighting Shah's regime. Turned against Khomeini in course of 1979 and came under attack from Hezbollahi.

Supported Bani Sadr in 1981. When demonstrations did not overthrow regime it turned to guerrilla methods, blew up the headquarters of the Islamic Republican Party, killing 70 key supporters of Khomeini, then fought alongside Iraq in the war against Iran.

Pasdaran See Revolutionary Guard.

Rafsanjani, Ali Akbar Hashemi (1934–) Cleric and organiser of underground activity on behalf of Khomeini under the Shah. Co-founder of the Islamic Republican Party. Speaker of parliament in 1980s. Defended mass execution of the Mujahedeen. Architect of Khamenei's appointment as Supreme Leader in 1989. President 1989-97. Defeated in second round by Ahmadinejad in 2005. Reputedly the richest man in Iran and described as "pragmatic conservative".

Revolutionary Guard Islamist military organisation created by Khomeini's supporters in aftermath of revolution. Played an important role during Iran-Iraq War.

Shorahs Factory councils thrown up by workers in the 1979 Revolution.

Tudeh Party The pro-USSR Communist party in Iran.

Velayat-e faqih Interpretation of Shia Islam doctrine by Khomeini which put political leadership in the hands of religious dignitaries.

Workers' House Regime-sponsored union.

the protest movement in a democratic, anti-capitalist and anti-imperialist direction.

The post-election crisis was a product of an unprecedented rupture in the ruling class on the one hand and a huge mobilisation from below on the other. This article aims to put both developments in a historical perspective and provide an understanding of the opportunities and pitfalls facing the revolutionary left.

Revolution and counter-revolution

In his speech inaugurating Ahmadinejad's second term, Supreme Leader Ali Khamenei described the protests as a "caricature" of the "great movement" of 1979.[1] This remark was politically significant because it conceded that a mass movement had erupted after the presidential elections and acknowledged that what was at stake was the legacy of the 1979 Revolution. The demonstrations were reclaiming the emancipatory potential of the revolution by repeating its slogans; those attacking them were also claiming the revolution for themselves, posing as its defenders against "liberal" and "Western" deviations. The two sides were in fact referring to different things—revolution and counter-revolution—which the leaders of the Islamic Republic have always presented as the same. These leaders were able to blur the transition from one to the other because of their own participation in the revolution and because mass mobilisation was a special feature of the counter-revolution. But the crackdown on millions of Iranians repeating the demands and slogans of 1979 was a powerful reminder that the existing regime had been born out of counter-revolution. To appreciate the significance of this twist, it is imperative to briefly revisit events from 1977 to 1983.

The revolutionary movement that emerged in 1977 was the culmination of a century of protests, which had three prominent moments.[2] The first, the Constitutional Revolution (1906-11), was led by merchants, clerics and intellectuals (among them Iran's first socialists) and challenged both domestic tyranny (the Qajar dynasty) and imperialism (Russia and Britain).[3] The second moment started with the blossoming of the labour movement, women's organisations and the pro-Moscow Tudeh Party in the 1940s and ended with the US and British sponsored coup d'état against

---

1:   "Iran Supreme Leader's Speech At President Ahmadinejad's Approval Ceremony", *Iranian Students New Agency*, 4 August 2009.
2:   See Abrahamian, 1982 and 2008, for overviews of this period.
3:   See Afary, 1996. Matin, 2006, has provided an excellent analysis from the perspective of uneven and combined development.

the nationalist government of Mossadeq. His crime was that he had nationalised the Anglo-Iranian Oil Company, which Winston Churchill called "a prize from fairyland beyond our wildest dreams" because of the huge profits it yielded for Britain.[4] After the fall of Mossadeq the Shah established an authoritarian regime with military and financial assistance from the US, which trained his secret service, the Savak, to repress secular nationalist and Communist forces. As a result of this repression it was the clergy, headed by Ruhollah Khomeini, that played a central role in the protests of 1963-4, and political Islam (Islamism) emerged as an important force in the next two decades without ever becoming hegemonic, even during the early years of the revolution.

The roots of the third moment, the 1979 Revolution, lie in the political and social contradictions that the Shah's rule had created.[5] These came to a head in 1977-9 as a relative loosening of repression gave the opposition an opportunity to protest and a recession mobilised the lower classes. It is important to note that the revolution was made by a broad coalition of socially and ideologically diverse forces. As Abrahamian writes, if "the traditional middle class" of the *bazaari* merchants and the clergy "provided the opposition with a nationwide organisation, it was the modern middle class that sparked off the revolution, fuelled it, and struck the final blows", while "the urban working class" was "its chief battering ram".[6]

Students, intellectuals and clerics had staged protests from early 1977. The mercantile bourgeoisie played an important role through their financial assistance, as did the urban poor (the "lumpenproletariat") through providing the masses on the streets, but it was the strike movement in the last months of 1978, especially in the oil industry, that broke the back of the regime. Despite the myth of a monolithic Islam, there were all shades of Islamic-inspired ideologies at work: Khomeini's clerical Islamism, the non-clerical Islamism of the radical intellectual Ali Shariati, the Islamic socialism of the Mujahedeen, the Islamic liberalism of Mehdi Bazargan and the traditionalist Islam of the clergy. There were also various secular forces with a mass following: Communists, liberals and nationalists.

The fall of the Shah's regime in February 1979 was greeted by millions of Iranians as the "spring of freedom". A flood of new publications were sold and discussed at the roadside. There were public meetings in the streets, universities and workplaces covering politics, religion, philosophy

---

4: Kinzer, 2003, p39.
5: See Poya, 1987; Marshall, 1988; Parsa, 1989, and Moaddel, 1993.
6: Abrahamian, 1982, pp533-535.

and art. Socialist parties grew fast and new ones were founded. Oppressed groups such as women and national minorities took centre stage and demanded equal rights. Peasants seized the land. Independent trade unions were founded and strike committees developed into *shoras* (workers' councils)—some of them taking over production in plants where the management had fled. Strikes also continued after the revolution. There were 350 disputes in 1979.[7] Everywhere there was a liberating excitement and a sense that a different future was possible.

In general the vision of the revolutionary movement was one of independence from foreign domination, social justice and liberty. It is not true, as is argued by some liberals and leftists, that the slogan *Azady* (freedom) had merely an anti-imperialist content as befitted a movement with a lack of democratic aspirations. This claim ignores the historical resonance of the word, going back to the Constitutional Revolution and the opposition to the Shah's dictatorship. "Independence, freedom, Islamic republic"—the slogan that became popular in the last weeks of the revolution—indicated that for many people there was no contradiction between the three elements. However, Khomeini had a different vision for the future and a specific definition of an "Islamic republic". Around 1970 he had developed a new interpretation of the Shia doctrine of *velayat-e faqih*, according to which a supreme interpreter of Islamic law must lead the believers politically and religiously. He and his close allies kept this idea in the background and instead stressed the fight against poverty and imperialism. Khomeini even promised that the clerics would function merely as religious guides and leave politics to laymen. After the revolution, however, he started to concentrate all power in the hands of a group of clerics and lay Islamists. The main vehicles were the Revolutionary Council that Khomeini established as a parallel centre of power to the Provisional Government headed by the liberal-religious Bazargan, the Islamic Republican Party and the Islamic Revolutionary Guard Corps, whose members were mainly recruited from the urban and rural poor.

Khomeini, exiled in Paris as the revolution began to unfold, symbolised for many the unity of the diverse forces in its early days. On his return he used his influence to establish his own dominant role in the post-revolutionary state. But he could only do so by manoeuvring between different forces in ways that led many to misunderstand the class interests he represented.

First Khomeini allied himself with the bourgeois forces around

---

7:    See Bayat, 1987, on the *shoras*.

Bazargan's Provisional Government to marginalise the left in the universities and suppress the *shoras*, which were replaced by Islamic Associations. The Khomeinists also moved against the organisations of the left, banning or attacking their demonstrations and headquarters. Women's rights came under attack and the veil was made compulsory. Gangs of *hezbollahi* (partisans of god) intimidated dissidents. The Revolutionary Guard's assault on the Kurdish national movement at the end of 1979 was meant to demonstrate its power. By that time, counter-revolution was uprooting all grassroots organisations or bringing them under the control of the Islamic Republic.

The seizure of the American Embassy in November 1979 by student followers of Khomeini who held its officials hostage for 444 days enabled him to assume an anti-imperialist posture to further sideline the left, while at the same time turning on his bourgeois allies and forcing Bazargan to resign as prime minister. It also provided a distraction from the massive formal power given to the clergy through the inclusion of *velayat-e faqih* in the constitution—put to a vote in December and approved by a majority. Then in early 1980 Khomeini set about purging the left from the universities, conducting this "cultural revolution" in alliance with the newly elected president, the liberal-religious Bani Sadr. The Iraqi invasion in September 1980 came as a godsend for the Khomeinists. They used the all-out mobilisation for war to consolidate their power and conquer the last centre of power—the presidency—by launching an attack on Bani Sadr.

The left were thoroughly confused by this sequence of events. The left Islamist guerrillas of the Mujahedeen sided with Bani Sadr and then started a campaign of assassinations. Finding themselves no match for Khomeini's army they then fled to Iraq and joined Saddam Hussein's onslaught against Iran. The Communists of the Tudeh Party and the "majority" faction of the secular Fedayeen guerrilla organisation continued their unconditional support for Khomeini. Other leftist organisations, such as the "minority" faction of the Fedayeen, openly confronted the Islamic Republic but were forced into exile. Then in 1983 it was the turn of Tudeh and the Fedayeen "majority" to be banned. Hundreds of their members were arrested. Some 12,000 opponents of the Islamic Republic were either executed or killed in the armed struggles from 1981 to 1985 and thousands of others were executed in the summer of 1988.

However, the counter-revolution was not accomplished by repression alone. It also created its own social base. The Iranian left's failure to acknowledge this led them to misunderstand the nature of the Islamic Republic and to underestimate its power. Before returning to this issue I shall first look at the left's strategic mistakes that allowed the Islamists to advance.

The tragedy of the left

Despite their courage and self-sacrifice, the left were not able to stop the Khomeinists from taking power. The common explanation on the Iranian left is still to blame imperialism. According to one account:

> The entire resources of the international and national bourgeoisie, orchestrated by the CIA, were mobilised to transfer power to Khomeini as the representative of the capitalist clergy, to safeguard and save the bourgeois state... This was one of the most (if not the most) important factors in placing Khomeini at the head of the mass movement.[8]

This explanation is not only mistaken; it has also prevented the left investigating its own mistakes and drawing lessons for the future.

The left made two strategic mistakes. The guerrilla strategy of the left organisations prevented them from building a national organisation rooted in the day to day struggles of workers, even though some of their activists tried to compensate for this after the revolution by creating "workers' fronts" alongside "student" and "women" fronts. When Khomeini turned on the *shoras* and the workers' movement he did not simply have to rely on the use of force; he could also look to the influence of his Islamist followers. The left lacked the organisational resources to counter these attacks, to link the *shoras* together and further their development.

The other strategic mistake by the largest part of the left (Tudeh and the Fedayeen's "majority" faction) was to support Khomeini unconditionally, seeing him as the representative of the "progressive"—ie anti-imperialist—bourgeoisie. Instead of organising the working class as an independent force, they encouraged it to follow Khomeini. This logic followed from the Stalinist "two stages" theory, according to which the national bourgeoisie must first complete the struggle for independence and democracy, and only then can the left launch the second stage of socialist revolution. Tudeh argued that the transition from the first to the second stages could proceed smoothly if the new state accepted the path of "non-capitalist development" by copying the Soviet Union's state capitalism and joining its camp.

Tudeh and the guerrilla organisations were two sides of the same

---

8:    Razi, 2009.

coin: they both substituted other forces for the working class, assigning class struggle to second place. Tudeh argued that the Islamic Republic should be supported because it was "anti-imperialist"; the rest of the left opposed it on the grounds that it was imperialism's "puppet".

While Tudeh recognised that Khomeini enjoyed popularity among the lower classes, it did nothing to challenge his leadership. This would have been possible only by building an independent workers' movement with a revolutionary left at its core, which could pull the urban poor and the lower middle class away from the Khomeinists. The "Marxist" left underestimated Khomeini's popularity and launched an open assault on the Islamic Republic from mid-1980 onwards and was subsequently crushed.

A historian of the Iranian Revolution has put it this way:

> While a number of Marxist organisations (the Tudeh amongst others) interpreted the political independence of the Islamic Republic of Iran as a sign of a possible drift towards an understanding with the Soviet Union, the overwhelming majority denied the obvious and attempted to depict the new regime as a disguised puppet of imperialism. The Marxists were outmanoeuvred by the Islamists because they refused to accept the independent nature of the new leadership at face value, a factor which played an important role in the movement's inability to cope, and ultimately led to its downfall.[9]

The left also lacked a strategy for connecting the struggle for democratic rights to socialist revolution (the strategy of permanent revolution). They had developed a view in which the two stood in opposition to one another. The disastrous consequences of this logic became first apparent when in March 1979 thousands of women protested against the new gender policies of Khomeini, in particular the decree that made wearing the *hijab* obligatory. The left gave lip-service to women's rights, but did not take concrete steps to defend them and called on supporters to refrain from those protests because most of the participants were from the middle and upper classes. Finally, the left were seriously weakened by their fragmentation and sectarianism. Each organisation set up its own front organisations for students, women and workers instead of creating unity between revolutionaries and non-revolutionary workers, students and women to fight for common goals such as freedom of expression and organisation.

9: Behrooz, 2000, p104.

Islamist populism

Lenin, reflecting on the dark days that followed the 1905 Russian Revolution, wrote, "One had to know how to retreat, and that one had absolutely to learn how to work legally in the most reactionary of parliaments, in the most reactionary of trade unions, co-operative and insurance societies and similar organisations".[10] Unfortunately, the Iranian left did not retreat like the Bolsheviks; they just fractured into ever smaller fragments that became dominated by what Lenin, in the same passage, called "phrase-mongers". The new regime's brutality was not the only cause; more significant was the left's failure to make a realistic assessment of the new balance of forces and to develop their strategy and tactics accordingly. Such a reorientation would have required the left to come to terms with the nature of the counter-revolution.

The common view on the Iranian left was that the main components of the Islamist bloc headed by Khomeini were the clergy and the traditional petty bourgeoisie.[11] This prompted two different expectations. Tudeh thought that diverging economic interests would pit the petty bourgeois against the big bourgeoisie and shift them closer to the working class and the Soviet Union. The rest of the left expected that the traditional middle class would not be able to steer a modern state and economy, and would line up with the bourgeoisie against the working class. This became the dominant view after Khomeini's attacks on the left and the *shoras*, which was interpreted as a bourgeois counter-revolution.[12] This kind of analysis led many Iranian Marxists to explain the regime's instability by the contradiction between the bourgeoisie's "modern" economic interests and the "pre-modern" political-religious system of the clergy embodied in *velayat-e faqih*.

These theories exaggerate the influence of the "mosque-bazaar alliance"; more significantly they ignore the crucial role of the new middle class in both the revolution and the formation of the Islamic Republic.[13] Large numbers of students, intellectuals, lawyers, doctors, engineers and professionals were attracted to political Islam, not so much as a religion, but as a political project. Tony Cliff provided a succinct explanation of the role of the intelligentsia in developing countries:

10: Lenin, 1966, p28.

11: See, for instance, Saleth, 2007

12: A much sounder, though problematic (see below), analysis was provided by Rahe Kargar, one of the smallest organisations in 1979, which regarded the Islamic Republic as a form of Bonapartist bourgeois state.

13: Keshavarzian, 2007 and 2009.

The intelligentsia is sensitive to their countries' technical lag. Participating as it does in the scientific and technical world of the twentieth century, it is stifled by the backwardness of its own nation. This feeling is accentuated by the "intellectual unemployment" endemic in these countries... They feel insecure, rootless, lacking in firm values... [They] combine religious fervour with militant nationalism... They care a lot for measures to drag their nation out of stagnation, but very little for democracy. They embody the drive for industrialisation, for capital accumulation, for national resurgence... All this makes totalitarian state capitalism a very attractive goal for intellectuals.[14]

The emergence of the group around Khomeini was not merely an expression of a traditional bazaar-based, parasitic merchant capital, as Chris Harman pointed out in an important article on Islamism. The new middle class formed the organisational backbone of the Islamist cadre of the revolution and the state apparatus. Nor was this simply a classic bourgeois counter-revolution. The Islamists "undertook a revolutionary reorganisa- tion of ownership and control of capital within Iran even while leaving capitalist relations of production intact, putting large-scale capital that had been owned by the group around the Shah into the hands of the state and parastate bodies controlled by themselves".[15]

The Khomeinist counter-revolution differed from classic bour- geois counter-revolution in the sense that it was not trying to restore a lost political and social order; it created a new one, while preserving capitalist relations of social production. Val Moghadam was referring to this phe- nomenon when she wrote that the period between 1979 and 1983 did not contain one but two revolutions.[16] Because of the continuity between the two phases, with different orientations, one could also speak of a "deflected permanent revolution".[17] This term was first used by Cliff to describe the revolutions in China (1949) and Cuba (1959), but it also applies to some other revolutions in backward countries. They all shared the following characteristics: (a) a social order that was decomposing under external pres- sures and internal crises; (b) revolutionary outbursts from below; (c) power equilibrium between bourgeois and working class forces; and (d) a relatively large and radicalised middle class. In these situations the middle class could

14: Cliff, 1963.
15: Harman, 1994, p45.
16: Moghadam, 1989.
17: Cliff, 1963.

give leadership to revolutionary movements and create a state that initiated industrialisation from above.

Viewed from a global and historical perspective, this kind of revolution is an instance of a "revolution of backwardness" of the type that arises in countries affected by uneven and combined development.[18] Such countries are witness to what Trotsky in his classical description of Russia called "a drawing together of the different stages" of development and lead to "a combining of separate steps, an amalgam of archaic with more contemporary forms".[19] The theory of uneven and combined development has no difficulty in understanding Khomeinism's combination of "traditional" and "modern" features, unlike the liberal modernisation theory and "Marxist" versions of it that view capitalism as a unidirectional, progressive and homogenising process. It also demystifies the "uniqueness" of Khomeinism by showing that it is universal and specific at the same time.

Historically "revolutions of backwardness" have appeared in different forms, depending on the specific configuration of national and international forces.[20] One form, prevalent in Latin America and the Middle East, is populism. Khomeinism, or Islamism in general, is a particular form of populism. As I hope to demonstrate below, it shares the general characteristics of populism as a political movement, an ideology, a strategy for socio-economic development and a form of rule.[21] However, it also has its distinguishable characteristics.

In the words of Abrahamian, populism is:

A [political] movement of the propertied middle class that mobilises the lower classes, especially the urban poor, with radical rhetoric directed against imperialism, foreign capitalism, and the political establishment. In mobilising the "common people", populist movements use charismatic figures and symbols, imagery, and language that have potent value in the mass culture. Populist movements promise to drastically raise the standard of living and make the country fully independent of outside powers. Even more important, in attacking the status quo with radical rhetoric, they intentionally stop short of threatening the petty bourgeoisie and the whole

18: Knei-Paz, 1977.
19: Trotsky, 1977, p27-28.
20: What Gramsci called passive revolutions and other Marxists have called bourgeois revolutions from above are specific examples. The Russian Revolution of 1917 is an example of the strategy that socialists advocate—permanent revolution.
21: See Colás, 2004, for an application of this argument to Islamism in Algeria, Morocco and Tunisia.

principle of private property. Populist movements, thus, inevitably emphasise the importance, not of economic-social revolution, but of cultural, national, and political reconstruction.[22]

Crafting a multi-class coalition, dominated by the middle class, was central to Khomeini's populism:

> We are for Islam, not for capitalism and feudalism, not for land-grabbers, but for the barefooted, for deprived classes. Islam originates from the masses, not from the rich. The martyrs of the Islamic Revolution were all members of lower classes, peasants, industrial workers, and bazaar merchants and tradesmen.[23]

Khomeini reconciled these contradictory elements by talking about an undifferentiated Islamic people (*ommat*) or the "deprived," in which he included the *bazaaris*! As soon as the Khomeinist movement became institutionalised, however, it fell apart in different political factions reflecting different class interests, and different ideological and religious orientations.

Ideologically Khomeinism did not represent a return to the past or a total rejection of the modern world. It was based on "ideological adaptability and intellectual flexibility, with political protests against the established order, and with socio-economic issues that fuel mass opposition to the status quo".[24] It was revolutionary *and* conservative. It espoused a mythical past *and* it wanted to transform society. Thus Khomeinism was not a continuation of the traditional Islam of the clergy but a reinterpretation to provide an Islamic response to modern political and socio-economic issues. This project was conducted from the early 1960s by Khomeini and other radical clerics, but also by lay Islamists such as Ali Shariati, whose lectures attracted many students and intellectuals critical of the hair-splitting of the traditional clergy. Arguing against traditionalists after the revolution, Ali Akbar Hashemi Rafsanjani—at that time a close collaborator of Khomeini—asked, "Where in Islamic history do you find parliament, president and cabinet ministers? In fact, 80 percent of what we now do has no precedent in Islamic history".[25]

After the revolution the leaders of the Islamic Republic did not have

---

22: Abrahamian, 1993, p17.
23: Saeidi, 2001, p224.
24: Abrahamian, 1993, p2.
25: Quoted in Abrahamian, 1993, p15.

a clear strategy for socio-economic development. Some favoured state intervention, while others argued for laissez-faire economics. The immediate need to save the economy from collapse and then mobilise all resources for the war with Iraq made the state interventionist tendency dominant. This had two sets of goals: wealth redistribution and social programmes to appease the lower classes, and the restoration of capital accumulation to build a modern economy. As a result the economy became dominated by state capitalist monopolies, such as nationalised industries and banks, and the huge conglomerates under the direction of *bonyads* (parastatal foundations).

The state in the Islamic Republic acquired relative autonomy from social classes, just like other populist regimes that are often associated with Bonapartism. This is, as Marx analysed in *The Eighteenth Brumaire of Louis Bonaparte*, a situation where a charismatic leader claims to stand above class divisions and to represent "the people" through the state apparatus and corresponding mass organisations. Because the relative autonomy of a Bonapartist state depends on the power equilibrium between the bourgeoisie and the working class, it is inherently unstable. However, this changes when the state bureaucracy creates its own independent socio-economic base through its control of the means of production and itself becomes a class. As Cliff explained, this is what happened in the Soviet Union from the late 1920s.[26] The Islamic Republic arose from a Bonapartist moment (1979-83) but then expanded the state bureaucracy, giving it control over large parts of the economy, most importantly oil revenues. In doing so, Islamism provided members of the new middle class with upward mobility and enabled them to combine religious devotion and material advance.

Directly after the revolution Islamist members of the new middle class filled 130,000 positions that became vacant after local and foreign managers and technicians left the country.[27] The number of ministries expanded from 20 employing 304,000 civil servants in 1979 to 26 in 1982 employing 850,000.[28] The nationalisation of industry, the creation of various parastatal organisations and the growth of the army expanded the directing layer of the bureaucracy. That is why the state bureaucratic class, or the state bourgeoisie, plays a significant role in Iran. The state affected class formation also in other ways, because of its central role in capital accumulation. A new bourgeoisie—the millionaire mullahs—grew in the interstices between the state sector, the *bonyads* and the bazaar.

26: See Cliff, 1988.
27: Harman, 1994, p44.
28: Abrahamian, 2008, p169.

The historical role of the clergy in these developments and the powerful position they achieved are embodied in a specific form of political rule, which is neither a republican democracy nor a theocratic dictatorship. It is a complex combination of both elements (see figure 1). Khomeini became Supreme Leader in accordance with the doctrine of *velayat-e faqih* enshrined in the constitution. The power of the clergy was also vested in the Assembly of Experts, which elects and supervises the Supreme Leader; the Guardian Council, which approves or rejects candidates for political offices and checks the compatibility of parliamentary legislation with Islamic law; and the Expediency Council, which was created in 1988 to mediate in disputes between the Guardian Council and the parliament. Parallel to these institutions, but in a subordinate power relation, are the republican institutions: the presidency, the parliament and the city councils. Their officials are elected, but first they have to be approved by the Guardian Council. The members of the Assembly of Experts are elected as well.

Analysis in these terms allows us to recognise the strengths and the weaknesses of the Islamic Republic. The Iranian left made a serious mistake in the early 1980s in regarding the Islamic Republic as an archaic, weak system that it could easily overcome or strike deals with. Its ideology, socio-economic strategy and political power made it more resilient than many thought. At the same time it contained from the beginning huge internal contradictions on all three terrains, which created factional power struggles in the elite and eroded its legitimacy and social base in society. This process created opportunities for social movements to organise according to their own interests.

The rise and demise of populism (1983-9)

As soon as the Islamic Republic had consolidated its power by repressing the liberal and socialist opposition, it became divided into left and right factions. The central issue was the orientation of the economy, but religious and cultural themes played a role as well.

The grouping within the regime known as the "Islamist left" was the dominant force in the 1980s. The majority of its members came from the radicalised new middle class but it included populist clerics as well. It had the majority in the parliament and several of its leading members had governmental posts. As the prime minister, Hossein Mousavi was the public face of this faction as it implemented populist economic policies to protect the lower classes against the effects of economic crisis and the war, which had cut per capita national income to half of its pre-revolution level by 1988. He argued, "The way of Islam is to attend to social justice," and "the

Figure 1: Structure of the Islamic Republic

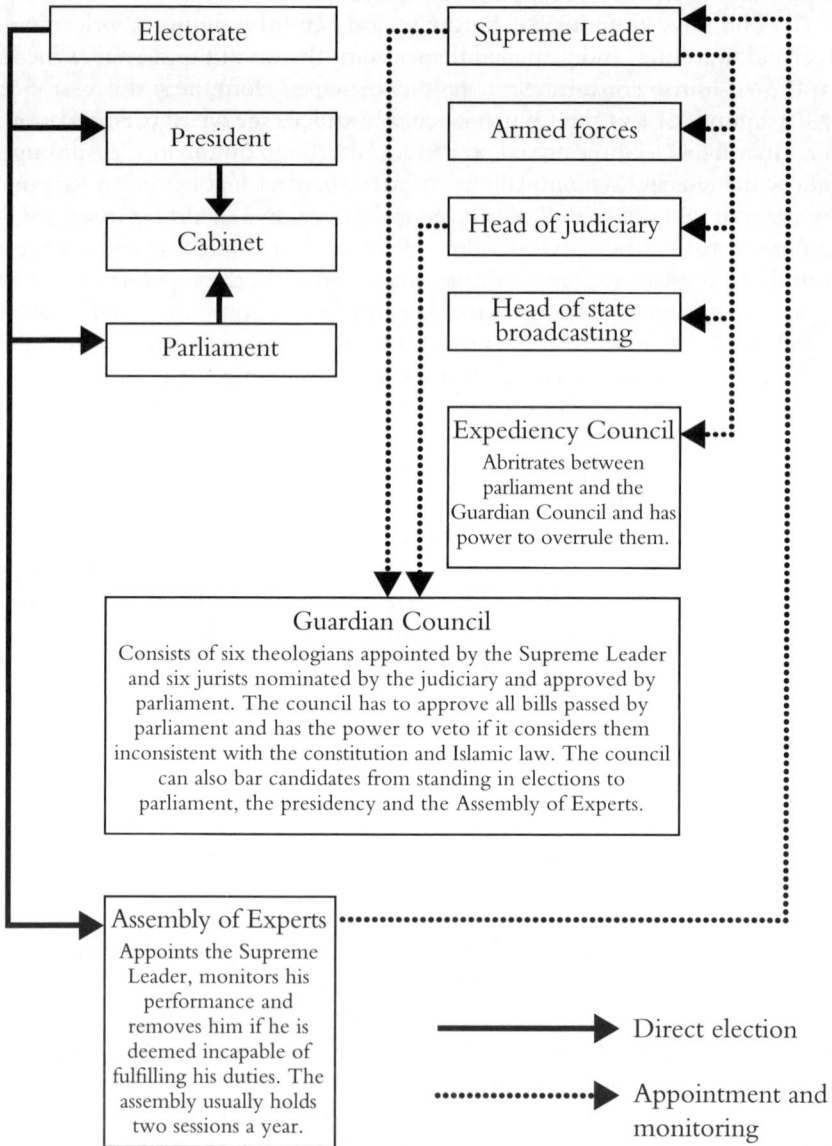

Electorate		Supreme Leader
President		Armed forces
Cabinet		Head of judiciary
Parliament		Head of state broadcasting

Expediency Council
Abritrates between parliament and the Guardian Council and has power to overrule them.

Guardian Council
Consists of six theologians appointed by the Supreme Leader and six jurists nominated by the judiciary and approved by parliament. The council has to approve all bills passed by parliament and has the power to veto if it considers them inconsistent with the constitution and Islamic law. The council can also bar candidates from standing in elections to parliament, the presidency and the Assembly of Experts.

Assembly of Experts
Appoints the Supreme Leader, monitors his performance and removes him if he is deemed incapable of fulfilling his duties. The assembly usually holds two sessions a year.

→ Direct election

······► Appointment and monitoring

security of the revolution lies in the eradication of poverty and serving the destitute... Capital must not rule and the priority of the regime should be the poor and not the well off".[29]

The government subsidised essential products, imposed price controls and rationing, and provided the social programs of the *bonyads*. One in every four Iranians, 12.4 million people, benefited from the social assistance of the Foundation of the Oppressed and Disabled, the Martyrs Foundation, the Imam Relief Committee and the 15 Khordad Foundation.[30] Although Iran remained highly unequal, the relative share of income going to poor and middle income households increased (see table 1). Furthermore, a significant section of the population benefited from state expenditures on education, healthcare, infrastructure and social welfare programmes, as can be seen in the rise of Iran's human development index from 0.559 in 1980 to 0.671 in 1990 (it further increased from 0.735 in 2000 to 0.770 in 2005 (comparable to Turkey's HDI).[31] The percentage of urban households with a refrigerator increased from 36.5 in 1977 to 92.4 in 1989. The percentage of rural households with access to electricity rose from 16.2 to 71.2 in the same period.[32] Moreover, some 220,000 peasant families received 850,000 hectares of land after the revolution. "They, together with the some 660,000 families who had obtained land under the earlier White Revolution, form a substantial rural class that has benefited not only from these new social services but also from state-subsidised cooperatives and protective tariff walls. This class provides the regime with a rural social base".[33]

Table 1: Income distribution[34]

	1977	1986	1991
Gini coefficient	0.515	0.466	0.456
Share of lower 40 percent	11.36%	12.71%	13.43%
Share of middle 40 percent	31.32%	36.51%	36.64%
Share of upper 20 percent	57.32%	50.78%	49.92%

29: Moslem, 2002, p120.
30: Saeidi, 2001, p232.
31: Available from http://hdr.undp.org
32: Salehi-Isfahani, 2009, p20.
33: Abrahamian, 2009.
34: Beheshti, 2003, table 8.1. The Gini coefficient, which lies between zero and one, is a measure of inequality. The lower the coefficient, the more equal the income distribution.

The Islamic Republic also gained the backing of sections of the rural and urban poor by engaging them in mass organisations and campaigns. The *Jahad-e Sazandegi* (Reconstruction Jihad), for instance, sent thousands of young people to rural areas to aid the poor with cheap or free housing. Membership of the Revolutionary Guard and its paramilitary wing, the *Basij*, was for many poor young people a way to attain social status and material benefits.

Populist economic policies were combined with state capitalist methods to industrialise the economy. The government in fact continued the import substitution strategy under the previous Pahlavi administration but called it, in Khomeini's words, *khod kafa'i* (self-sufficiency). This sought to bring foreign trade under its control with import licences, tariffs and regulation of foreign exchange.

Despite some moderate successes in industrialisation, the government's state capitalist strategy faltered as the 1980s progressed. Partly this was because of the burden of the war with Iraq, particularly when oil prices nose-dived from 1986. But it was also because Iran's economy had become secluded from, yet remained dependent on, the world market, which allowed for intermediate and capital imports and the export of oil and gas.[35]

The failure of state capitalism enhanced the position of the Islamist right, which favoured free market politics. Its supporters were mainly among the traditional clerics and the mercantile bourgeoisie of the bazaar. Their political bulwark was the conservative Guardian Council, which "raised objections to 102 out of 370 bills proposed by the first parliament and 118 out of 316 bills passed by the second parliament on the pretext of their being un-Islamic or unconstitutional".[36] Eventually factional struggles paralysed the Islamic Republic Party, forcing Khomeini to dissolve it in May 1987. It also paralysed the Society of Combatant Clergy, with a group of clerics belonging to the Islamist left splitting away to form the Association of the Combatant Clergymen. Among them were future leaders of the reformists, such as Khatami and Karrubi.

Supreme Leader Khomeini had sought to keep both factions balanced. But he often tilted towards the left, declaring before the 1988 parliamentary elections that people should "vote for candidates who work for the barefooted and not those adhering to capitalist Islam". In his Friday prayer speech of 1 January 1988 he gave the government, controlled by the left, a free hand in conducting affairs of state, asserting that

---

35: See Amid and Hadjkhani, 2005.
36: Moslem, 2002, p62.

government is "one of the primary injunctions of Islam and has priority over all other secondary injunctions, even prayers, fasting, and *hajj*".[37] He introduced the concept of *maslehat* (expediency), arguing that all matters should be judged by what is best for the Islamic state. If anyone thought that Khomeinism meant Islamising politics, this should convince them that it meant precisely the opposite.

The timing of Khomeini's renewed populism was no coincidence. It was an attempt to win public support. But at the same time, under the pressure from falling oil revenues and a disgruntled mercantile bourgeoisie, Mousavi's government made some concessions to the pro-market right faction. The Tehran stock exchange reopened in September 1988 and in April 1989 the government announced a privatisation policy.

The enthusiasm among the population for the Islamic Republic was fading fast after a decade of devastating war that had killed 300,000 and wounded 700,000 Iranians.[38] An estimated 1.6 million people had fled their homes along the border with Iraq. The end of the war with Iraq in August 1988 followed by Khomeini's death in July 1989 meant the disappearance of two major factors that had rallied a majority of the population around the Islamic Republic. Ali Khamenei was chosen by the Assembly of Experts as the new Supreme Leader, but he lacked the authority of Khomeini among both the general population and the clergy. Without the centripetal effects of the war and Khomeini's authority, the factional fight intensified.

The regime was also facing problems of ideological legitimacy. After a decade of "Islamification", there was still a huge gap between its official ideology and the variety of social values and attitudes in society at large—a gap that secularisation was to increase in the following decades. The ideological differences among the Islamists themselves were far from resolved and started to lead them in different directions.

The end of the war was a significant turning point, as many committed Islamists who had left their poor families for the army returned to see that there was still a huge gap between the rhetoric of social justice and the reality of the rise of a new class of rich clerics and *bazaaris*. This disillusionment was brilliantly captured by Mohsen Makhmalbaf in his movie *The Marriage of the Blessed* (1989), in which Hadji, a young soldier, returns from war with psychological scars and finds it difficult to adapt to the new situation. In the opening scene the camera catches the revolutionary slogans

37: Moslem, 2002, p74.
38: Hiro, 2005, p233.

on the wall through the logo of a Mercedes. The driver turns out to be his future father in law, a rich cleric. Outraged by the hypocrisy of the religious rich, Hadji stands up at his wedding to "welcome" the guests with these cynical words: "Those who have come with different socks on their feet [because they are poor], be welcome! Also those who have come with different cars, be welcome!"

Over the subsequent decade some of these Islamists, such as the film-maker Makhmalbaf, opted for reforming the system, while others turned towards neoconservatism. The various political projects that were initiated in the years that followed—Rafsanjani's economic liberalisation, Khatami's political reforms and Ahmadinejad's neopopulism—can each be regarded as a response from a section of the ruling class to the crisis of legitimacy faced by the regime.

Economic liberalisation (1989-97)

No one in the ruling class understood better than Rafsanjani, who was elected president in 1989, that the economic precipice facing the Islamic Republic meant it could not be business as usual if it were to survive. His rise to power reflected the emergence of a new political faction, the Islamist modern right ("the pragmatists"), and a new social group of technocrats and nouveau rich. They shared the pro-market politics of the traditional right ("the conservatives") but instead of relying mainly on the bazaar economy they favoured a modern industrial based economy. They also had less rigid socio-cultural attitudes and sought better relations with the West.

Rafsanjani's call for post-war reconstruction had some initial appeal to the population. He replaced *khod kafa'i* (self-sufficiency), the catchword of the 1980s, with *towse'eh* (development) and *islahat* (reforms), which basically meant orienting the economy towards the free market. The reception of the World Bank/IMF mission to Iran in June 1990 symbolised this turn. Rafsanjani's reforms very much followed these institutions' recipe for economic "restructuring": foreign trade liberalisation; decontrolling prices and eliminating subsidies; privatisation; deregulation; foreign borrowing; encouragement of foreign investment; establishment of free trade zones; stimulation of the Tehran stock exchange; and the reorganisation of the banking and financial services.

With these pro-market policies Rafsanjani was reorienting the Islamic Republic towards the bourgeoisie by providing them with new opportunities to make profits. Rafsanjani, his family and relatives certainly did make a fortune themselves. The investigative journalist Klebnikov reported in 2003 how a new group of capitalists emerged after the revolution:

The 1979 revolution transformed the Rafsanjani clan into commercial *pashas*. One brother headed the country's largest copper mine; another took control of the state-owned TV network; a brother in law became governor of Kerman province, while a cousin runs an outfit that dominates Iran's $400 million pistachio export business; a nephew and one of Rafsanjani's sons took key positions in the ministry of oil; another son heads the Tehran Metro construction project (an estimated $700 million spent so far). Today, operating through various foundations and front companies, the family is also believed to control one of Iran's biggest oil engineering companies, a plant assembling Daewoo automobiles, and Iran's best private airline... Rafsanjani's youngest son, Yaser, owns a 30-acre horse farm in the super-fashionable Lavasan neighbourhood of north Tehran, where land goes for over $4 million an acre. Just where did Yaser get his money? A Belgian-educated businessman, he runs a large export-import firm that includes baby food, bottled water and industrial machinery.[39]

This liberalisation benefited the *bazaaris* as well:

Asadollah Asgaroladi exports pistachios, cumin, dried fruit, shrimp and caviar, and imports sugar and home appliances; his fortune is estimated by Iranian bankers to be some $400 million. Asgaroladi had a little help from his older brother, Habibollah, who, as minister of commerce in the 1980s, was in charge of distributing lucrative foreign trade licences.[40]

Rafsanjani offered the middle and working classes an "economic bargain" in return for their political support—consumerism. He allowed the *bazaaris* to flood the Iranian market with import products and justified this by saying, "Why should you forbid yourself things that god made permissible?... God's blessing is for the people and the believers. Asceticism and disuse of holy consumption will create deprivation and a lack of drive to produce, work and develop".[41]

In reality, however, economic liberalisation undermined support among the working class and the urban poor. Rafsanjani's policies raised the consumer price index from 23 in 1993 to 60 in 1994.[42] Foreign debt increased from 7.6 percent of GNP in 1990 to 58.2 percent in 1995, and

---

39: Klebnikov, 2003.
40: Klebnikov, 2003.
41: Moslem, 2002, p144.
42: Nomani and Behdad, 2006, p52.

in 1994 the government had to slash imports compared to their 1991-2 levels. The gap between rich and poor increased, while privatised companies laid off their workers, pushing up the unemployment rate. The poorest sections of society were also hurt by cutbacks in subsidies.

The populist relationship of the 1980s between the state and the lower classes was being dismantled. Even the access of the official trade union, the Workers' House, to the corridors of power was tightened and it became increasingly alienated.[43] The discontent among the lower classes increased, leading to at least seven riots from 1991 to 1995.[44] According to Bayat:

> Riots in Tehran in August 1991 and in Shiraz and Arak in 1992 were carried out by squatters because of demolition of their shelters or forced evictions. Even more dramatic unrest took place in the city of Mashhad in 1992 and Tehran's Islamshahr community in 1995. In Mashhad, the protests were triggered by the municipality's rejection of demands by city squatters to legalise their communities. This massive unrest, on which the army failed to clamp down, left more than a dozen people dead. The three-day riots in Islamshahr, a large informal community in South Tehran, in April 1995 had to do with the post-war economic austerity—notably increases in bus fare and fuel prices—under President Rafsanjani.[45]

Despite Rafsanjani's pro-market policies, Iran did not become "neoliberal", nor did it fully integrate with world capitalism as is sometimes claimed on the left. Despite the intention to reduce the state sector by 8 percent, it grew by 3 percent in the early 1990s.[46] The management of just 48 companies was transferred to shareholders. The whole process was accompanied by corruption and fraud as the enterprises were cheaply sold to people with government connections. Reminiscent of what has happened in other developing countries, privatisation became what Joseph Stiglitz has called "briberisation". The state bureaucratic class maintained its central role in the economy, opening it to the domestic and foreign private sector where its interests required it to do so, and keeping it closed where they didn't. The resurgent bourgeoisie in the private sector resented the privileges of the state-owned enterprises and the businesses of the *bonyads* but at the same time depended on the state for protection from foreign

---

43: See Habidzadeh, 2008.
44: For a detailed account see Mirza'i, 2002, pp69-74.
45: Bayat, 2002, p4.
46: Khajehpour, 2000, p583.

industries and hoped to gain access to oil revenues in the form of subsidised foreign currency and cheap loans. What emerged in Iran was thus, by analogy with David Harvey's conceptualisation of China, "neoliberalism with Iranian characteristics" or, in the words of Kaveh Ehsani, "neoliberal state capitalism".[47] The central role of the state in the economy did not disappear; it was simply oriented away from providing protection to the poor towards promoting capital accumulation.

Rafsanjani's administration created several hundred semi-public enterprises. "The procurement department of a given ministry would function as a company, selling supplies acquired with the ministry's funds to the ministry, for profit. The profits were then distributed among shareholders, who were mostly the same ministry's personnel".[48] Those who controlled this process could make huge profits. The case of the Foundation of the Oppressed and Disabled is illuminating. Its main goal was to assist "deprived sections" of society through charitable activities but it also developed huge economic interests. By a conservative estimate it had 800 subsidiaries and employed 700,000 people, with profits amounting to $430 million between 1990 and 1995. A significant portion of these were used to buy stocks or privatised companies. Some profits also flowed to the Revolutionary Guard and some to *bazaaris*. Corruption was part and parcel of this process. The brother of the director was found guilty in 1995 of embezzling $450 million.

Rafsanjani's economic policies intensified the political faction fight. Supreme Leader Khamenei and the traditional right had initially supported Rafsanjani. The conservative Guardian Council helped him to marginalise the left faction in parliament by rejecting the candidacy of its members for the parliamentary election of 1992. However, they turned away from Rafsanjani in 1994. Some *bazaaris* and their allies in the right faction resented policies that harmed the traditional economy, such as increased taxes and the growth of modern trade centres. More importantly, Khamenei feared that growing discontent among the lower classes and the increasing personal power of Rafsanjani would destabilise the regime and threaten his own position.

Khamenei invested heavily in building a support base among commanders of the Revolutionary Guard. He made connections to a younger generation of Islamists who had played a subordinate role during the revolution but a leading role during the war with Iraq. They formed the core of

---

47: Ehsani, 2009.
48: Karbassian, 2000, p637.

a new faction that emerged a decade later as a political force—the neocon-servatives. Khamenei also started to undermine Rafsanjani's government, using his influence among the conservatives in parliament and the Guardian Council. In addition he sought personal support among the wider popula-tion. The central plank of his strategy was to promise the restoration of "Islamic values" and a fight against the "cultural onslaught" of the West. The moral police intensified their control on the dress code, while satellite dishes that were becoming popular at that time were taken down from the roofs and destroyed.

The attempt to rally the country to conservative values backfired. Society had changed by the mid-1990s, becoming less receptive to the con-servative message. The regime's gender policies had contradictory results. After being pushed away from public life in the early 1980s, women's par-ticipation in the labour market and education started to increase. By 1996 the proportion of women in employment had reached pre-revolutionary levels. Female participation in universities, just 12 percent before the revo-lution, was at 40 percent by 1996. Women managed to progress through their individual perseverance and collective struggles that brought both reli-gious and secular women together around concrete goals.

Society was rapidly urbanising and secularising. By the mid-1980s 61 percent of the population were living in the cities. A survey showed that only 6 percent of the young Iranians who regularly watched television tuned in to religious programmes. Of those reading books only 8 percent were interested in religious literature. Almost 80 percent of the youth held a "neutral" or "negative" attitude towards the clergy and 86 percent were not saying daily prayers.[49] This did not mean that the youth were becoming anti-religious or even less religious. The overwhelming majority were finding ways to combine personal religious beliefs with social practices that ignored the rules of the conservative clergy. Another development was the emergence of the "new religious thinkers" among Islamic intellectuals. Soroush, Kadivar and Shabastari among others argued that Islam should be interpreted according to the time and place, and that it was compat-ible with democracy. The trajectory of their thinking is a testimony to the huge contradictions of Islamism. Ironically, Soroush and other Islamists who spent much time studying Marx, Weber and other political thinkers in order to fight for their influence in the universities became influenced by them. There were also signs of the revival of the students' and workers' movements, to which I will return below.

49: Bayat, 2007, p61.

By the mid-1990s all these changes had created a dynamic, self-conscious and resistant society that increasingly collided against the rigid political system and its conservative values. Near the end of Rafsanjani's second term as president (1993-7) it became clear that his economic liberalisation had not stablised the regime but had instead destabilised the populist class alliance underpinning it.

Euphoria to disillusion: political reforms (1997-2005)

The presidential election of May 1997 marked the beginning of a new phase after the reformist candidate Mohammad Khatami won a landslide victory, receiving 70 percent of the votes. In his inaugural speech of 4 August 1997 he explained his reform programme, which he considered to be a contract "between the president and the nation":

> Protecting the freedom of individuals and the rights of the nation, provision of the necessary conditions for the realisation of the constitutional liberties, strengthening and expanding the institutions of civil society and preventing any violation of personal integrity, rights and legal liberties [are the president's obligation]. The growth of legality will provide a favourable framework for the realisation of social needs and demands... In a society well acquainted with its rights and ruled by law, the rights and limits of the citizens are recognised.[50]

Khatami's message, that politicians ought to respect the people, was well received by the voters, many of whom detested both the growing distance between themselves and the wealthy political elite (represented by Rafsanjani), and the conservative offensive of the previous years. Khatami's message was also attractive for some in the ruling elite who saw political reforms as necessary to regulate the internal faction fight. Thus Khatami's reform project was a response to both pressures from below and the contradictions at the top. Its unifying logic was to manage change inside the Islamic Republic, not to transform it. This is most evident if we look to its central idea, "political development" (towse'e-ye siyasi). This concept was developed in the early 1990s by a think-tank led by Saeed Hajjarian, the strategic brain of the reformists. Hajjarian argued that political development was crucial, "first because it was a precondition for economic development and second, because it could contain the repercussions of economic growth—inequality and social unrest".[51]

50: *Ettela'at*, 5 August 1997.
51: Bayat, 2007, p95.

Khatami's reforms created a relatively more open political space for critical newspapers, books and movies. Students' and women's organisations blossomed and expanded their activities. For the first time since the early 1980s independent labour militants organised meetings and rallies, and produced publications.

Conservatives reacted with rage. They used the support of Supreme Leader Khamenei and their leading positions in the judiciary, the armed forces and the Guardian Council to undermine the government. In April 1998 the head of the Revolutionary Guard told his men in Qom that he had warned "Mr Mohajerani" that "your way [allowing press freedom] is endangering national security," adding, "I am after uprooting anti-revolutionaries everywhere. We must behead some and cut out the tongues of others." Some months later a number of intellectuals and political dissidents were killed. The judiciary closed down the prominent reformist paper *Salaam* and when some 500 students staged a protest in July 1999 there was a violent crackdown by *hezbollahi*. In the following days students organised protests in 22 cities.

The student uprising of July 1999 marked a turning point. Khatami's image as a defender of democratic rights was damaged when he failed to defend the students against the conservatives and, even worse, called the students' slogans "demagogic, provocative, and a danger for the national security".[52] The conservatives realised that allowing political space to the reformists would unleash social movements that neither they nor the reformists could control. It later emerged that 24 commandants of the Revolutionary Guard had warned Khatami that they would take action themselves if he would not stop the "violence" against the system.[53]

After the July 1999 protests the reformist leaders ordered their followers to avoid demonstrations and concentrate on winning the parliamentary elections of 2000 and the presidential elections of 2001. Despite the Guardian Council disapproving 10 percent of the reformist candidates, they won 189 of the 290 seats in parliament and Khatami was elected for a second term as president. The conservatives intensified their counter-attacks, closed down more newspapers and arrested reformist intellectuals. This led to a growing disillusion among intellectuals and activists who had supported Khatami. While a majority of them became apathetic, a minority were radicalising, becoming increasingly attracted to Marxist politics and looking towards struggle from below to provide a

---

52: *Iran Times*, 16 July 1999.
53: Hiro, 2005, p311.

way forward. They were now demanding that Khatami should keep his promises or resign.

The city council elections of 2003 reflected the growing disillusion with the reformists. The overall turnout was low for Iran, 48 percent, and in Tehran only 12 percent of the voters participated. The low turnout enabled the neoconservatives to win a majority on the city council of Tehran and elect Mahmoud Ahmadinejad as the new mayor. It was even easier for the neoconservatives to win the parliamentary elections of 2004, because the Guardian Council barred the candidacies of 2,400 reformists, among them almost all the sitting parliamentarians. The erosion of Khatami's electoral basis continued and enabled Ahmadinejad to win the presidential elections of 2005.

There were two main reasons for the failure of the reformists. The reformist strategist Saeed Hajjarian has hinted at both: "While reformists with seats in the *Majlis* were often thinking of compromise, those outside, the rank and file, were thinking of challenging the system in an extremist way... We should have struck a balance between challenge and compromise which we did not." He added that the reformist electoral coalition represented the interests of the new middle class and asked, "So what is our relationship with the working class?"[54]

The reformists had pursued "compromise" because they feared that the movement from below would escape from their control and challenge the whole system. Khatami made this clear as he was leaving office: "We believed that internal clashes and chaotic conditions were a fatal poison for the country's existence and the Islamic Republic sovereignty." For the same reason Rafsanjani's modern right faction withdrew its public support for Khatami, fearing that political instability would hurt the interests of the bourgeoisie. This claim is supported by a non-Marxist—the close observer of Iran's private sector, the director of Tehran-based Atieh Bahar Financial and Investment Consulting. He commented that domestic and foreign businessmen were relieved with the end of the political crisis after the conservatives won the municipal elections in 2003.[55] Hajjarian recognised in May 2005:

> During Khatami's first term, the private sector was a mainstay of the reformist movement, but that is no longer true. The private sector is more concerned with stability and order than with democratic reform, and some

---

54: *Vagha'ye Etefaghiye*, 22 July 2004.
55: Farhadian, 2004.

elements of it have now formed links with the conservatives… The private sector is now part of the problem facing democracy in Iran.[56]

His point was lost on most progressive intellectuals who were affected by the worldwide anti-Marxist climate that emerged after the fall of "Communism". They turned en masse to the magic power of "civil society", which is, of course, itself a terrain on which class divisions operate in complex ways, through ideologies, institutions and, most importantly, the workings of the capitalist market itself. They swallowed the liberal myth that it is the bourgeoisie that hands down democracy to a thankful people, ignoring the historical role of the working class.[57] As Bayat has pointed out, the "intellectual baggage of reformist thinkers carried simply too much of Habermas and Foucault and not enough of Marx and Gramsci".[58] They were looking in all the wrong places for the agents of democracy.

This suggests the second reason why the reform movement failed: it remained confined to the middle class. However, contrary to Hajjarian's suggestion, it did have a relationship with the working class—one characterised by animosity. Khatami continued Rafsanjani's economic liberalisation by reducing the system of subsidies and social protection and increasing the rate of privatisation. According to the data provided by the Privatisation Organisation that Khatami established, privatisation amounted to over $16 billion from 1991 to 2007. More than 25 percent of this amount was realised during Rafsanjani's presidency, 43.3 percent was realised during Khatami's presidency and 30.7 during Ahmadinejad's first full year of presidency. According to the parliamentary statistical bureau, 50 percent of the rural population and 20 percent of the urban population lived under the Iranian poverty threshold.[59] The 2006 data from the World Bank show that the share of the wealthiest tenth in the national income was 33.7 percent, compared to the 2 percent of the poorest tenth; the wealthiest 20 percent enjoyed about 50 percent of the national income, while the poorest 20 percent received just 5.1 percent.[60] High levels of inequality are a special source of discontent among the lower classes in a country where the political elite tries to legitimise its rule through the discourse of social justice.

56: Khojasteh Rahimi and Sheibani, 2005.
57: For a demolition of this myth see Rueschemeyer and others, 1992.
58: Bayat, 2007, p134.
59: www.baztab.com, 6 February 2005.
60: Data available from www.devdata.worldbank.org

In February 2000 Khatami's government exempted all establishments with five or fewer employees from observing the labour law. Two years later this policy was extended to companies with ten or fewer workers.[61] This affected just under half of all workers employed in small workplaces. The government also took measures to limit the influence of Workers' House, prompting some of its members to set up the Islamic Labour Party. The daily paper of Workers' House published a manifesto against the minister of labour in January 2003, which demanded among other things "the recognition of the legal right of workers to strike", "opposition to globalisation as a new form of exploitation" and "a stop to privatisation".[62] Workers had voted in large numbers for Khatami. One can imagine how disillusioned and frustrated they were after eight years of his government.[63]

The rise of social movements

As we have seen, Khatami's political reforms were partly a response to pressures from below and, in turn, opened up a space in which students, women and workers could create new networks and fight for their own demands. To the outside world the student movement has played the most visible role. In the 1990s students utilised the official student union (*Daftar-e Tahkim-e Vahdat*, the Bureau for Strengthening Unity) to organise activity on campuses. Like other Islamists who had developed reformist ideas, the leading members of this organisation became active supporters of Khatami and some of them moved to the left after they became disillusioned with him. The re-emergence of student activism provided the conditions for the growth of independent and socialist student networks in the universities.

Unfortunately, some of the leftists on campus developed a sectarian attitude towards students who looked towards the reformists. Despite their courageous defiance of the authorities they were as a result unable to develop a broad student movement to defend democratic rights against the conservative onslaught. This sectarian approach led to tactics that made it easier for the authorities to harass and arrest left activists, who were also weakened by various splits. Some student activists started a re-evaluation of this experience which has opened the way for non-sectarian socialist politics in the universities.

The movement that is probably most widespread and active is the

---

61: Malm and Esmailian, 2007, p56.

62: Habibzadeh, 2008, p102-112.

63: A survey found that workers in establishments with fewer than five workers had voted overwhelmingly for Khatami. See Khosravi, 2001, p6.

women's rights movement. The revolution had a profoundly contradictory effect on the position of women in society. Women's rights activists
have tried to use these contradictions to demand reforms. They argue that
it is absurd, for instance, that, while women's judgement is good enough
to elect the president, it is not good enough to be used in court as they
are not allowed to be judges. Secular socialist women's rights activists have
been successful in creating common platforms with Islamic feminists. This
has allowed a broad movement to emerge, which has engaged thousands
of women and won some reforms. For instance, in August 2006 women's
rights activists launched the One Million Signatures Campaign "in support
of changes to discriminatory laws against women", which campaigns to
collect one million signatures by going door to door, holding meetings
and using the internet.

The workers' movement began a slow comeback from the late
1990s. This was in part stimulated by the relative recovery of the
economy. Many workers who had swollen the ranks of the petty bourgeoisie in the 1980s found jobs in the expanding manufacturing and
service sectors. According to Nomani and Behdad, the share of the
working class in the working population rose from 24.6 percent in 1986
to 31.1 percent in 1996. The figures should in fact be higher, as they
exclude those workers in education and healthcare. The working class
became also relatively less fragmented as the share of workers in large
private enterprises (50 or more employees) increased from 35.3 percent
in 1986 to 40.2 percent in 1996. These percentages would be higher still
if they included the public sector, which has the largest establishments.
These trends have since continued.

There were 90 cases of labour protests reported in large industries alone in 1998, including strikes in the Isfahan Steel plant, Behshahr
Textiles, the Hamedan Glass manufacturing plant, and several strikes and
demonstrations by workers in the oil industry at the Abadan Refinery.
One survey recorded 266 strikes from April 1999 to April 2000. About
half them were triggered by non-payment of wages and 10 percent by
layoffs. In 1999, under pressure from the rank and file, Workers' House
was forced to organise a public celebration of May Day. Some workers
seized the opportunity to protest against the plans to reform the labour
law. In 2000 similar protests saw greater participation. Over the following
years the May Day celebration became a symbol of defiance, which was
increasingly organised by workers themselves.

From 2004 a number of high profile strikes gave the emerging
workers' movement a national profile. The first of these occurred in

January 2004 with the massacre of Khatounabad, a small city where con-struction workers were building a copper melting plant. Just before the plant opened all but 250 of them were sacked. Workers, joined by their families, blockaded the building. Then in clashes with security forces who opened fire several workers were killed and 300 were wounded. During the same month there was another important strike by workers in Iran Khodro demanding job security, an end to temporary contracts, and overnight pay for night shifts. The strike was ignited by the death of two workers in their twenties from heart attacks. In May and June 2005 workers went on strike again after a similar incident, then again at the end of 2005 and in March 2006. Since then Iran Khodro has remained an important site of protests.

The best known workers' struggle internationally is that of the Union of Workers of the Tehran and Suburbs Bus Company, which was set up in 2004 as an independent union. Many of its members, including its leader, Ossanlou, have been physically attacked and imprisoned.

With 140 strikes reported in October 2005, followed by 120 in November, it was clear that by the end of Khatami's presidency workers' militancy was becoming a major concern for the government and employers, especially as the protests were becoming politicised. In 2005 *Reuters* reported, "Thousands of banner-wielding Iranian workers rallied in Tehran, marking Labour Day with sharp criticism of the Islamic republic's ambitious privatisation plans. 'Stop privatisation, stop temporary contracts,' workers chanted."

The farce of neopopulism (2005–)

Khatami's political reforms, the intensification of factional fights within the regime, the rise of the social movements and imperialist threats invigorated the neoconservatives, personified in Ahmadinejad. In the 2005 election campaign he revived the populist rhetoric of the 1980s, attacking the rich "oil mafia". His election broadcasts promoted his image as a simple "man of the people" who would keep his promise to put the "oil money on the table of the people".

This, together with high levels of voter abstention, allowed him to defeat Rafsanjani in the second round with 62 percent of the votes. The result represented a "no" against Iran's rich and corrupt elite, and a "yes" for social justice and national independence. The threats from the White House and the presence of American troops on Iran's borders stirred up nationalist sentiments and convinced many voters that Iran needed a president who could defend the country. They remembered that

George Bush had included Iran in the "Axis of Evil" in 2002. The US did Ahmadinejad a great service by denying Iran the right to develop nuclear energy, something that had become a matter of national pride among Iranians of all political convictions. The rise of Ahmadinejad signalled the ascendency of the security personnel. Having made his own political career in part through the Revolutionary Guard, he opened the corridors of power to the military. Of the 21 ministers in his first cabinet nine were members or former members of the Revolutionary Guard or the *Basij*. More than the half of the 30 provincial governors that he appointed came from these organisations.[64]

Once he was in office Ahmadinejad's promise to revive the populist economics of the 1980s did not come anywhere close to being fulfilled. His policies were aimed at a section of the poor in a clientelist way. During his government's first two years an estimated $10 million was handed out in cash by the presidential office[65] at a time when the overall effect of his socio-economic policies hurt the lower classes. Statistics from Iran's central bank show that in the period from March 2005 to March 2007 social expenditures, such as those on education, healthcare, welfare and housing, did not rise at all when corrected for inflation, while oil revenues increased dramatically.[66] Ahmadinejad's financial policies created a housing bubble, making it impossible for the working and middle classes to buy a house, while the rich benefited. The government tried to take off the pressure by providing cheap loans for the retired, young couples, house buyers and agricultural businesses, but these were already heavily indebted. The burden on working class families became almost unbearable when inflation peaked at 29 percent in September 2008. The living costs for an urban family have almost doubled in the past four years, rising faster than wages. The estimated monthly wage for a worker is $223, which is well below the poverty line. Unemployment was officially nearing 13 percent in 2009 but according to one of Ahmadinejad's ministers, Mohammad Abbas, it reached four million, which amounts to 18 percent, and this is probably a conservative estimate.

Nothing proves the hollowness of Ahmadinejad's populism better than the fate of privatisation policy under his government. Ahmadinejad's government privatised more from 2006 to 2007 than Rafsanjani did from 1989 to 1997. Even more revealing is how privatisation has proceeded and

---

64: Ehteshami and Zweiri, 2007.
65: *Asia Times*, 24 August 2007.
66: *Sarmayeh*, 18 August 2009.

who it has benefited. A parliamentary investigation of the Privatisation Organisation concluded that many of its activities "cannot be considered privatisation. After some companies have been passed on, the buyer has fired the workers, changed the zoning and speculated on the land after having sold the assets".[67] Privatised companies have often been bought by government institutions, the *bonyads* or the Revolutionary Guard. One recent example is the "privatisation" of Tehran's International Expo Centre. Just a few weeks after Ahmadinejad's re-election Etemaad-e Melli reported that the Privatisation Organisation had transferred 95 percent of the Expo Centre's lands and assets to the Armed Forces Social Security Organisation, without other buyers being able to make a bid. Another example is the "privatisation" of the National Iranian Copper Industries Company in 2007 for the price of $1.1 billion. In this case the buyers were other state-owned companies, including the pension funds of the state steel and broadcasting companies.

Ahmadinejad tried to camouflage all this by presenting privatisation as promoting "social justice" . His government allocated 40 percent of the assets marked for privatisation to low-income people under the rubric of "justice shares". According to one account, some five million recipients among the poorest tenth of the population were supposed to be organised in 337 cooperatives in order to receive roughly $3 billion of shares of state companies:

> As the Russian experience has shown, however, these cooperatives can easily be formed by the well-connected. Low income people will be all too willing to sell their small shares to individuals (or companies) with the wherewithal to scoop up fortunes in bits and pieces.[68]

Privatisation has been just one channel for profit-making by privileged sections of the bureaucratic state class, including those in the *bonyads* and the Revolutionary Guard.

Ahmadinejad has also secured the capitalist interests of the military apparatus. As *The Economist* reported in 2007, it is:

> No coincidence that in the past two years the Guard's (the *Pasdaran*) commercial interests have prospered. Their engineering arm, known as Ghorb, has been granted juicy slices of big state projects, including the

67: *Sarmayeh*, 18 August 2009.
68: Ehsani, 2006.

building of gas pipelines and a new section of the Tehran metro. Sayeed Laylaz, a former government official and now a private economist in Tehran, says simply that the Guards are "Iran's *nomenklatura*—a new class formed by domination of the economy". Within ten months of Mr Ahmadinejad's election, he reckons the value of civil contracts awarded to the Guards, many of them without going to competitive tender, had trebled from $4 billion to $12 billion.[69]

According to one extensive study, "From laser eye surgery and construction to automobile manufacturing and real estate, the [Revolutionary Guard] has extended its influence into virtually every sector of the Iranian market".[70] The process by which sections of the state bureaucracy developed their own economic interests had already begun in the late 1980s, and accelerated under Rafsanjani and Khatami. The same period witnessed the emergence of a bourgeoisie that operates in a shady space between the state sector, the *bonyads* and the private sector, with some of its members operating purely in the private sector. Competition for control over the economic resources came to a head under Ahmadinejad and fed into existing factional fights.

Lost in translation: the meaning of the election fallout

This situation formed the backdrop against which the presidential elections took place on 12 June 2009. The preceding weeks witnessed the most lively election campaign since the early days of the revolution. One critical factor that raised the political temperature in the final weeks was the live televised debates between the four candidates. Ahmadinejad called the other candidates henchmen of the powerful former president Akbar Hashemi Rafsanjani, who he described as corrupt. Mousavi argued that Ahmadinejad had ruined the economy, created poverty and isolated Iran internationally. He also accused Ahmadinejad of taking the country towards dictatorship. Mousavi promised political freedoms and rights for women and minorities. The damage to the president's image was considerable in these debates, in which he portrayed the state of the economy as healthy, for instance, by downplaying the high rate of inflation which was palpable for many Iranians. This provided Mousavi's campaign with a last-minute push, bringing tens of thousands onto the streets and raising expectations that he could reach the second round.

69: *Economist*, 19 July 2007.
70: Wehrey and others, 2009, p55.

The official election results came as a shock. They gave Ahmadinejad almost 63 percent, way ahead of Mousavi's 34 percent. Post-election analyses have found evidence suggesting the results were manipulated.[71] But some on the left internationally have claimed the election results were free from manipulation. One central piece of evidence is an opinion poll conducted by the American NGO Terror Free Tomorrow just three weeks before the elections. This showed Ahmadinejad leading by a margin of more than two to one.[72] However, this ignores the fact that only 51 percent of respondents made their choice clear (34 percent for Ahmadinejad, 14 percent for Mousavi, 2 percent for Karrubi and 1 percent for Rezai). The remaining 49 percent had either answered, "I don't know," (27 percent) or had refused to give an answer at all (24 percent). More disturbing than the fact that some on the left became obsessed with speculation over vote-rigging was the fact that some simply dismissed the protests that demanded the annulment of the election result and free elections as "imperial destabilisation".[73] The demonstrators were described as "liberal elites on the streets", who opposed Ahmadinejad because he "commands the loyalty of the poor, the working class and the rural voters whose development he has championed". Thus the political crisis was reduced to a question of pro- or anti-imperialism and pro- or anti-neoliberalism.

These arguments totally ignored the social and political realities in Iran. The election fallout reflected real divisions in Iran's ruling class. As argued above, while Ahmadinejad had retained the loyalty of sections of the lower classes, the persistence of poverty, inequality, high unemployment and political repression had reduced his popularity. At the same time, Mousavi was not seen by voters as a hardcore neoliberal. Like the rest of the Islamist left faction he had moved to the right in the 1990s, accepting the role of the free market. However, he was also strongly associated with the egalitarian economics of the 1980s. The reformists' choice of Mousavi as their candidate was a tactical move, as they were aware of their failure to attract the votes of the working and lower classes under Khatami.

The location of Mousavi's first public appearance in the election campaign was carefully chosen. He held a speech in Nazi Abad, a working class district in southern Tehran, where he was greeted with the chant "*Mir Hossein ghareman—hamiye mostazafan*" ("Mir Hossein

71: www.chathamhouse.org.uk/files/14234_iranelection0609.pdf
72: Available from www.terrorfreetomorrow.org
73: Petras, 2009.

hero—supporter of the downtrodden"). He said that "in this chaotic world, the independence of the Islamic Republic is a great achievement" and added that "before the revolution there were foreign military advisers in every sector of our country and Iran was considered a central link in the West's security system in the region". In an attempt to claim part of Iran's success in developing nuclear technology he said this wouldn't have been possible without "independence" and the "holy defence" against the Iraqi invasion, in which he played a central role. Referring to the legacy of Khomeini he argued that true Islam belongs to the poor, adding that "we oppose the wealthy that show off their belongings while society suffers from so many problems... Imam [Khomeini] did not want to disturb the relations between employers and employee, but he didn't want commercialisation either."

Mousavi's promise of a "future without poverty" attracted voters from the working class, but workers were not indifferent to the message that under his presidency they would acquire more democratic rights. They had first hand experience of repression whenever they staged demonstrations and strikes. Many of them also had the experience of collecting their children from police offices because they had violated the "moral rules". So when the protests erupted, they attracted not only the middle class but also many workers who were seeking an outlet for their accumulated frustration and anger. As Robert Fisk reported from the protests, those participating were not just "the trendy, young, sun-glassed ladies of northern Tehran. The poor were here, too, the street workers and middle aged ladies in full chador".[74]

The protests were not about the clash between religious and non-religious people, as many participants in the protests consciously made clear with slogans that exposed the lies that both Ahmadinejad and neoconservatives in the West were spreading. They shouted "*Allaho akbar*" and "With chador and without chador, down with the dictator." Nor was the dividing line between pro- and anti-imperialists. The protests did not demand foreign intervention or the squandering of Iran's independence—still seen as an achievement of the 1979 Revolution and cherished by the overwhelming majority. Another myth is that there was a sharp division between urban and rural areas. It is true that Ahmadinejad and Khamenei have more support in the rural areas but it is also true that almost 70 percent of the population live in urban areas (defined as cities with more than 5,000 inhabitants).

74: Fisk, 2009.

The meaning of the election fallout does not reside in these supposed contradictions. It should be rather interpreted as a qualitative transformation that has made divisions inside Iran's ruling class, which were previously regulated through elections, unmanageable and has turned discontent into mass mobilisation from below.

The post-election crisis also signified the emergence of an alliance between Ahmadinejad, Supreme Leader Khamenei and Revolutionary Guard commanders, who moved to concentrate all political power in their own hands and eliminate the reformists from the centres of power. This has fundamental consequences for the nature of the Islamic Republic, because the permanent tensions that have always existed between the elected and unelected institutions are being resolved by giving the latter absolute power. This was justified by Ahmadinejad's religious mentor, the ultra-conservative ayatollah Mesbah-Yazdi, who said, "When a president is endorsed by the *vali-ye faqih* [Khamenei], obeying the president is like obeying god." This tendency is resisted by Mousavi and other reformists, as well as various ayatollahs, most importantly Montazeri, who have said that only the people can legitimise political power.

What is at stake in Iran is not only the nature of the political system, but also the distribution of power among sections of the ruling class. The political conflict between Rafsanjani and Ahmadinejad has much to do with the economic conflict between an emerging bourgeoisie in the private sector and the monopolies controlled by the state, the *bonyads* and the Revolutionary Guard. This is why Rafsanjani sided with Mousavi during and immediately after the elections. However, his support has vacillated as he fears that protests might grow out of control and destroy any possibility of striking a deal with Khamenei. Rafsanjani's concern is not for democracy but to open up oil revenues and new channels for profit-making to Iran's capitalist class. Mousavi's firm roots in the political establishment—he was prime minister when thousands of socialists were executed in the 1980s—and his commitment to the Islamic Republic and a free market economy also rule him out as an ally of the working class.

However, the election fallout is not simply about the rupture in the ruling class. The clash between different factions of the ruling class has unleashed social forces that none of them control. In the first weeks after the 12 June elections semi-spontaneous protests erupted in Tehran, Isfahan, Shiraz, Tabriz, Mashad, Babol, Rasht, Orumiyeh and other major cities to demand the annulment of the election results. On Monday 15 June more than a million people responded to a call by Moussavi's party for a march, even though it hadn't received permission. In fact, Moussavi only showed up to give a speech after his advisers told him hundreds of thousands had gathered.

In the days that followed, the movement demanded leadership from Moussavi, yet still marched when he discouraged them. They courageously stood firm against state repression, chanting, "Tanks, guns, *Basiji* have no effect any more," and continued into the night with cries of "God is great" from the roofs—reviving the slogans of the 1979 Revolution. Marchers also shouted, "People, why are you silent? Iran has become like Palestine," and, "Don't be afraid. We are all together." More than a million people marched on 18 June in Tehran wearing black to commemorate the deaths of the previous days. On the same day more than 200,000 protested in Shiraz. The size of the demonstrations created a new sense of self-confidence. Some were shouting, "*Akhare hafte, Ahmadi rafteh*" ("By the end of the week, Ahmadinejad will be gone"). Older people said that the atmosphere felt like the days of the revolution.

From 19 June the climate changed. Ayatollah Khamenei endorsed Ahmadinejad during Friday prayers and announced that the authorities would no longer tolerate demonstrations. That was the green light for the Revolutionary Guard to crack down violently on the protests. In the following days thousands of young people defied the *Basij* and the security forces. Dozens were killed and more than 2,000 were arrested, some of whom endured rape and violence. To further intimidate the protest movement the authorities organised show trials against about 100 reformist intellectuals, journalists and politicians who were considered to be the leaders of the protest movement. Despite all of this, protests have continued, although on a smaller scale.

The causes of the mass discontent have not disappeared and the consequences of the post–election crisis will continue to destabilise the government. If it chooses to continue the clampdown, it risks deepening the crisis of legitimacy. Many more people will draw the conclusion that they cannot change their fate through elections and will radicalise. The nature of the political system has been exposed dramatically. At the same time, socio-economic conditions are worsening. Two months before the election the government boosted the salaries of some public sector workers and retirees. Just a month later these workers were shocked to discover that their pay checks indicated their wages had dropped back to the same level as before the elections.[75]

75: *Sarmayeh*, 30 July 2009.

There is no doubt that all sorts of political forces will try to push the movement in a direction that benefits their own class interests. Western powers will also try to take advantage of the political crisis in Iran to push through their own interests in the region. Barak Obama has not withdrawn the "democracy" promotion programme that the US began under George Bush. The current bourgeois and middle class leaders of the protests—Mousavi and Rafsanjani—will try to use the movement as leverage to strengthen their own positions against other factions.

The pro-democracy struggle can only move forward if the working class movement begins to challenge the capitalist logic of the Islamic Republic. This does not mean, however, that revolutionary Marxists should abstain from the current protests until a pure working class movement appears. As Marx and Engels wrote in the *Communist Manifesto*, "Communists everywhere support every revolutionary movement against the existing social and political order of things. In all these movements, they bring to the front, as the leading question in each, the property question, no matter what its degree of development at the time." In other words, the working class needs to win hegemony by playing a leading role in the struggle for democracy and taking the movement in an anti-capitalist direction. This is, in a nutshell, the strategy of permanent revolution that can arm a new generation of socialists in Iran to build a revolutionary movement.

References

Abrahamian, Ervand, 1982, *Iran between two Revolutions* (Princeton University).

Abrahamian, Ervand, 1993, *Khomeinism: Essays on the Islamic Republic* (University of California).

Abrahamian, Ervand, 2008, *A History of Modern Iran* (Cambridge University).

Abrahamian, Ervand, 2009, "Why the Islamic Republic Has Survived", *Middle East Report 250*, www.merip.org/mer/mer250/abrahamian.html

Afary, Janet, 1996, *The Iranian Constitutional Revolution 1906-1911: Grassroots Democracy, Social Democracy and the Roots of Feminism* (Columbia University).

Amid, Javad, and Amjad Hadjkhani, 2005, *Trade, Industrialisation and the Firm in Iran: The Impact of Government Policies on Business* (IB Taurus).

Bayat, Asef, 1987, *Workers and Revolution* (Zed Books).

Bayat, Asef, 1997, *Street Politics: Poor People's Movements in Iran* (The American University in Cairo).

Bayat, Asef, 2002, "Activism and Social Development in the Middle East", *International Journal of Middle East Studies 34*, www.merip.org/mer/mer226/226_bayat.html

Bayat, Asef, 2007, *Making Islam Democratic: Social Movements and the Post-Islamic Turn* (Stanford University).

Behdad, Sohrab, 2000, "From Populism to Liberalism: The Iranian Predicament", in Parvin Alizadeh (ed), *The Economy of Iran: Dilemma's of an Islamic state* (IB Taurus).

Beheshti, Mohammad B, 2003, "Iran's Economic Development and Structural Change in Human Resources", in Ali Mohammadi (ed), *Iran Encountering Globalisation: Problems and Prospects* (Routledge Curzon).

Behrooz, Maziar, 2000, *Rebels with a Cause: The Failure of the Left in Iran* (IB Taurus).

Cliff, Tony, 1963, "Deflected Permanent Revolution", *International Socialism 12* (first series), www.marxists.org/archive/cliff/works/1963/xx/permrev.htm

Cliff, Tony, 1988, *State Capitalism in Russia* (Bookmarks), www.marxists.org/archive/cliff/works/1955/statecap/

Colás, Alejandro, 2004, "The Re-Invention of Populism: Islamist Responses to Capitalist Development in the Contemporary Maghreb", *Historical Materialism*, volume 12, number 4.

Ehsani, Kaveh, 2006, "Iran: The Populist Threat to Democracy", *Middle East Report 241*, www.merip.org/mer/mer241/ehsani.html

Ehsani, Kaveh, 2009, "Survival Through Dispossession: Privatisation of Public Goods in the Islamic Republic", *Middle East Report 250*, www.merip.org/mer/mer250/ehsani.html

Ehteshami, Anoush, and Mahjoob Zweiri, 2007, *Iran and the Rise of its Neoconservatives: The Politics of Iran's Silent Revolution* (IB Taurus).

Farhadian, Mahdy, 2004, "Beyond Khatami's Reform Era: Economic Talibanisation or Liberalisation?", *Iran Analysis Quarterly*, volume 1, number 3.

Fisk, Robert, 2009, "Iran's Day Of Destiny", *Independent*, 16 June 2009, www.independent.co.uk/opinion/commentators/fisk/robert-fisk-irans-day-of-destiny-1706010.html

Habibzadeh, Afshin, 2008, *Mosharekat-e Siyasi Tabagheh Kargar* (Kavir).

Harman, Chris, 1994, "The Prophet and the Proletariat", *International Socialism 64*, http:// pubs.socialistreviewindex.org.uk/isj64/harman.htm

Hiro, Dilip, 2005, *Iran Today* (Politicos).

Karbassian, Akbar, 2000, "Islamic Revolution and the Management of the Iranian Economy", *Social Research*, volume 67, number 2, http://findarticles.com/p/articles/mi_m2267/is_2_67/ai_63787346/

Keshavarzian, Arang, 2007, *Bazaar and State in Iran: The Politics of the Tehran Marketplace* (Cambridge University).

Keshavarzian, Arang, 2009, "Regime Loyalty and Bazari Representation under the Islamic Republic of Iran: Dilemmas of the Society of Islamic Coalition", *International Journal of Middle East Studies 41*.

Khajehpour, Bijan, 2000, "Domestic Political Reforms and Private Sector Activity in Iran", *Social Research*, volume 67, number 2, www.iranchamber.com/government/articles/political_reform_private_sector_iran.php

Khojasteh Rahimi and Sheibani, 2005, "Gerdhamai Roshanfekran Bara-ye Democracy", *Shargh*, 18 May 2005.

Khosravi, Khosro, 2001, "Jame'e Shenasiye Entekhabate Iran", *Andishe Jame-e*, numbers 17 and 18.

Kinzer, Stephen, 2003, *All the Shah's Men: An American Coup and the Roots of Middle East Terror* (Wiley).

Klebnikov, Paul, 2003, "Millionaire Mullahs", *Forbes* (July 2003), www.forbes.com/forbes/2003/0721/056_print.html

Knei-Paz, Baruch, 1977, "Trotsky, Marxism and the Revolution of Backwardness", in Shlomo Avineri (ed), *Varieties of Marxism* (Jerusalem Van Leer Foundation).

Lenin, Vladimir Ilyich, 1966, *Left-Wing Communism: an Infantile Disorder*, in *Collected Works*, volume 31 (Progress), www.marxists.org/archive/lenin/works/1920/lwc/

Malm, Andreas, and Shora Esmailian, 2007, *Iran on the Brink: Rising Workers and Threats of War* (Pluto).

Marshall, Phil, 1988, *Revolution and Counter-Revolution in Iran* (Bookmarks).

Matin, Kamran, 2006, "Uneven and Combined Development and 'Revolution of Backwardness': the Iranian Constitutional Revolution, 1906-1911", in Bill Dunn and Hugo Radice (eds), *100 Years of Permanent Revolution: Results and Prospects* (Pluto).

Mirza'i, Morteza Mohammad, 2002, *Tragedi-ye Shoraha* (Rowzaneh).

Moaddel, Mansoor, 1993, *Class, Politics and Ideology in the Iranian Revolution* (Columbia University).

Moghaddam, Val, 1989, "One Revolution or Two? The Iranian Revolution and the Islamic Republic", *Socialist Register 25*, http://socialistregister.com/index.php/srv/article/view/5560/2458

Moslem, Mehdi, 2002, *Factional Politics in Post-Khomeini Iran* (Syracuse University).

Nomani, Farhad, and Sohrab Behdad, 2006, *Class and Labour in Iran: Did the Revolution Matter?* (Syracuse University).

Parsa, Misagh, 1989, *Social Origins of the Iranian Revolution* (Rutgers University).

Petras, James, 2009, "Iranian Elections: the 'Stolen Elections' Hoax", 18 July 2009, http://petras.lahaine.org/articulo.php?p=1781&more=1&c=1

Poya, Maryam, 1987, "Iran 1979: Long Live Revolution!... Long live Islam?", in Colin Barker (ed), *Revolutionary Rehearsals* (Bookmarks).

Razi, Maziar, 2009, "Why Revolutionary Marxists Should not Support Islamic Fundamentalists", www.pishtaaz.com/english/fundamentalism2.htm

Rueschemeyer, Dietrich, Evelyne Huber Stephens and John D Stephens, 1992, *Capitalist Development and Democracy* (Polity).

Saeidi, Ali, 2001, "Charismatic Political Authority and Populist Economics in Post-Revolutionary Iran", *Third World Quarterly*, volume 22, number 2.

Salehi-Isfahani, Djavad, 2009, "Oil Wealth and Economic Growth in Iran", in Ali Gheissari (ed), *Contemporary Iran: Economy, Society and Politics* (Oxford University).

Saleth, Torab, 2007, "Class Nature of the Iranian Regime", *Critique*, volume 35, number 3, www.informaworld.com/openurl?genre=article&issn=0301%2d7605&volume=35&issue =3&spage=435

Saleth, Torab, 2009, "On the 30th Anniversary of the Iranian revolution", available at www.critiquejournal.net/torab-iranrev.html

Trotsky, Leon, 1977 [1930], *The History of the Russian Revolution* (Pluto), www.marxists.org/ archive/trotsky/works/1930-hrr/

Wehrey, Frederic and others, 2009, *The Rise of the Pasdaran: Assessing the Domestic Roles of Iran's Islamic Revolutionary Guards Corps* (Rand).

On party democracy

John Molyneux

It really needs to be said that the first things to be forgotten are just the first points, the most elementary things… The first point is that there do in fact exist rulers and ruled, leaders and led… In the formation of leaders the premise is fundamental: does one wish there always to be rulers and ruled, or does one wish to create the conditions where the necessity for the existence of this division disappears?… Nevertheless, it needs to be understood that the division of rulers and ruled, though in the last analysis it goes back to divisions between social groups, does in fact exist, given things as they are, even inside the bosom of each separate group, even a socially homogeneous one…and it is mainly on this question that the most serious "errors" come about… It is believed that when the principle of the group is laid down obedience ought to be automatic…or even that it is beyond discussion… So it is difficult to rid the leaders of dictatorial habits, that is, the conviction that something will be done because the leader thinks it is correct and rational that it should be done: if it is not done, the "blame" is put on those who "ought to have" etc.[1]

This article examines the much disputed issue of internal party democracy in the light of the Marxist tradition and past and recent experience. It considers the challenge offered to the Marxist theory of the party by the German sociologist Robert Michels, in the belief that facing and attempting to answer this challenge yields insights into the real nature of the problem. On this basis it seeks to reformulate the issue of party

---

1: Gramsci, 1970, pp143-144.

democracy in a way different from that in which it is usually posed on the left, namely as a goal continuously to be striven for rather than a norm simply to be observed.

The tradition

When, in 1847, Karl Marx and Frederick Engels joined the League of the Just, an international secret society composed mainly of German artisans, which duly became the Communist League and for which they composed the *Communist Manifesto*, it was on condition that, among other things, "the organisation itself was thoroughly democratic, with elective and removable authorities".[2]

This condition was central to the new worldview and political practice that they had persuaded the League to adopt, namely the doctrine of class struggle outlined in the Manifesto, in which the transformation of society—the revolution—was to be accomplished by the working class itself. Prior to Marx and Engels, and prior to the emergence of the modern working class, the dominant form of revolutionary organisation was the secret club or conspiracy—a model inherited from the French Revolution of 1789—which envisaged the transformation of society from above following a coup d'etat by a dedicated and enlightened few. Marx and Engels considered party democracy a crucial means for combating this, essentially bourgeois, concept of revolution. "This alone [a democratic party structure] barred all hankering after conspiracy, which requires dictatorship".[3]

The commitment to party democracy was inscribed in our tradition from its inception and has been reinscribed many times since.

"Unity of action, freedom of discussion and criticism. Only such discipline is worthy of the democratic party of the advanced class…the proletariat does not recognise unity of action without freedom to discuss and criticise," wrote Lenin.[4] Leon Trotsky wrote of the Bolshevik Party:

> The party took watchful care not only that its boundaries should always be strictly defined, but also that all those who entered these boundaries should enjoy the actual right to define the direction of the party policy. Freedom of criticism and intellectual struggle was an irrevocable content of the party democracy. The present doctrine that Bolshevism does not tolerate factions is a myth of the epoch of decline. In reality the history of Bolshevism is

---

2:   Engels, 1970, p195.
3:   Engels, 1970, p196.
4:   Lenin, 1965a, pp230-231.

a history of the struggle of factions. And, indeed, how could a genuinely revolutionary organisation, setting itself the task of overthrowing the world and uniting under its banner the most audacious iconoclasts, fighters and insurgents, live and develop without intellectual conflicts, without groupings and temporary factional formations?[5]

Similarly, Duncan Hallas in 1971:

[A revolutionary socialist party] cannot possibly be created except on a thoroughly democratic basis; unless, in its internal life, vigorous controversy is the rule and various tendencies and shades of opinion are represented, a socialist party cannot rise above the level of a sect. Internal democracy is not an optional extra. It is fundamental to the relationship between party members and those amongst whom they work.[6]

It should be added that this is not just a question for Marxist revolutionary parties. The overwhelming majority of working class organisations—trade unions, parties, campaigns, cooperatives, tenants associations, etc—are at least established with democratic constitutions and aspirations. The working class is the socialist class because, among other things, it is the democratic class. The economic role and position of the working class, making and operating the decisive means of production, producing the bulk of its wealth, concentrated in large workplaces and towns and integrated into a global division of labour, gives it (a) the power to defeat the capitalist class; (b) the ability to inaugurate the transition to a fully classless society because it can be both the producing and the ruling class at the same time. In other words, it can create structures (the Paris Commune, soviets, factory councils, etc) that enable it to control production and govern society democratically.

The experience
And yet... And yet everyone who knows something of the history of the socialist movement and anyone who has had any experience of it over the last 30 or 40 years knows that the question of inner party democracy has been an ever-recurring issue.

The Stalinist parties provide the most obvious example. In the Communist Party of the Soviet Union every shred and semblance of democracy was extinguished by Stalinist counter-revolution. Communist

---

5:   Trotsky, 1936, chapter five.
6:   Hallas, 1971.

parties in Eastern Europe, China, North Korea, Vietnam, etc more or less followed suit, and if the Communist parties of Western Europe had a less draconian character, not having a secret police to hand, they nevertheless were not remotely democratic.

However, for us now, the undemocratic nature of the Stalinist parties poses the least theoretical problems. It is clear that in the Stalinist states the Communist parties had become instruments of rule, not of the working class, but of new bureaucratic ruling classes and therefore had to be undemocratic in the extreme. This was the only way of overcoming the contradiction between their actual function and their declared aims.[7]

Something similar applies to the traditional social democratic parties with their dual character as bourgeois workers' parties (as Lenin put it)—ie as parties with working class membership, and bourgeois leadership and policy. In these cases their mass working class bases obliged these parties to retain some elements of democracy (conferences with some real debate, elected leaders, etc) but also to develop mechanisms capable of preventing the worker majority from asserting itself. In the case of old Labour (New Labour became even less democratic) the two most important of these mechanisms were the block vote in the hands of the trade union bureaucrats and the ability of the parliamentary leadership to ignore decisions of party conference.[8]

More theoretically challenging is the recurrence of the democracy issue in avowedly non-Stalinist, non social democratic or libertarian organisations. Let us take a few examples drawn from throughout the history of the socialist movement. First there was the conflict between Marx and the anarchist Mikhail Bakunin in the First International. Bakunin denounced Marx's authoritarianism and called him a "dictator over the proletariat". Marx replied by accusing Bakunin of operating a secret society inside the International (the International Brotherhood, also known as the International Alliance of Socialist Democracy) in which there was no democracy of any kind but rather an unelected "collective and invisible dictatorship" of Bakunin.[9] During debates over the split between the Bolsheviks and the Mensheviks in 1903 Trotsky attacked Lenin, saying, "In the internal politics of the party these methods lead…to the party organisation 'substituting' itself for the party, then the central committee substituting itself for the

---

7: Clearly I am here taking for granted the analysis of the Stalinist states and the Comintern by Trotskyists and, later, Tony Cliff in his theory of state capitalism.

8: The best analysis of how such parties work is provided by Cliff and Gluckstein, 1988.

9: See Molyneux, 1978, p28.

party organisation; and finally the dictator substituting himself for the central committee".[10] At the same time Rosa Luxemburg upbraided Lenin for his "overanxious desire to establish the guardianship of an omniscient omnipotent central committee".[11]

The international Trotskyist movement in the 1930s was plagued with complaints, disputes and splits over real or alleged violations of inner party democracy, and Trotsky was frequently led wearily to lament petty bourgeois elements who wanted to debate and discuss forever. In the most important of these splits, that in the American Socialist Workers Party in 1939-40, the question of the "party regime" presided over by James P Cannon played a considerable role.[12]

After the Second World War the pattern on the Trotskyist left remained broadly the same. In virtually every faction fight or split, and they were far too numerous to document here, the issue of inner party democracy would raise its none too beautiful head. At one end of this particular spectrum lay the Socialist Labour League/Workers Revolutionary Party, which, from reasonably promising beginnings around 1956, degenerated into the ever more erratic personal dictatorship of its "philosopher" thug leader Gerry Healy. Healy deployed a combination of an idealist version of the dialectic and highly materialist fists to terrorise intellectuals and worker militants alike until it all fell apart in 1986, amid accusations of the systematic sexual abuse of female comrades. At the other end was the "ultra-democratic" International Marxist Group (IMG), British section on the Unified Secretariat of the Fourth International, and followers of Ernest Mandel. The IMG went so far in the opposite direction that by the 1970s there were institutionalised permanent factions (at least three at any one time), none of which had a working majority. At this point ultra-democracy seems to have turned into its opposite in that the majority of the members were unable to assert any kind of stable strategy or line.

Between these extremes lay a multitude of small Trotskyist or semi-Trotskyist groups with a wide variety of organisational practices and internal regimes. However, the general isolation of such groups from the mass of the working class meant that the tendency to become a sect, dominated in practice by a few individuals, was pretty strong.

10: Trotsky, 1979, p77.

11: Luxemburg, cited in Molyneux, 1978, pp98-99.

12: For Trotsky's side of this dispute see Trotsky, 1975. For Cannon's see Cannon, 2001. Commentators from this journal's tradition have tended to side with Trotsky and Cannon, but to have some sympathy with the opposition on the "regime" question—see Cliff, 1993; Bambery, 1987.

The most promising development in these years (in my opinion, of course) in terms of its politics, growth and democratic openness was the International Socialists (IS), which later became the Socialist Workers Party (SWP), in Britain. I had joined the Socialist Labour League Young Socialists in January 1968, only to leave shortly thereafter, repelled by its terrifying authoritarianism. I joined the IS in about June of that year and at my first conference found the organisation divided into at least *five* (!) short-lived tendencies or factions. Despite some serious splits in the leadership in 1975-6 and 1979 (basically over coming to terms with the downturn in industrial struggle) the overall tendency was for the central committee steadily to increase its hegemony within the organisation. But there were always concerns being raised, rightly or wrongly, about the issue of internal democracy—at one point there was actually a Faction for Revolutionary Democracy (known as FRED).

The purpose of this brief and superficial survey is not to engage in retrospective "democratic" judgment (for Marx against Bakunin, with Lenin against Trotsky and Luxemburg, or 0/10 for Healy, 6/10 for Mandel, or whatever) but simply to demonstrate that the problem of inner party democracy is a recurring one and it is therefore necessary to consider its social basis.

The problem

For Marxists, as historical materialists, this ought to be the obvious starting point but this aspect of the problem has received relatively little attention. On the one hand, it has frequently been asserted that the leadership of small revolutionary group X do not constitute a materially privileged bureaucratic stratum—in the sense that the trade union and Labour leaders, or the Communist Party leaders in Stalinist states, clearly do—and that therefore it is unmaterialist to think there can be a serious problem over democracy in such a group. On the other hand, Trotsky provided a sociological explanation as to why "petty bourgeois elements" would be prone to make unreasonable demands for excessive democracy:

A worker spends his day at the factory. He has comparatively few hours left for the party. At the meetings he is interested in learning the most important things: the correct evaluation of the situation and the political conclusions. He values those leaders who do this in the clearest and the most precise form and who keep in step with events. Petty bourgeois, and especially declassed elements, divorced from the proletariat, vegetate in an artificial and shut-in environment. They have ample time to dabble in politics or its substitute.

They pick out faults, exchange all sorts of tidbits and gossip concerning happenings among the party "tops". They always locate a leader who initiates them into all the "secrets". Discussion is their native element. No amount of democracy is ever enough for them.[13]

In contrast Duncan Hallas provided an illuminating account of how the degeneration of inner party democracy can result from a false perspective. He showed how the aforementioned Socialist Labour League ruined itself through its continued adherence to a perspective of imminent economic catastrophe (drawn directly from Trotsky's 1938 writings) throughout the prolonged boom of the 1950s and 1960s:

Discussion, which is dangerous to the leadership, can be checked by hyperactivity; and this, in turn, is justified by the nearness of crash. The membership, driven at a frenzied pace, has a high casualty rate. A large proportion is always new—and therefore does not remember the non-fulfilment of past prophecies. A vicious circle is set up which makes the correction of the line more and more difficult. "Building the leadership"—which is, of course, identified with the organisation—becomes a substitute for serious political and industrial work. Serious militants are repelled and the "revolutionary youth" come to make up an ever-larger proportion of the activists. The leadership, which alone has much continuity, becomes unchallengeable and finds it less and less necessary to check its policies and practice.[14]

The tendency that manifested itself in grotesque form in the case described by Hallas could also manifest itself in more moderate forms in much saner organisations. The argument, however, can be reversed and used to defend complacency. Since the perspective is "correct" it can be said that there is no need to worry about democracy. If the function of party democracy is to achieve a correct perspective, the claimed existence of a correct perspective could either render democracy superfluous or constitute proof of its good health.

But this line of argument is flawed. The causal relation may flow, not from false perspective to lack of democracy, but from lack of democracy to false perspective. Also it is mistaken to base the case for party democracy solely on its providing the necessary inputs and checks to control the perspective. Democracy is also necessary to educate and train the members to

---

13: Trotsky, 1975.
14: Hallas, 1969.

argue for socialism in the class[15] and to retain "ownership" of the party by its members and, ultimately, the working class.

The challenge from Michels
A different but interesting light is thrown on this whole question by Robert Michels in his book *Political Parties*, first published in 1911. Michels was a pupil of Max Weber and a member of German Social Democracy prior to the First World War who, after the war, became a supporter of fascism. In *Political Parties* Michels propounded his so-called "iron law of oligarchy" according to which any large-scale political party or organisation will inevitably be ruled by a small self-perpetuating elite at its centre: "It is organisation that leads to the domination of the elected over the electors... Who says organisation says oligarchy".[16]

Hallas comments:

> The equation "centralised organisation equals bureaucracy equals degeneration"...leads to profoundly reactionary conclusions. For what is really being implied is that working people are incapable of collective democratic control of their own organisations. [This] is to argue that socialism is impossible because democracy, in the literal sense, is impossible. This is precisely the conclusion that was drawn by the "neo-Machiavellian" social theorists of the early 20th century [eg Michels] and which is deeply embedded in modern academic sociology.[17]

Hallas is absolutely right (and in becoming a fascist Michels was, in a sense, following his own logic) but pointing out the reactionary conclusions of an argument is not the same as refuting it, and the fact is that Michels makes a powerful case, based precisely on his knowledge of the socialist movement, particularly in Germany.

Michels argues that there exists a "mechanical and technical impossibility of direct government by the masses" and observes:

15: This point was powerfully made by Isaac Deutscher: "When the European Communist went out to argue his case before a working class audience, he usually met there a social democratic opponent whose arguments he had to refute... Most frequently he was unable to do this, because he lacked the habits of political debate, which were not cultivated within the party, and because his schooling deprived him of the ability to preach to the unconverted"—cited in Hallas, 1971, p21.

16: Michels, 1968, p15.

17: Hallas, 1971.

It is easier to dominate a large crowd than a small audience...enormous public meetings commonly carry resolutions by acclamation or by general assent, whilst these same assemblies, if divided into small sections, say, of 50 persons each, would be much more guarded in their assent... The impotence of direct democracy, like the power of indirect democracy, is a direct outcome of the influence of number...in the great industrial centres where the labour party sometimes numbers its adherents by tens of thousands, it is impossible to carry on the affairs of this gigantic body without a system of representation. The great socialist organisation of Berlin...has a member roll of more than 90,000.[18]

He then describes the tendency of the representatives to establish their independence from and hegemony over the represented. He notes "the establishment of a customary right to the office of delegate" and the need for leadership felt by the masses including "the cult of veneration among the masses".[19] Michels cites especially Ferdinand Lassalle, but also Giuseppe Garibaldi, Jules Guesde and Marx; today, of course the list could be much longer and more grotesque.

Michels notes the general cultural and educational superiority of the professional leaders over the rank and file, and he comments, "No one who studies the history of the socialist movement in Germany can fail to be greatly struck by the stability of the group of persons leading the party".[20]

Moreover, he argues, the leaders actively strive to maintain their position:

As the chiefs become detached from the mass they show themselves more and more inclined, when gaps in their own ranks appear, to effect this not by popular election, but by co-optation, and also to increase their own effectiveness wherever possible by creating new posts upon their own initiative. There arises in leaders a tendency to isolate themselves, to form a sort of cartel, and to surround themselves, as it were, with a wall, within which they will admit those only who are of their own way of thinking.[21]

Michels analyses the role of "bourgeois elements in the socialist leadership" and "labour leaders of proletarian origin",[22] while noting the "psychological metamorphosis of the leaders":

18:   Michels, 1968, pp63-65.
19:   Michels, 1968, pp81, 93.
20:   Michels, 1968, pp107, 117.
21:   Michels, 1968, p126.
22:   Michels, 1968, pp238, 277.

The average leader of the working class parties is morally not lower, but on the whole higher, in quality than the average leaders of the other parties... Yet it cannot be denied that the permanent exercise of leadership exerts upon the moral character of the leaders an influence which is essentially pernicious.[23]

Michels also explains why neither syndicalism nor anarchism, for all their rhetoric, are able to overcome these oligarchic tendencies, citing, among others, the familiar example of Bakunin and his secret unelected dictatorship inside the First International.[24] However, underpinning all Michels' observations, acute as many of them are, and running like a thread throughout *Political Parties* is what he calls "the formal and real incompetence of the mass".[25] The "iron law of oligarchy" is, for him, an iron law because the masses are inherently incapable of running their own organisations or democratically controlling their leaders:

The incompetence of the masses is almost universal throughout the domains of political life, and this constitutes the most solid foundation of the power of leaders. The incompetence furnishes the leaders with a practical and to some extent a moral justification.[26]

And we should be clear, for Michels this incompetence is innate and general, as is the drive of leaders to dominate. It is a question of human nature. Almost certainly, we see here the influence of Friedrich Nietzsche's "will to power":

The apathy of the masses and their need for guidance has as its counterpart in the leaders a natural greed for power. Thus the development of the democratic oligarchy is accelerated by the general characteristics of human nature... The desire to dominate for good or evil, is universal...every human power seeks to enlarge its prerogatives.[27]

The Marxist response
This, of course, is where a Marxist response to, and critique of, Michels must begin. The various facts, tendencies and patterns of behaviour

---

23: Michels, 1968, p205.
24: Michels, 1968, p327.
25: Michels, 1968, p107.
26: Michels, 1968, p111.
27: Michels, 1968, pp205-206.

observed by Michels are not universal or general characteristics of human nature but products of class society in general and capitalist society in particular. And it is precisely on this point that the Bolshevik Nikolai Bukharin took issue with him:

> What constitutes an eternal category in Michels' presentation, namely, the "incompetence of the masses", will disappear, for this incompetence is by no means a necessary attribute of every system; it likewise is a product of the economic and technical conditions, expressing themselves in the general cultural being and in the educational conditions. We may state that in the society of the future there will be a colossal overproduction of organisers, which will nullify the stability of the ruling groups.[28]

But here Bukharin is treating Michels' book, which he describes as "very interesting", primarily as an objection to the possibility of a future classless society. However, in relation to the *transition* to full socialism Bukharin accepts that Michels points to real problems, though he remains confident they can be overcome.

But the question of the transition period from capitalism to socialism, ie the period of the proletarian dictatorship, is far more difficult. The working class achieves victory, although it is not and cannot be a unified mass. It attains victory while the productive forces are going down and the great masses are materially insecure. There will inevitably result a tendency to "degeneration", ie the excretion of a leading stratum in the form of a class-germ. This tendency will be retarded by two opposing tendencies: first, by the growth of the productive forces; second, by the abolition of the educational monopoly. The increasing production of technologists and of organisers in general, out of the working class itself, will undermine this possible new class alignment. The outcome of the struggle will depend on which tendencies turn out to be the stronger.[29]

Clearly, writing in 1921, the question of the transition to socialism was uppermost in Bukharin's mind, but for our purposes he is not addressing the key point. To argue that the oligarchic pressures derive from capitalism, not human nature, and will therefore be overcome post-capitalism, in the

---

28: Bukharin, 1925, chapter 8. As far as I know Bukharin is the only major Marxist to have attempted a rebuttal of Michels, though there is also a brief response in Sidney Hook, 1933, p312.
29: Bukharin, 1925, chapter 8.

transition to socialism, is all well and good, but the revolutionary socialist party has to be built *under* capitalism.

Of course, it would be possible to claim that Michels' analysis was based on the parties of the Second International—mass reformist parties built in a period of relative social peace in which a bureaucratic hierarchy of paid officials developed. In that case it would be of no relevance to small revolutionary groups, where no substantial materially privileged bureaucracy exists. However, although the anti-democratic pressures are less powerful in small revolutionary groups than in mass reformist parties, they still exist. The workers who join such groups are still products of the profoundly anti-democratic socialisation received in capitalist society, which is reinforced by every defeat we suffer at the hands of the bosses or the government.

The pressures generated by bourgeois society are also a factor in the cult-like features exhibited by some small groups. In order to maintain the loyalty and discipline of a tiny number of adherents in more or less total opposition to wider society they develop the sort of characteristics typical of small religious sects such as the veneration of "the leader" and the establishment of shibboleths. A shibboleth was originally a code word or phrase whose use distinguished the member of a group from an enemy or spy. In our context a shibboleth is a belief or doctrine whose principal function is to separate the true believer from the common herd and reinforce their loyalty. This is, for example, the function of the ban on blood transfusions for Jehovah's Witnesses or support for Israel for the Alliance for Workers' Liberty. With the Socialist Labour League it was the perennial call for a general strike. These sect practices are highly anti-democratic because they strongly inhibit free and rational debate of policies and perspectives.

The adoption of a false perspective, especially an exaggerated ultra-left perspective, greatly intensifies the need for a leadership cult and shibboleths, but this does not make the false perspective the sole source of undemocratic tendencies. Rather we need to understand that the social origin of real democracy in the socialist movement is the struggle of the working class. Party democracy is likely to suffer in so far as the party is cut off from that source—whether because it has set itself above the class (labour and trade union bureaucrats), because it has been driven to the margins of the class (Trotskyism in the 1930s), because it has cut itself off from the class or because the level of class struggle is low.

When I first considered the challenge posed by Michels (while researching for *Marxism and the Party* in the early 1970s) I concluded that, while the iron law of oligarchy was generally valid for social democratic type parties, trade unions and similar organisations, it did *not* apply to

Bolshevik-type parties. This was because central to the Bolshevik model was the restriction of party membership to (a) those who placed the overall interests of the working class above any sectional interest (ie were internationalist, anti-racist, anti-sexist and non-sectionalist), (b) militant activists working under the discipline of party organisations. Such a membership, though necessarily a minority of the class, would not be "incompetent" and would be able to democratically control its leadership. This seemed to me sound in theory and confirmed in practice by the example of the Bolshevik Party, which was highly democratic, especially in 1917.

In making this judgement I was much influenced by Tony Cliff who argued that the trade union bureaucracy, with its conservative and undemocratic practices, rested on the passive majority of the union membership as opposed to the active minority. Chris Harman also argued in his 1969 article "Party and Class" that there was a fundamental difference between the Leninist and social democratic models of organisation. And, he argued:

> Within Lenin's conception those elements that he himself is careful to regard as historically limited and those of general application must be distinguished. The former concern the stress on closed conspiratorial organisations and the need for careful direction from the top down of party officials, etc: "Under conditions of political freedom our party will be built entirely on the elective principle. Under the autocracy this is impracticable for the collective thousands of workers that make up the party."

> Of much more general application is the stress on the need to limit the party to those who are going to accept its discipline. It is important to stress that for Lenin (as opposed to many of his would-be followers) this is not a blind acceptance of authoritarianism. The revolutionary party exists so as to make it possible for the most conscious and militant workers and intellectuals to engage in scientific discussion as a prelude to concerted and cohesive action. This is not possible without general participation in party activities…

> Centralism for Lenin is far from being the opposite of developing the initiative and independence of party members; it is the precondition of this… "Discipline" means acceptance of the need to relate individual experience to the total theory and practice of the party. As such it is not opposed to, but a necessary prerequisite of the ability to make independent evaluations of concrete situations. That is also why "discipline" for Lenin does not mean

hiding differences that exist within the party, but rather exposing them to the full light of day so as to argue them out.[30]

At that time Harman's perspective, and mine, was to build Leninist parties of this kind in Britain and internationally, in the belief that the objective conditions had developed which made this possible. Unfortunately experience, nearly 40 years of it, has shown this to be a rather complicated business, and this in turn has implications for the question of party democracy. Between Bolshevism's birth as a faction of the Russian Social Democratic Labour Party in 1903 and its conquest of power as a mass party in October 1917 lay only 14 years. Those years included a revolution in 1905, a catastrophic world war and the revolutionary overthrow of Tsarism in February 1917. In contrast the IS/SWP tradition has endured almost 60 years, 40 since our emergence as a mini-party in 1968, without any comparable experiences. In Russia the period of reaction (which was intense and nearly destroyed the Bolsheviks) began in 1907 and lasted five years before being swept aside by mass strikes from 1912. In Britain class struggle entered a downturn in the mid to late 1970s and, with some fluctuations and partial recovery, has remained at a low level to this day. Moreover, while the level of struggle has generally been low, there has not been any sustained or generalised repression. And, of course, similar conditions have applied for all left organisations in Western Europe and North America over this period.

Lenin devotes the early chapters of *Left Wing Communism—An Infantile Disorder* to expounding the relationship between Russian conditions and experience and Bolshevik organisational principles (Lenin focuses on "discipline" but, as we have seen, discipline and democracy are intimately connected):

As a current of political thought and as a political party, Bolshevism has existed since 1903. Only the history of Bolshevism during the *entire* period of its existence can satisfactorily explain why it has been able to build up and maintain, under most difficult conditions, the iron discipline needed for the victory of the proletariat… Bolshevism…went through 15 years of practical history (1903-17) unequalled anywhere in the world in its wealth of experience. During those 15 years, no other country knew anything even approximating to that revolutionary experience, that rapid and varied succession of different forms of the movement—legal and illegal, peaceful

---

30: Harman, 1971, pp59-61.

and stormy, underground and open, local circles and mass movements, and parliamentary and terrorist forms.[31]

And Georg Lukács comments:

The Bolshevik concept of party organisation involved the selection of a group of single-minded revolutionaries, prepared to make any sacrifice, from the more or less chaotic mass of the class as a whole... *Lenin's concept of party organisation presupposes the fact—the actuality—of the revolution...* Had the historical predictions of the Mensheviks been correct, had a relatively quiet period of prosperity and of the slow spread of democracy ensued, in which— at least in backward countries—the feudal vestiges of "the people" had been swept aside by the "progressive" classes, the professional revolutionaries would have necessarily remained stranded in sectarianism or become mere propaganda clubs. The party, as the strictly centralised organisation of the proletariat's most conscious elements—and only as such—*is conceived as an instrument of class struggle in a revolutionary period.* "Political questions cannot be mechanically separated from organisation questions," said Lenin, "and anybody who accepts or rejects the Bolshevik party organisation independently of whether or not we live at a time of proletarian revolution has completely misunderstood it".[32]

Unfortunately the times we have lived through have not, a few exceptional moments apart, been a revolutionary period and the revolution has been "actual" only in the most abstract sense. It has therefore not been possible to restrict party membership to "a group of single-minded revolutionaries, prepared to make any sacrifice", or even to people prepared to be consistently active in party organisations. When Harman wrote, "The party is not to be made up of just anybody who wishes to identify himself as belonging to it, but only those willing to accept the discipline of its organisations. In normal times the numbers of these will be only a relatively small percentage of the working class; but in periods of upsurge they will grow immeasurably",[33] he and the rest of us envisaged a party of many thousands, perhaps tens of thousands, growing in time of revolution to hundreds of thousands (the Bolsheviks were about 26,000-strong in February 1917 and between 200,000 and 400,000 by October),

---

31: Lenin, 1964, chapter 2.
32: Lukács, 1970, chapter 3.
33: Harman, 1971.

not a group of tens or a few hundred. To have restricted the membership of the SWP to the criteria of commitment required by the Bolsheviks would, in our non-Bolshevik conditions, have reduced the party to the low hundreds at best and would anyway have been false "toy bolshevism", since such fanatical "revolutionaries" would have lost the other key pillar of Leninism: the ability to "maintain the closest contact, and—if you wish—merge, in certain measure, with the broadest masses of the working people".[34] Consequently circumstances obliged us to operate with a substantial proportion of members who were not sufficiently engaged to exercise democratic control over the party.

The question of repression and illegality plays an interesting and contradictory role here. On the one hand, conditions of illegality create huge obstacles to the proper formal functioning of party democracy, to the convening of regular meetings and conferences, to the holding of regular elections, to the provision of accurate party statistics and so on. Moreover, illegality may strengthen the claims of discipline over democracy, insofar as sometimes they can conflict. On the other hand, repression resolves the problem of an engaged membership: if the penalty for party membership is possible exile to Siberia, or imprisonment, torture and death, the passive armchair member is taken care of and members have a massive, perhaps life or death, stake in the determination of party policy. Of course, this in itself offers no guarantee of democracy, as the example of many Stalinist parties shows, but it does help with one aspect of the problem.

Another factor that has to be considered here is the long timescale involved. Gramsci commented in his *Prison Notebooks* that a prolonged siege is always debilitating, and many people capable of intense resistance and extreme sacrifice for a short time are unable to sustain the same commitment over a long period. To this must be added the crucial role played by the level of the class struggle. A major element in Michels' "incompetence of the masses" is not lack of technical competence but lack of confidence, which the capitalist socialisation process breeds in working class children as surely as it breeds confidence in the children of the bourgeoisie. The principal antidote to this lack of confidence, and therefore vital for internal party democracy, is the experience of collective resistance and struggle, of organising and leading strikes, picket lines, occupations, demonstrations, workplace branches and the like (in the case of students, speaking at mass union meetings, leading college occupations, etc). Not only does participation in such activity raise members' confidence as individuals but it also

---

34: Lenin, 1964, chapter 2.

means that when they take up an issue inside the party they often do as a representative of a collective in their workplace or college. In conditions of downturn, when party members' typical experience at work is of defeat or isolation, their confidence to challenge the party's leadership is undermined. Even if they remain active revolutionary socialists, the feeling may develop that in addition to fighting the bosses, the government, the system, the media and probably their own union leaders, all as a small minority, arguing in their own party is just too much.

In these conditions the counterpart to a passive rank and file, a leadership that becomes accustomed to leading unchallenged, is virtually certain to develop or at least begin to develop.

Having so strongly stressed the anti-democratic pressures at work on and in any would-be revolutionary party, it is necessary also to note that there is a major countervailing tendency. In opposition to Michels' "iron law of oligarchy" there exists, in any party or organisation whose leadership does not wield the combined sticks and carrots of state power, an almost universal "law of democracy". In any voluntary organisation where membership does not itself confer material privilege (even the British Tory party or the Nazi BNP) there is an element of democracy in that the leadership requires the consent of the rank and file in the form of its continuing membership and support. So even right wing union leaders, such as Joe Gormley of the National Union of Mineworkers in 1972-4 or Derek Simpson of Unite today, are obliged to defend their members' interests and respond to their demands to some degree, on pain of losing members (and with them the dues that pay the leaders' salaries).

This democratic pressure from below is all the stronger in a small far-left socialist party, even if it remains overtly passive, because (a) the leaders are plainly not motivated by desire for material privilege, there being none on offer (though sometimes the desire to maintain material security may be a factor); (b) the rank and file are motivated overwhelmingly by conviction; and (c) it is not difficult for them to vote with their feet and leave. To give an example from the organisation I know best, namely the SWP, it is well known that the party's leadership remained pretty stable through the 1990s and early part of this decade, and was seldom subject to serious challenge. But this was on condition that it ran the party within the narrowly prescribed limits of Trotskyist revolutionary socialism. If the SWP leadership had, as opposed to making strategic or tactical errors, ever clearly crossed class lines or contravened basic socialist principles or made moves to renounce Marxism, there would undoubtedly have been an outcry and, if the outcry was not rapidly successful, a mass exodus. This is not to suggest that the SWP leadership ever wanted to do any of these things. I know of no evidence of this whatsoever. Nevertheless, the objective pressure was there and it was a democratic pressure—a pressure to lead the organisation in conformity with the wishes of its members. Moreover it is clear that in general this inherent democratic pressure will, given favourable conditions, be capable of considerable expansion.

Some conclusions

What conclusions follow from this analysis? First and foremost that the case for party democracy made by all the classical Marxists and cited at the start of this article retains all its validity, but it must be understood that the achievement of this democracy in a capitalist society is far from easy.

From a Marxist perspective it is possible not only to integrate the anti-democratic pressures cited by Michels but also to elaborate on them. Capitalist socialisation, through the family and school, instills obedience and subservience in working class children, practically from birth. A "good" baby is one who sleeps and feeds to order; a "good" child is "no trouble" and does what its parents tell it. A successful pupil is one who accepts the agenda of the school and its teachers.[35] A "deviant" teenager has "a problem with authority". Ruling class children are likewise trained to obey the rules but, especially via the public schools, their education also contains a significant stress on developing leadership qualities.

The world of work is invariably hierarchical and undemocratic. Working class occupations consist overwhelmingly of following orders, ruling class ones of giving them and middle class ones of enforcing decisions from above on those below. What is completely lacking from most people's lives is any experience of democracy other than the extremely limited business of voting every so often in parliamentary or local elections. By far the most important exception is trade unionism, which does provide some working people with the experience of saying "no" to those in authority over them, but, as we know only too well, this is a highly uneven and fluctuating process and offers an ongoing regular democratic engagement to only a minority.

The act of joining a revolutionary organisation constitutes a major rebellion against society's conditioning but it does not eliminate it. The anti-democratic pressures continue to operate on and within the party. This is why party democracy is not something that can be guaranteed by any constitution or set of institutional arrangements (which is not to gainsay the necessity of democratic constitutions and institutional arrangements)

35: Willis, 1977; Bowles and Gintis, 1976.

but also requires the development and maintenance of a democratic culture based on frank and open debate in which party members are encouraged to speak their mind. Such a culture has to be embodied in institutions and practices, of course, the most important and permanent of which is the principle of the party conference or congress as the party's sovereign body. But the precise nature of these institutions and practices must necessarily be adapted to specific circumstances and change over time.

Nor is party democracy a political or moral norm that can be established simply by the will or good behaviour of its leaders (or members). For every would-be revolutionary party internal democracy is a goal, a relationship between members and leaders, that has to be continually striven for in the same sense that the correct relationship of party to class has to be continually striven for—indeed the two relationships are intimately connected. Deficiencies in democracy, like errors in perspective and tactics, are inevitable, but not reasons for despair. The point is to correct them.

In this ongoing struggle there are no grounds whatsoever for renouncing either the Leninist concept of the vanguard party or democratic centralism. On the contrary, the Leninist democratic centralist party is *both* necessary for the success of the revolution *and* the *most* democratic form of political organisation.

The case for the Leninist party rests on arguments in no way limited in their validity to Russia or to the historical period of the Russian Revolution. Rather these arguments refer to features of capitalist society and the working class struggle which are pretty much universal and permanent: (a) the centralised nature of the capitalist class and its state which demands centralisation on the part of its adversary; (b) the bourgeoisie's ideological hegemony which requires the waging of an ideological struggle in society and within the working class, a struggle that can only be conducted by a party based on ideological and political clarity; (c) the unevenness in the levels of working class consciousness, confidence, organisation and struggle which require the welding together of the most advanced elements in the class to defeat the reactionary, scab elements and increase their influence over the vacillating majority; (d) the existence, on the basis of this unevenness, of mass reformist (or Stalinist or nationalist) parties which will hold back or betray the revolution, and which must be combated by a revolutionary party which retains its political and organisational independence. Moreover, these theoretical arguments, powerful in themselves, have been confirmed in practice positively, by the role of the Bolshevik Party in the victory of the Russian Revolution and, negatively, by the defeats in Italy, Germany, Spain and elsewhere precisely for the want of such a party.

As far as democracy is concerned, all other forms of political organisation—the social democratic party, the trade union, the "loose" anarchist or autonomist federation or clique, the single-issue campaign—are subject to exactly the same anti-democratic "oligarchic" pressures from capitalist society without the same resources to resist them. No other form of organisation compares with the Leninist party in terms of its ability to equip its members with the political education that enables them to assess the overall political situation and their own party's work. No other form of organisation practises a comparable level of intervention in such a variety of issues, campaigns and struggles, thus potentially training its members as political generalists able to hold its leaders to account. I do not doubt that SWP branches have many defects but one would only have to compare the topics discussed at a typical SWP weekly branch meeting with those at an average Labour Party ward (do they still meet?) to get the point. At the former you might get the economic crisis one week, Palestine the next, followed by fascism and the BNP the week after; at the latter it would be more likely to be the jumble sale, the local pavements and who contests which seat in the local elections, if that.

Furthermore the element of party discipline inherent in democratic centralism—the notion of unity in action in implementing party policy—far from undermining or infringing democracy, is an essential democratic provision. Without it the party could engage in the most democratic process of debate and decision making only to see those decisions come to nothing when they were ignored or flouted by the party leadership, as was routinely the case with old Labour. This element in a revolutionary party is particularly important at decisive moments in the class struggle, especially that of insurrection, when the political and psychological pressures on party leaders are most intense.[36]

If the case for the Leninist party remains compelling, it would, however, be wrong to identify Leninism with one narrowly defined organisational model or set of practices. Lenin himself, in his last speech to the Comintern in 1922, while insisting on the international importance of the Bolshevik experience, warned against the mechanical imitation of Russian organisational methods.[37] For example, on the question of factions there have been at least two views taken in recent years by avowed Leninist

---

36: Trotsky, 1937, for an analysis of how such pressures affected even the Bolshevik leadership in October 1917. This work was also an oblique commentary on the failure of the German party to seize the revolutionary opportunity in autumn 1923.
37: Lenin, 1965b, p430.

Parties—namely the British SWP and the French Ligue Communiste Révolutionnaire (LCR). Both would accept Trotsky's statement, quoted earlier, that "the present doctrine that Bolshevism does not tolerate factions is a myth of the epoch of decline".

But whereas the SWP has permitted only temporary factional organisation, partly to try to avoid the ingrained tendency of Trotskyist groups to split, the LCR has taken the opposite view and sought to maintain unity by allowing permanent tendencies to coexist in the party. I have alluded above to the fact that this policy did not work well for the LCR's co-thinkers in Britain, the IMG, but the LCR, with their recent electoral success and launch of the New Anticapitalist Party, have fared much better. One important objection to their model is that it might lead to paralysis of the party leadership in crucial situations where speedy and decisive action is required. Nevertheless this is a debate which can be had between Leninists and which depends on concrete circumstances.

This last proviso applies to much of this debate. The principle of the need to struggle to realise and improve democracy in the revolutionary party is permanent but the precise means of achieving it vary over time. In general what is needed is, in Gramsci's words, organic centralism, not bureaucratic centralism: "democratic centralism that is 'centralism' in movement, so to speak, that is, a continuous adjustment of the organisation to the real movement".[38] This means working, at each stage in the class struggle, to establish a political culture and set of political practices that facilitate democratic debate and decision making, and develop the political knowledge and confidence of the rank and file.

This is a problem that has to be solved and re-solved not on paper but in practice—and it will never be fully resolved this side of the overthrow of capitalism. Nevertheless a clear statement of the problem and an awareness of the challenge involved may help. That has been the aim of this article.

38: Gramsci, 1970, p178.

References

Bambery, Chris, 1987, "The Politics of James P Cannon", *International Socialism 36* (autumn 1987).

Bowles, Samuel, and Herbert Gintis, 1976, *Schooling in Capitalist America* (Routledge).

Bukharin, Nikolai, 1925 [1921], *Historical Materialism: A System of Sociology* (International Publishers), www.marxists.org/archive/bukharin/works/1921/histmat/

Cannon, James P, 2001 [1940], *The Struggle for a Proletarian Party* (Pathfinder), www.marxists.org/archive/cannon/works/1940/party/

Cliff, Tony, 1993, *Trotsky: volume four—The Darker the Night the Brighter the Star* (Bookmarks), www.marxists.org/archive/cliff/works/1993/trotsky4/

Cliff, Tony, and Donny Gluckstein, 1988, *The Labour Party: A Marxist History* (Bookmarks).

Engels, Frederick, 1970 [1847], "On the History of the Communist League", in Karl Marx and Frederick Engels, *Selected Works*, volume three (Progress), www.marxists.org/archive/marx/works/1847/communist-league/1885hist.htm

Gramsci, Antonio, 1970, *The Modern Prince and Other Writings* (International Publishers).

Hallas, Duncan, 1969, "Building the Leadership", *International Socialism 40*, first series (October-November 1969), www.marxists.org/archive/hallas/works/1969/xx/building.htm

Hallas, Duncan, 1971, "Towards a Revolutionary Socialist Party", in Tony Cliff and others, *Party And Class* (Pluto), www.marxists.org/archive/hallas/works/1971/xx/party.htm

Harman, Chris, 1971, "Party and Class", in Tony Cliff and others, *Party and Class* (Pluto), www.marxists.de/party/harman/partyclass.htm

Hook, Sidney, 1933, *Towards the Understanding of Karl Marx* (John Day).

Lenin, Vladimir, 1964 [1920], *Left Wing Communism—An Infantile Disorder*, *Collected Works*, volume 31 (Progress), www.marxists.org/archive/lenin/works/1920/lwc/

Lenin, Vladimir, 1965a [1906], "Party Discipline and the Fight Against the Pro-Cadet Social Democrats", *Collected Works*, volume 11 (Progress), www.marxists.org/archive/lenin/works/1906/nov/23d.htm

Lenin, Vladimir, 1965b [1922], "Five Years of the Russian Revolution", *Collected Works*, volume 33 (Progress), www.marxists.org/archive/lenin/works/1922/nov/04b.htm

Lukács, Georg, 1970 [1924], *Lenin: A Study of the Unity of his Thought* (New Left Books), www.marxists.org/archive/lukacs/works/1924/lenin/

Michels, Robert, 1968 [1911], *Political Parties* (Free Press). An alternative version of the book is available online: http://socserv2.socsci.mcmaster.ca/~econ/ugcm/3ll3/michels/polipart.pdf

Molyneux, John, 1978, *Marxism and the Party* (Pluto).

Trotsky, Leon, 1936, *The Revolution Betrayed*, http://www.marxists.org/archive/trotsky/1936/revbet/

Trotsky, Leon, 1937 [1924], *Lessons of October* (Pioneer), www.marxists.org/archive/trotsky/1924/lessons/

Trotsky, Leon, 1975 [1942], *In Defence of Marxism* (New Park), www.marxists.org/archive/trotsky/idom/dm/

Trotsky, Leon, 1979 [1904], *Our Political Tasks* (New Park), www.marxists.org/archive/trotsky/1904/tasks/

Willis, Paul, 1977, *Learning to Labour* (Ashgate).

Shock and awe
Neil Davidson

*A review of Naomi Klein, **The Shock Doctrine: The Rise of Disaster Capitalism** (Allen Lane, 2007), £25*

Authors with both talent and a theme of topical importance are still not guaranteed to seize the public imagination: they also require good timing. More precisely, they require a mass audience predisposed to sympathetically listen to what they have to say. This means that the writers concerned must be, if not exactly ahead of their potential audience, at least attuned to shifts in popular consciousness that are perhaps not yet fully formed. Several classics of socialist literature appeared too early to have an immediate impact. George Orwell's 1938 work *Homage to Catalonia*, for example, is now rightly regarded as one of the outstanding autobiographical accounts of the Spanish Civil War and a merciless critique of the bankruptcy of the Popular Front strategy. But by the time of Orwell's death in 1950 it had failed to sell even the initial print run of 1,500.[1] The very defeats which Stalinism had helped bring about meant that the majority of socialists were simply not open to the arguments it contained. Its popularity came later, in the wake of Orwell's fame as the author of *Nineteen Eighty-Four* and the emergence of a New Left after 1956.

The Canadian radical journalist Naomi Klein has been rather more fortunate in her timing. Between 1995 and 1999 Klein worked to expose how giant multinational brands dominated the world economy. The resulting book, *No Logo*, appeared early in 2000, only months after the

---

1:     Davison, 1998, p135.

November 1999 demonstrations against the World Trade Organisation in Seattle signalled the coalescence of new forms of collective opposition to capitalist globalisation.

According to Klein's own account, her book went to the printers as the protesters took to the streets: "I consider myself lucky that I happened to write a book just at a movement's moment." Klein herself did not fully appreciate the scale and extent of the movement—although, to be fair, no one else did either. Indeed, before starting the book she was only aware of "small-scale activism" such as "culture jamming" and "ad busting", and saw these as having an important future only as "an act of faith".[2] No Logo itself concludes by listing the fragmented groups which she hoped together might "wrest" globalisation "from the grasp of the multinationals": "Ethical shareholders, culture jammers, street reclaimers, McUnion organisers, human-rights activists, school-logo fighters and internet watchdogs are at the early stages of demanding a citizen-centred alternative to the international rule of the brands".[3] Nevertheless, No Logo caught a mood and, once a relatively cohesive movement did emerge, it rapidly achieved classic status, elevating Klein to a pre-eminent position in the movement. Contributors to International Socialism have disagreed with her support for decentralisation and opposition to the resolution of strategic differences through hard political argument. But there is no doubt that Klein has played a serious participatory role, refusing the temptation to become a mere radical celebrity offering detached commentary on events.[4]

From global brands to disaster capitalism

Seven years lie between No Logo and Klein's latest book, The Shock Doctrine, during which time her only substantive publication has been a collection of journalism written between Seattle and 9/11.[5] The latter event and the various responses to it on the left seem to have been the catalyst for a change in her perspective. In particular, as she recently explained in conversation with the Marxist geographer Neil Smith, she was concerned about the way in which 9/11 divided what had, until then, been a movement finding its way towards opposing the system as a whole: into oppositions focused respectively on war and capitalism, without seeing the connections between the two.[6] What Klein is attempting in The Shock Doctrine is to

---

2: Klein, 2008a.
3: Klein, 2000, pp445-446.
4: See, for example, Harman, 2000, pp53-56.
5: Klein, 2002.
6: Klein and Smith, 2008, pp589-590.

integrate events like wars—not least the "Global War on Terror"—but also supposedly "natural" disasters, into an account of how contemporary capitalism works. *The Shock Doctrine* is in other respects a very different type of book from *No Logo*. Rather than a series of contemporary snapshots, the approach is historical, tracing the unfolding of the neoliberal era from the Chilean coup of 1973 onwards, occasionally moving further back in time to search for precedents. But the differences are not merely structural. A more sombre tone has replaced the vibrant optimism with which she first caught the movement's attention. It is as if the longer perspective she adopts here has brought home the extent of the violence committed against humanity during a period which has now lasted nearly 40 years.

We now think of that period as one dominated by neoliberalism, although Klein tends to treat neoliberalism and neoconservatism as interchangeable terms for a particular way of organising capitalism, which she prefers to call "corporatism", characterised by "huge transfers of public wealth to private hands, often accompanied by exploding debt, an ever-widening chasm between the dazzling rich and the disposable poor and an aggressive nationalism that justifies bottomless spending on security".[7] Whatever terminology is employed for the current form of capitalist organisation (I will continue to refer to neoliberalism in what follows) Klein rightly distinguishes it from capitalism itself.[8] As we shall see, however, this avoids one error, only to open up the possibility of another—that "another capitalism is possible" shorn of the inhumanity of neoliberalism. I will return to this point below; but first, what is Klein's argument?

She begins with the way in which theoretical support for free markets was kept alive by a small band of thinkers, above all Milton Friedman (who features as her main intellectual adversary here), after the tide began to turn against free market capitalism with the Great Crash of 1929:

During these dark days for laissez-faire, when Communism conquered the East, the welfare state was embraced by the West and economic nationalism took root in the postcolonial South, Friedman and his mentor, Friedrich

---

7:   Klein, 2007, pp14-15. See also Klein, 2007, p253.
8:   Neoconservatism is often wrongly regarded simply as a US foreign policy doctrine based on military intervention. In fact, it is the inescapable domestic complement to neoliberalism across the capitalist world, in the sense that the social division and fragmentation caused by marketisation, commodification, privatisation and the rest require massive increases in the repressive and surveillance apparatus of the state in the name of restoring social discipline. For that reason, although the two ideologies are inextricably linked, we should maintain an analytic distinction between them. For a longer discussion, see Davidson, 2009a.

Hayek, patiently protected the flame of a pure version of capitalism, untarnished by Keynesian attempts to pool collective wealth to build more just societies.[9]

But the coming to power of rulers either searching for economic answers or already committed to market solutions—initially the Chilean military, then the Thatcher and Reagan governments—provided the first opportunities for these ideas to be put into practice. Coincident with the preservation of neoliberal theory at Chicago University by Friedman and his acolytes, a form of Electro Convulsive Therapy ("electroshock treatment") was being developed by Ewen Cameron at McGill University with CIA funding. Ostensibly to help psychiatric patients, this was in fact used by his paymasters to reduce prisoners to a vegetative state of blankness and receptivity. Klein claims that this form of psychological torture, "coercive interrogation", although in actual use, most recently in the aftermath of 9/11, also acts as a metaphor for a broader social process: "Like the terrorised prisoner who gives up the names of his comrades and renounces his faith, shocked societies often give up things they would otherwise fiercely protect".[10]

Social shock treatment and neoliberal economics have been linked, in the sense that the former has been used to pave the way for the introduction of the latter, in a conjoined process Klein calls "disaster capitalism". She twice quotes Friedman's statement that "only a crisis—actual or perceived—produces real change" and argues that neoliberalism is a "shock doctrine" which takes advantage of disaster to impose the idea of the new market order.[11] The notion of "shock" therefore works on three levels: first, "countries are shocked—by wars, coups d'état and natural disasters"; second, "they are shocked again—by corporations and politicians who exploit the fear and disorientation of this first shock to push through economic shock therapy"; and third, "people who resist are, if necessary, shocked again—by police, soldiers and prison interrogators".[12]

Putting this argument to work, Klein is able to demonstrate that, contrary to the neoliberal claim that free markets and parliamentary democracy are mutually dependent systems, "this fundamentalist form of capitalism has consistently been midwifed by the most brutal forms of coercion, inflicted on the collective body politic as well as on countless individual bodies".

9:   Klein, 2007, p17.
10:   Klein, 2007, p17.
11:   Klein, 2007, pp6-7, 140-141.
12:   Klein, 2007, pp24-25. See also Klein, 2007, p71.

And not only the introduction but the maintenance of neoliberal regimes requires at the very least the severe curtailment of democracy, in all respects other than the most formal—the bare right to vote for virtually indistinguishable parties. As this suggests, Klein regards neoliberalism from the beginning as a project reliant on state power. Rather than markets being "freed" from the state as the ideology proclaims, we have instead witnessed the formation of a new, but equally close, relationship between the two:

> In every country where Chicago School policies have been applied over the last three decades, what has emerged is a powerful ruling alliance between a few very large corporations and a class of mostly wealthy politicians—with hazy and ever shifting lines between the two groups.[13]

Klein supports her argument with a series of individual country by country case studies, which constitute the core of the book and which have an undeniable cumulative power.

The critique I want to offer here differs from the attacks by self-deluded liberals such as Will Hutton.[14] Whatever problems there are with Klein's work, her position is infinitely more realistic about the workings of capitalism than the vacuous waffle about "civil society", "democratic governance" and the like which Hutton has been promoting for decades. Above all, Klein is on the side of those who are fighting back against capitalism; Hutton is committed to defending the system against which they struggle, despite its "excesses". Klein has also been criticised for her unsparing accounts of organisations such as Solidarity in Poland and the ANC in South Africa which once embodied popular aspirations but have since capitulated to neoliberalism. Ronald Suresh Roberts, for example, has accused Klein of condescension towards black South Africans who re-elected the ANC with ever bigger majorities until 2004.[15] To argue that criticism of post-colonial regimes is a refusal of solidarity, regardless of what these regimes have done or failed to do after taking power, is a piece of moral blackmail that has been used all too often in the past to whip Western liberals and even some would-be revolutionaries into line. It is to Klein's credit that she refuses to bow to it, rightly understanding that the solidarity we owe is to the exploited and oppressed, not to parties or states which claim to represent them while betraying their interests at every turn.

13: Klein, 2007, p15.
14: Hutton, 2007.
15: Roberts, 2008, p7.

The limitations of a metaphor

The real problems with *The Shock Doctrine* lie elsewhere. The detail which Klein provides of how neoliberalism has become the dominant form of capitalist organisation is far more convincing than the organising metaphor within which it is presented. Klein presents neoliberalism as the manifestation of the inner logic of corporate capitalism (although perhaps not of capitalism itself) and "shock" as the means by which it can be realised. She therefore treats every geopolitical event (using that term in its broadest sense) since 1973 as one either consciously undertaken or opportunistically manipulated to impose neoliberalism, a fixation which inevitably produces unnecessarily conspiratorial undertones to her work. (As Joseph Stiglitz remarks, "There are no accidents in the world as seen by Naomi Klein".[16]) There are three problems with the "shock" metaphor as an aid to understanding contemporary capitalism.

First, how necessary was "shock" to the introduction of neoliberalism? "There are huge Third World economies that have been ravaged by neoliberalism that haven't endured 'the shock doctrine'," notes Alexander Cockburn.[17] He specifically mentions India in this context, but could just as easily have mentioned Mexico or Egypt. Klein does not discuss either of these countries, even though they are in the neoliberal vanguard of their respective regions and are at least as important in geopolitical and geoeconomic terms as Chile or Iraq, which receive detailed attention because they appear to confirm her thesis.[18] More damaging still is the absence of credible examples of "shock therapy" in the cases of the two states of the developed world where neoliberalism has taken deepest root: the UK and the US.

Klein identifies the Falklands War of 1982 as the decisive moment for Thatcher in implementing her programme in the UK: "The disorder and nationalist excitement resulting from the war allowed her to use tremendous force to crush the striking coal miners and to launch the first privatisation frenzy in a Western democracy".[19] In fact, the popular impact of the Falklands victory was relatively short-lived and did not feature particularly prominently in Conservative electoral material during the 1983 campaign, although it certainly helped to consolidate Thatcher's leadership over her party.[20] The Conservative victory that year had a far less epochal and far

---

16: Stiglitz, 2007.
17: Cockburn, 2007.
18: India and Mexico receive one passing reference each, Egypt receives none. See Klein, 2007, pp399, 452.
19: Klein, 2007, p10. See also Klein, 2007, pp136-140.
20: See Sanders, Marsh and Ward, 1987.

more conjunctural basis. In electoral terms, they faced a compromised and incoherent Labour Party, a section of whose voting base had shifted to the newly formed Social Democratic and Liberal Party. But equally significant was the state of the working class—disillusioned with the previous Labour government, weakened by unemployment but offered some relief by the emergence of the economy from the depths of the 1981-2 slump.

Far from the Falklands being the shock that made Thatcher's victory over the miners and everything that followed possible, the outcome of the subsequent miners' strike was itself the turning point in establishing the neoliberal regime in Britain. The key to Thatcher's triumph was the failure of other unions and the TUC to deliver effective solidarity with the National Union of Mineworkers. The British working class was temporarily defeated in a way that had serious consequences (from which it has yet to fully recover) but it was scarcely shocked into a condition of psychological collapse.

Klein's account of the USA is even more implausible, focusing as it does on the aftermath of 9/11:

> What happened in the period of mass disorientation after the attacks was, in retrospect, a domestic form of economic shock therapy. The Bush team, Friedmanite to the core, quickly moved to exploit the shock that gripped the nation to push through its radical vision of a hollow government in which everything from war fighting to disaster response was a for-profit venture.[21]

Reading this one might almost believe that the US had been spared the neoliberal onslaught until the fall of the Twin Towers. In fact it suffered, from the late 1970s, longer and more intensively than anywhere in the West apart from the UK. In the case of the US too the key was the weakening of the labour movement, a task made easier by the fact that the US labour movement did not even enjoy the collective successes of the British in the early 1970s. The retreat started much earlier than the American equivalent of the miners' strike, the defeat of the Patco air traffic controllers in 1981.[22]

Second, was "shock" always applied for the purpose of introducing neoliberalism? In general Klein makes far too direct a link between economics and politics.[23] Take, for example, the two central events which

---

21: Klein, 2007, p298.
22: Moody, 2007, pp106-114.
23: For a discussion of how the links might be made, without reducing one to the other or treating them as autonomous, see Davidson, 2009b.

dominate *The Shock Doctrine*, and which she explicitly links: the Chilean coup of 1973 and the invasion of Iraq in 2003.[24]

Klein is, of course, right to say that in Chile it was only in the aftermath of a violent seizure of power by the military that the neoliberal regime could have been put in place. But this was not the motivation for the coup, which was carried out to crush the political aspirations of the working class movement which had looked to Allende and which was by 1973 beginning to organise on its own behalf. In fact the generals initially had little idea what economic policies to introduce and in other circumstances might well have looked to the Catholic corporatist model applied by Franco in Spain after 1939, which had been followed more or less faithfully by previous Latin American dictatorships. In retrospect, the arrival of the "Chicago Boys" to oversee the implementation of Pinochet's programme of privatisation and deregulation has a wider significance, but initially it appeared to have no resonance elsewhere and subsequent coups to that in Chile did not immediately adopt neoliberalism. Klein herself notes that the Argentinian dictatorship that came to power in 1976 did not follow its Chilean predecessor in privatising social security or natural resources: in fact these were achieved decades later under civilian governments.[25]

In relation to Iraq, Klein quotes Bush the Father at the head of one chapter denying accusations that Bush the Son "invaded Iraq to open up new markets for US companies", a denial which she regards as self-evidently preposterous.[26] However, painful though it is to admit, the elder Bush is simply speaking the truth. The US did not invade and occupy Iraq in order to create profit opportunities for private security firms but for strategic reasons connected to Middle Eastern oil—not to guarantee price or even supply for American use, but to control the supply in relation to competitors, above all China.[27]

Third, even accepting that neoliberals have opportunistically intervened to take advantage of disaster situations in recent decades, why was it only at a certain stage in post-war history that crises were manipulated to produce these outcomes? Two examples will illustrate the problem.

One is from the core of the world system. At the end of the Second World War it quickly became apparent that Britain had unresolved economic problems. These were not helped by a massive rearmament

---

24: Klein, 2007, pp7-8.
25: Klein, 2007, pp88, 165-168.
26: Klein, 2007, p308.
27: Brzezinsky, 1997, pp158-173; Callinicos, 2003, pp93-98; Harvey, 2003, pp18-25, 74-86.

programme that began to erode the welfare state within years of it being initiated. When the Conservative Party was returned to office in 1951, some members of the new administration led by Rab Butler drafted a proposal to float the pound, which would have immediately led to it falling in value against the dollar. The central intention here was to put an end to balance of payments difficulties which were already characteristic of the British economy. Exports would be given a massive boost, while at the same time imports would fall; domestic prices would be high, but wages would have to be held down to avoid inflationary pressures, not least by allowing unemployment to rise. In effect, the government would be forced to cut funding of the welfare state, especially the housing programme, as well as its overseas military commitments.

The plan was dropped, largely as a result of Churchill's nervousness over the likely consequences in electoral terms.[28] Historians have tended to treat this episode as a typical example of the consensual thinking which supposedly prevented deep-seated problems from being tackled before the advent of the Thatcher regime.[29] The point, however, is that an experiment of this sort would have been, in capitalist terms, both destructive and unnecessary at this time. Destructive because it was contrary to the type of economic structures being put in place in the advanced capitalist West— most obviously it would have destroyed the Bretton Woods agreement, the only components of which to have been put in place were fixed exchange rates. Unnecessary because from the end of the Korean War in 1953 the British economy began to take off in a boom which meant that any attempt to limit trade union power or redefine the limits of the welfare state could be postponed. British capitalism did indeed have serious underlying problems, but in conditions of generalised expansion few members of the British ruling class felt it was necessary to take action. Those who did argue for proto-Thatcherite solutions in the late 1950s, such as Enoch Powell, were marginalised.

My other example is from the developing world. The Indonesian coup of 1965 was a successful attempt by a section of the local ruling class, backed by the US and the UK, to destroy the power of the Communist Party and the left more generally, in what was at that point the most extreme use of counter-revolutionary violence since the Second World War. But neither internal nor external forces sought to impose what was then thought of as a neoclassical economic programme on the country. Klein draws parallels between the group of Indonesian economists trained at the University

---

28: Hennessey, 2006, pp199-217.
29: See, for example, Marr, 2007, p131.

of California, the so-called "Berkeley Mafia" who advised the military both before and after the coup, with the "Chicago Boys" who played a similar post-coup role for the Chilean junta ten years later. She rather elides, however, the nature of the economic policies followed in the former case, which were quite different from the latter.[30] Indonesia under Suharto was regarded as a reliable ally of the West in the Cold War, but continued the strategy of state-led economic development initiated by the pre-coup regime. Its economic policies were similar to those of the other newly industrialising countries of East Asia, particularly Taiwan, Singapore and South Korea.

What these examples suggest is that neoliberalism was far from being the application of a doctrine which capitalists, state managers or politicians had been waiting to apply since the introduction of the New Deal in the 1930s or the creation of the post-war welfare states. In other words, if Klein's thesis was correct, the policies we now associate with neoliberalism would have been introduced much earlier in the 20th century than they in fact were. Instead even the most ferociously counter-revolutionary regimes followed the dominant economic model of state intervention.

It is certainly the case that in the Global South the military repression of regimes reflecting the reformist aspirations of the working class and the oppressed opened up opportunities for multinational corporations to play a greater role but the latter have not themselves always pursued neoliberal policies, nor have they always demanded them from the states with which they have had to deal. Klein writes that "Friedman's vision coincided with the interests of the large multinationals, which by nature hunger for vast new unregulated markets".[31] But the interests of the multinationals have changed over time. During the long post-war boom there was general support for state intervention among the larger businesses and corporations, while small businesses retained their traditional hostility to it. These differences expressed the relative security of their positions within the market. Corporations were protected from the worst exigencies of price competition and were able to plan for longer-term investment and growth, and often in alliance with the state. Small businesses were much more vulnerable, and the state simply represented a source of demands for predatory taxation and bureaucratic regulation.

Neoliberal globalisation has changed the relative position of the corporations so that all but the largest transnational corporations are in a similar position in terms of size to the small businesses of the post-war period:

30: Klein, 2007, pp67-70.
31: Klein, 2007, p57.

"The process of globalisation has sharply increased the degree of competitive pressure faced by large corporations and banks, as competition has become a worldwide relationship." Corporations still need a home state to act as a base, but they require it to behave differently. Increased competition "pushes them towards support for any means to reduce their tax burden and lift regulatory constraints, to free them to compete more effectively with their global rivals".[32]

Explaining the neoliberal moment

In many respects Klein's position is close to David Harvey's. Although he is only mentioned once in the text (in a footnote about the introduction of neoliberalism to China after the Tiananmen Square massacre), Klein refers in her acknowledgements to him as one of "several thinkers and chroniclers of neoliberalism [who] have shaped my thinking".[33] More recently she has said that her object, "using David Harvey's parameters", was to track "the counter-revolution against Keynesianism and developmentalism and the period from the 1930s through to the end of the 1960s, where there was a period when there was a response to another crisis which was the market crash of 1929".[34] There is, however, one central problem with the concept of a neoliberal "counter-revolution" shared by Harvey and Klein: it perpetuates the neoliberal myth that socio-economic developments in the post-war period were fundamentally detrimental to capital. It is certainly true that a number of concessions were granted to the working class, and it is for this reason that the reputation of "the golden age" remains high, particularly in contrast to what Eric Hobsbawm calls "the landslide" that followed. This reputation rests on two main factors.[35] One was high, indeed for practical purposes full, employment. The other was the expansion of the "social wage" through the provision of education, health and social security, particularly unemployment benefits and pensions.[36]

Both of these were necessary to capital, to gain the support of the labour force, helping to ensure social stability and to aid increases in productivity, thus contributing to international competitiveness. As Hilde Nafstad and her colleagues write, "Welfare states should not be understood

32: Kotz, 2001, p104.
33: Klein, 2007, pp190, 532.
34: Klein and Smith, 2008, p583.
35: Hobsbawm, 1994, pp403-416.
36: Although, as Perry Anderson rightly remarks, the period since 1973 has seen dramatic, if uneven, improvements in the living conditions of millions in the Global South who were excluded from the prosperity of the long boom. See Anderson, 2005, p301.

simply as a protective reaction against modern capitalism, but as varieties of modern capitalism".[37] Consequently, these measures were not necessarily dependent for their introduction on Social Democratic or even Liberal Democratic governments. As Tony Judt has correctly noted:

> Outside of Scandinavia—in Austria, Germany, France, Italy, Holland, and elsewhere—it was not socialists but Christian Democrats who played the greatest part in installing and administering the core institutions of the activist welfare state. Even in Britain, where the post-World War Two Labour government under Clement Attlee indeed inaugurated the welfare state as we knew it, it was the wartime government of Winston Churchill that commissioned and approved the report by William Beveridge (himself a Liberal) that established the principles of public welfare provision: principles—and practices—that were reaffirmed and underwritten by every conservative government that followed until 1979.[38]

Klein rightly rejects the USSR and its satellites and imitators as a model for the contemporary radical left, but nevertheless considers them to be "post-capitalist" societies, which consequently required an entirely new capitalist class to be created after their demise. However, as this journal has argued since its inception, rather than view these societies as being fundamentally different from those of the West it is better to see them as existing on a continuum of state intervention, with two extremes—the US and the USSR—at opposite ends of the scale.

The real roots of neoliberalism are to be found in the end of the period of exceptional growth that followed the Second World War. The precise causes of the return to crisis after 1973 have been widely debated but some key features are highlighted by most analysts. Increased price competition from West Germany and Japan within the advanced world was made possible by intensive investment in technology and relatively low wages. This forced their hitherto dominant rivals, above all the US, to lower their own prices in a situation where production costs remained unchanged. American corporations were initially prepared to accept a reduced rate of profit in order to maintain market share but, ultimately, they too undertook a round of new investments, thus raising the capital-labour ratio and increasing the organic composition of capital, leading to consequent further pressure on the rate of

---

37: Nafstead and others, 2007, p314.
38: Judt, 2008, p10.

profit.[39] As Al Campbell writes, neoliberalism was therefore a solution to "a structural crisis of capitalism" in which "policies, practices and institutions" that had hitherto served capital accumulation no longer did so: "More narrowly, one can say that capitalism abandoned the Keynesian compromise in the face of a falling rate of profit, under the belief that neoliberalism could improve its profit rate and accumulation performance".[40]

But the inadequacy of Keynesian policies was itself the result of changes to the nature of the world economy which had taken place during the long boom—an unprecedented three-fold expansion of international trade, the advent of cross-border production, the increase in large-scale foreign direct investment and the creation of "offshore" banking and flows of money capital unlimited by national boundaries—all of which made these policies increasingly difficult to apply with any possibility of success. States had not become completely powerless in the face of markets—that is, the myth of globalisation assiduously cultivated by politicians seeking to shift responsibility for neoliberal policies onto what T S Eliot once called "great impersonal forces" over which they had no control. In that sense neoliberalism represented a choice, but it was a choice increasingly difficult to avoid so long as the goal was the preservation and expansion of capitalism at all costs.

The economic roots of neoliberalism were therefore decisive. The one condition that was universally required in order to impose the neoliberal regime was to eliminate or at least reduce the power of the organised working class. The real reason for the attack on the ability of unions to effectively defend their members was threefold. The first was to enable corporate restructuring, the closing of "unproductive" units and the imposition of "the right of managers to manage" within the workplace. The second was to ensure that wage costs fell and stayed down so that the share of profits going to capital was increased. This also extended to the social wage. The main source of funding for the post-war welfare states came from redistribution within the working class itself. However, to the extent that it was also a cost to capital, it was one that capitalists were only prepared to pay so long as the system was expanding. When it began to contract, as it did after 1973, these costs had to be reduced, either by attacking provisions directly in the hands of employers (pensions, health insurance) or by shifting the burden of

---

39: Harman, 1984, pp99-102; Brenner, 2006, pp99-101. Harman argues that an increase in the organic composition of capital (as a result of declining effectiveness of the permanent arms economy as a countervailing tendency) was the reason for the falling rate of profit. Brenner rejects this explanation (see Brenner, 2006, pp14-15, note 1), but both he and Harman agree that the latter process is central to the crisis.
40: Campbell, 2005, p189.

taxation even more decisively onto the working class. The third, more long-term tactical consideration, was to assist social democracy as it adapted to neoliberalism by weakening the main source of countervailing pressure from the broader labour movement, thus ensuring that fiscal and other changes in favour of capital would not be reversed.

Only very rarely did these attacks involve destroying the trade union movement. The Chilean coup of 1973 is exceptional in this respect and it was only possible on a temporary basis. At the time, however, it was regarded as a tragic reversal of the reformist strategy adopted by Allende and Popular Unity, not as foreshadowing any new development. Latin America had, after all, experienced numerous coups in the 20th century, albeit few as violent as this. In the important case of China, the ruling class was fortunate in that there was no movement to be destroyed: the reality of this so-called "workers' state" being an atomised labour force presided over by official trade unions that were an arm of the state. (Ironically, the emergence of a genuine labour movement in China has been in response to the regime's neoliberal turn.) In most cases, apart from simply allowing mass unemployment to weaken worker confidence and combativity, the attack on trade union power involved two strategies.

One was to provoke a decisive confrontation between a state-backed employer and one or two important groups of unionised workers (air traffic controllers in the US in 1981, textile workers in India in 1982, miners in the UK in 1984-5), whose defeat would act as an example to the others, against a background of multiplying legal restraints and increasing employer intransigence. In these circumstances politicians gambled that most sections of the trade union bureaucracy would give priority to the continued existence of their organisations, however much reduced in power, rather than mount effective resistance. Looking back at the refusal of other unions or federations such as the AFL-CIO and the TUC to give effective support to unions under attack, the bet appears to have involved a limited amount of risk.

The other strategy was to establish new productive capacity, often virtually new industries in geographical areas with low or non-existent levels of unionisation, and to prevent the culture of membership from becoming established. The classic example of this strategy was the movement of productive capital from the old "rustbelt" industrial regions of the north east US to the southern "sunbelt".[41] Actual geographical shifts within nation-states were more common and more damaging to trade union organisation than the threatened geographical shifts to locations in the Global South, which were often made by employers but far less frequently carried out, not least

41: Moody, 2007, pp43-47.

because of their lack of technological infrastructure and the cost in abandoning fixed capital which such relocations would involve. However, as Graham Turner notes, "it is the threat of relocation that proves just as powerful as the reality of a transfer somewhere cheaper".[42]

The emergence of neoliberalism as a conscious ruling class strategy, rather than the esoteric ideological doctrine associated with Friedman and Co, therefore took place in response to the end of the post-war boom, but in changed conditions created by that boom. Politicians and state managers began to implement some of the policies long advocated by Hayek and Friedman, not because individual opportunities to do so which had previously been missing finally presented themselves, as Klein claims, but because the changed conditions of accumulation required changed strategies. Given the limited number of strategies available (assuming these were to be in the interests of capital), it is unsurprising that theory and practice began to overlap. The failure of Keynesianism and other forms of state capitalism predisposed many capitalists, state managers and politicians to embrace theories which they would have rejected earlier as eccentric, or even dangerously destabilising. But it is important to place the spread from economic to ideological crisis in the right order and, even then, to appreciate that the shifts which followed were as much pragmatic as ideological. As Andrew Gamble writes, neoliberalism as "a global ideology" was less significant than "the competitive pressures of capital accumulation in forcing the convergence of all capitalist models and all national economies towards neoliberal institutions and policies".[43] Even then neoliberalism as a system only emerged in a piecemeal fashion.

Conclusion

Neoliberalism is mutating in response to the current crisis. The precise character of this new capitalist organisation is not yet settled. We can, however, be sure that in the absence of a boom comparable to that of the post-war period (which seems unlikely, to say the least) any new formation will prove to be no more beneficial to the working class than its predecessor. Understanding neoliberalism is therefore not a historical issue, but one of urgent practical concern. It has shaped the conditions under which the working class still has to fight, conditions which extend beyond economic structures, or even the immediate situation in the workplace, to the types of political representation and the forms of consciousness with which

42: Turner, 2008, p10.
43: Gamble, 2001, p133.

workers will enter the struggles to come. Yet despite the crucial importance of the issue there is no wholly satisfactory account of this most recent
period in the history of capitalism. The book which comes nearest from a
Marxist perspective is Harvey's *A Brief History of Neoliberalism*, but theoretically it is highly eclectic and consequently misleading on several key points,
several of which have already been discussed in *International Socialism*.[44]
Furthermore, although it is markedly more readable than the average work
of Marxist political economy (including most of Harvey's earlier works), it
presents a formidable challenge to anyone not already familiar with a series
of complex theoretical debates.

For this reason alone, *The Shock Doctrine* is an important work.
Although, as we have seen, it draws on Harvey in some respects, it presents
an argument about neoliberalism in terms far more comprehensible to
non-academic activists than the jargon of, say, "the spatial fix". The very fact
of its popularity does, however, place an onus on Klein's fellow members of
the radical left to draw friendly but critical attention to its weaknesses. In the
end, these do not stem so much from the metaphor which provides Klein
with her title and structure but from the understanding of capitalism which
underlies it. Above all, Klein does not reject markets:

> I am not arguing that all market systems are inherently violent. It is eminently
> possible to have a market-based economy that requires no such brutality and
> demands no such ideological purity. A free market in consumer products can
> coexist with free public health care, with public schools, with a large segment
> of the economy—like a national oil company—held in state hands... Keynes
> proposed exactly that kind of mixed, regulated economy after the Great
> Depression, a revolution in public policy that created the New Deal and
> transformations like it around the world.[45]

But it was the propensity for a system run along the lines described
here to enter crisis that opened up the very period her book describes.
Indeed, economic crisis barely features in her account, unless as something
consciously created by ruling classes to change economic structures to their
advantage. The idea that capitalism enters into involuntary convulsions as
a result of the internal mechanisms of the mode of production is almost

---

44: Harman, 2008, pp89-92, 100-104. See also Davidson, 2009a.
45: Klein, 2007, p20. Klein is, of course, not alone on the left in seeing Keynesian solutions
as the only realistic alternative to neoliberalism, either from principle or because of the
supposed impossibility of making more radical change under current conditions. Compare
the liberal Stiglitz, 2002, pp249-250, with the Marxist Harvey, 2005, pp183-184, 206.

entirely absent from *The Shock Doctrine*, yet paradoxically it is in this fact that hope actually lies.

If neoliberalism was indeed the essence of capitalism then we would expect the bourgeoisie to endlessly seek to reimpose that model, whenever conditions are apt. This is certainly what Klein expects based on her response to the outbreak of the current crisis:

> During boom times it is profitable to preach *laissez-faire* because an absentee government allows speculative bubbles to inflate. When these bubbles burst, the ideology becomes a hindrance and goes dormant while government rides to the rescue. But rest assured: the ideology will come roaring back once the bail-outs are done.[46]

But if this is so, where does the impetus for her desired Keynesian welfare state come from? Surely not from capitalists since, according to Klein, they are merely waiting to reimpose free market conditions. But equally, how can the oppressed and exploited force a change on the capitalist class if the latter have been able to suppress the possibilities of democracy to the extent that her account reveals? Something of this dilemma is apparent in Klein's final chapter, where she offers some tentative reasons for optimism, which (apart from the Lebanese general strike of 2006) mainly amount to small-scale attempts at post-disaster "community reconstruction".[47] Her failure to understand the role of crisis, rather than some omnipresent capitalist urge towards free markets, as the motivation behind neoliberalism, also blinds her to the possibilities that a renewed period of crisis presents for both sides in the class struggle. Neoliberalism was founded on the weakening of the labour movement. If what replaces neoliberalism is to be in the interests of the exploited and oppressed, the labour movement must be rebuilt. That task will have to involve much more than projects of reconstructing what we had before the neoliberal catastrophe. We know, not least because Naomi Klein has shown us in this flawed but immensely valuable book, what our enemies are capable of if we fail.

46: Klein, 2008b.
47: Klein, 2007, pp443-466.

References

Anderson, Perry, 2005, "The Vanquished Left: Eric Hobsbawm", in *Spectrum: From Right to Left in the World of Ideas* (Verso).

Brenner, Robert, 2006, *The Economics of Global Turbulence: the Advanced Capitalist Economies from Long Boom to Long Downturn, 1945-2005* (Verso).

Brzezinski, Zbigniew, 1997, *The Grand Chessboard: American Primacy and its Geostrategic Imperatives* (Basic).

Callinicos, Alex, 2003, *The New Mandarins of American Power* (Polity).

Campbell, Al, 2005, "The Birth of Neoliberalism in the United States", in Alfredo Saad Filho and Deborah Johnston (eds), *Neoliberalism: A Critical Reader* (Pluto).

Cockburn, Alexander, 2007, "On Naomi Klein's *The Shock Doctrine*", *Counterpunch* (22/23 September 2007), www.counterpunch.org/cockburn09222007.html

Davidson, Neil, 2009a (forthcoming), "Introduction: What was Neoliberalism?" in Neil Davidson, Patricia McCafferty and David Miller (eds), *Neoliberal Scotland: Class and Society in a Stateless Nation* (Cambridge Scholars).

Davidson, Neil, 2009b (forthcoming), "Many Capitals, Many States: Contingency, Logic or Mediation?", in Alexander Anievas (ed), *Marxism and World Politics: Contesting Global Capitalism* (Routledge).

Davison, Peter, 1998, editorial note to George Orwell, *Homage to Catalonia*, in *Complete Works, volume two, Facing Unpleasant Facts, 1937-1939* (Secker and Warburg).

Gamble, Andrew, 2001, "Neo-liberalism", *Capital and Class 75* (autumn 2001).

Gowan, Peter, 2009, "Crisis in the Heartland: Consequences of the New Wall Street System", *New Left Review 55* (January/February 2009).

Harman, Chris, 1984, *Explaining the Crisis: A Marxist Analysis* (Bookmarks).

Harman, Chris, 2000, "Anti-capitalism: Theory and Practice", *International Socialism 88* (autumn 2000), http://pubs.socialistreviewindex.org.uk/isj88/harman.htm

Harman, Chris, 2008, "Theorising Neoliberalism", *International Socialism 117* (winter 2008), www.isj.org.uk/?id=399

Harvey, David, 2003, *The New Imperialism* (Oxford University).

Harvey, David, 2005, *A Brief History of Neoliberalism* (Oxford University).

Hennessey, Peter, 2006, *Having it So Good: Britain in the Fifties* (Allen Lane).

Hobsbawm, Eric, 1994, *Age of Extremes: The Short Twentieth Century, 1914-1991* (Allen Lane).

Hutton, Will, 2007, "Her Ranting Obscures Her Reasoning", *Observer*, 23 September 2007.

Judt, Tony, 2008, "Introduction: The World we have Lost", in *Reappraisals: Reflections on the Forgotten Twentieth Century* (William Heinemann).

Klein, Naomi, 2000, *No Logo: Taking Aim at the Brand Bullies* (Flamingo).

Klein, Naomi, 2002, *Fences and Windows: Dispatches from the Front Lines of the Globalization Debate* (Harper Perennial).

Klein, Naomi, 2007, *The Shock Doctrine: The Rise of Disaster Capitalism* (Allen Lane).

Klein, Naomi, 2008a, "This Much I Know", interview by Stephanie Morritt, *Observer*, 1 June 2008.

Klein, Naomi, 2008b, "After A Week Of Turmoil, Has The World Changed?", interview by Emily Butsellaar, *Guardian*, 20 September 2008.

Klein, Naomi, and Neil Smith, 2008, "*The Shock Doctrine*: A Discussion", *Environment and Planning D: Society and Space*, volume 26, number 4.

Kotz, David, 2001, "The State, Globalisation and Phases of Capitalist Development", in Robert Albritton, Makoto Itoh, Richard Westra and Alan Zuege (eds), *Phases of Capitalist Development: Booms, Crises and Globalisations* (Palgrave).

Marr, Andrew, 2007, *A History of Modern Britain* (Macmillan).

Moody, Kim, 2007, *US Labour in Trouble and Transition: The Failure of Reform from Above, the Promise of Revival from Below* (Verso).

Nafstad, Hilde, and others, 2007, "Ideology and Power: The Influence of Current Neo-Liberalism in Society", *Journal of Community and Applied Social Psychology*, volume 17, number 4.

Roberts, Ronald Suresh, 2008, "Beware Electrocrats: Naomi Klein on South Africa", *Radical Philosophy 150* (July/August 2008).

Sanders, David, David Marsh and Hugh Ward, 1987, "Government Popularity and the Falklands War: A Reassessment", *British Journal of Political Science*, volume 17, number 3 (July 1987).

Stiglitz, Joseph, 2002, *Globalization and Its Discontents* (Penguin).

Stiglitz, Joseph, 2007, "Bleakonomics", *New York Times*, 30 September 2007.

Turner, Graham, 2008, *The Credit Crunch: Housing Bubbles, Globalisation and the Worldwide Economic Crisis* (Pluto).

A note on Goldman Sachs and the rate of profit

Joseph Choonara

A recent paper produced by Goldman Sachs (GS) claims to shed new light on the trajectory of the global economy in the run-up to the current crisis.[1] As well as discussing the "global savings glut",[2] the paper presents new research on the "return on physical capital". The latter is of interest to Marxists because it bears some resemblance to the "rate of profit", and Marx famously placed the tendency of this rate to fall at the centre of his analysis of capitalism and crisis.[3] For Marx this ratio between profits and investment is crucial to the dynamic of capitalism because it governs the potential rate of expansion of capital.

The GS paper claims that "far from declining...the global return on capital...has trended up over the past decade or so. Even in 2008, by which stage the financial crisis had begun to hit profits materially, the global [return on capital] remained above its long-term average."

1: Daly and Broadbent, 2009. There are many problems with the paper, but here I look only at the one of most interest from a Marxist perspective. I have based my criticisms on the rather brief and unsatisfactory account of the methodology provided in the paper itself. Thanks to Graham Turner for his input on some of the technical issues and for providing me with data on the breakdown of the capital stock depreciator.

2: A concept that will be familiar to readers of this journal. See, for instance, Callinicos, 2009, and Harman, 2008, for our analysis.

3: Harman, 2007. Note, however, that Marx's rate of profit does not feature in economic statistics. Various proxies that might be expected to show a similar pattern are used by Marxists.

The authors of the GS paper in fact provide two measures of the return on capital. The first, which they call the "yield on capital", is calculated using a method similar to that of the Marxist theorist Robert Brenner, who argues that capitalism has faced a long-term crisis of profitability.[4] However, the GS paper's authors would not agree with Brenner's conclusion. They argue that the genuine return on capital has to be formed by adding a second quantity, the "capital gain", to the yield on capital. So, we have:

Return on capital = yield on capital + capital gain

The capital gain is measured by the "fractional changes in real capital prices" over a given period, relative to the changes in prices of goods consumed by households.[5] They seek to justify this through the argument that we must "consider a representative household…facing a choice of consuming" a quantity of capital "or investing it", and that we must look at the total return the household receives through "forgoing consumption".

But capital stock is not capital derived by households abstaining from consumption.[6] In the real world capitalists tend to expand investment by using profits obtained from previous production, and ultimately from the exploitation of workers, or by borrowing money gathered together by banks. In neither case is the cost of capital goods relative to household consumption goods especially relevant. The essential question is whether the profits made on past investment can sustain future accumulation. In this context a rise in the price of capital stock is a bane as much as a blessing because capitalists have to purchase these goods in order to accumulate.

The yield on capital, though far from perfect, is a better proxy for the potential rate of expansion of the system. If this is understood, three interesting results emerge from the GS paper:
(1) The yield on capital for the US economy matches quite closely the pattern found in Robert Brenner's work (see figure 1). But the GS paper misses out the crucial long-term trend because it only goes back to the early 1980s. If we track the yield figures back to the start of the post-war period, using Brenner's method, we see that profit rates tended to decline *up to* the 1980s. After that time they stabilised, rising and falling through successive business cycles, probably trending upwards slightly. Crucially,

---

4: See Choonara, 2009, for a brief discussion of Brenner's work.
5: Technically, the capital stock deflator deflated by the household consumption deflator. This is the ratio of the price indices of capital goods and household consumption goods.
6: About 170 years ago Marx castigated Nassau Senior for just such an "abstinence theory".

we remain caught in a period of problematic profitability. In other words, the GS paper does not undermine Brenner's analysis or that developed by this journal.[7]

Figure 1: Two methods of calculating the US profit rate

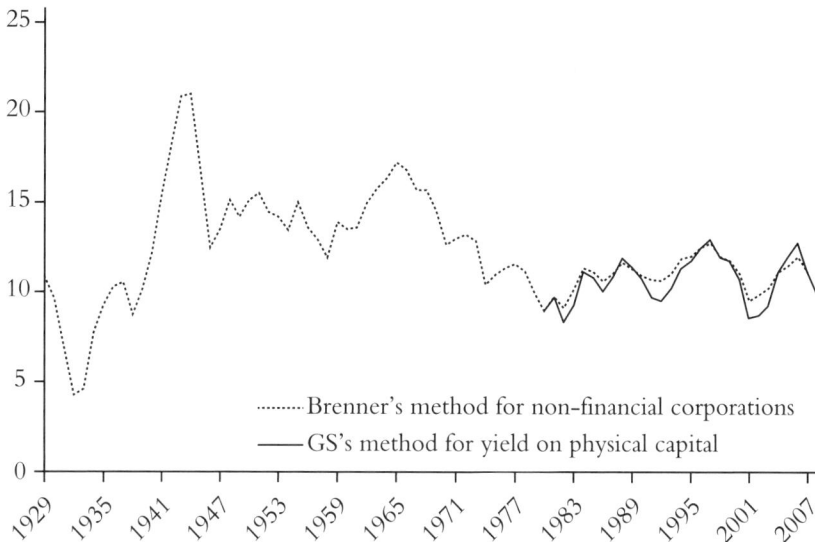

Brenner's method for non-financial corporations

GS's method for yield on physical capital

(2) The global yield measured by GS follows a roughly similar pattern to that of the US yield over recent decades (see figure 2). This is important because most major discussions of profitability among Marxists have focused on the US profit rate. The GS research ought to give us more confidence that global patterns broadly follow US patterns.

(3) The gap between GS's "return on capital" and their "yield on capital" is of interest (see figure 3). Recall that the former differs from the latter only in that it takes into account capital gains or losses. Taking the US figures, we see that the price of capital stock falls in the recessions of the early 1980s, 1990s and 2000s—examples of the depreciation of capital through crisis that Marx described. As the yield recovers from these recessions, the return on

---

7:    Although there remains debate between Marxists on how best to measure profit rates. For instance, Brenner's method, like that of GS, values capital stock at its current cost rather than its historical cost. Andrew Kliman has argued, for instance in his article in this journal, that the historical cost (ie the amount actually required to purchase the capital stock) should be used.

capital generally draws close to the yield, occasionally rising slightly above it. The exception, in which the return on capital soars above the yield, is the period 2004–7.

Figure 2: Global and US yield on physical capital calculated by GS.

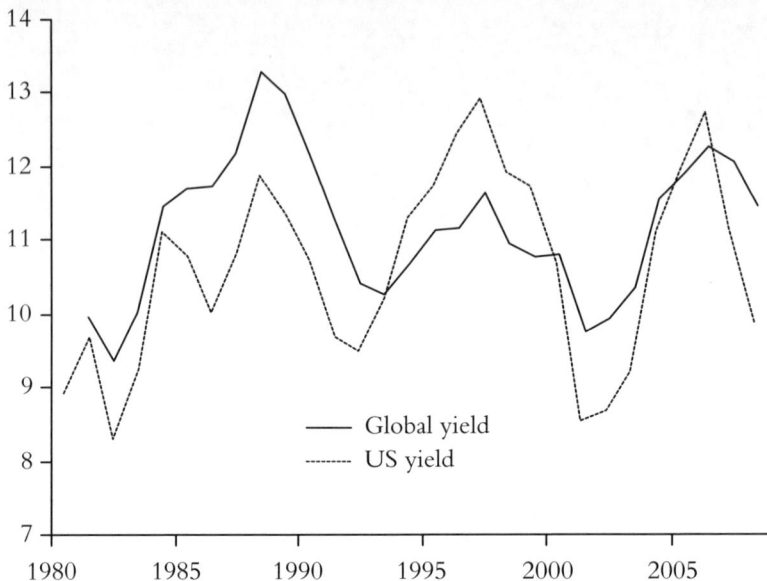

A similar, but less extreme, trend emerges from their analysis of the EU5 economies[8] and the global economy as a whole, though not China, where the boom was based on a genuinely high yield, with the return on capital lagging slightly below. This suggests that from 2004 there was, in the US and Western Europe at least, something of an investment frenzy, even in the non-financial sector, creating a temporary surge in capital costs without producing a sustained rise in profitability. And by 2008 the return on capital had, unsurprisingly, collapsed back below the yield.

8:    Germany, UK, France, Italy and Spain.

Figure 3: US yield and return on physical capital as calculated by GS

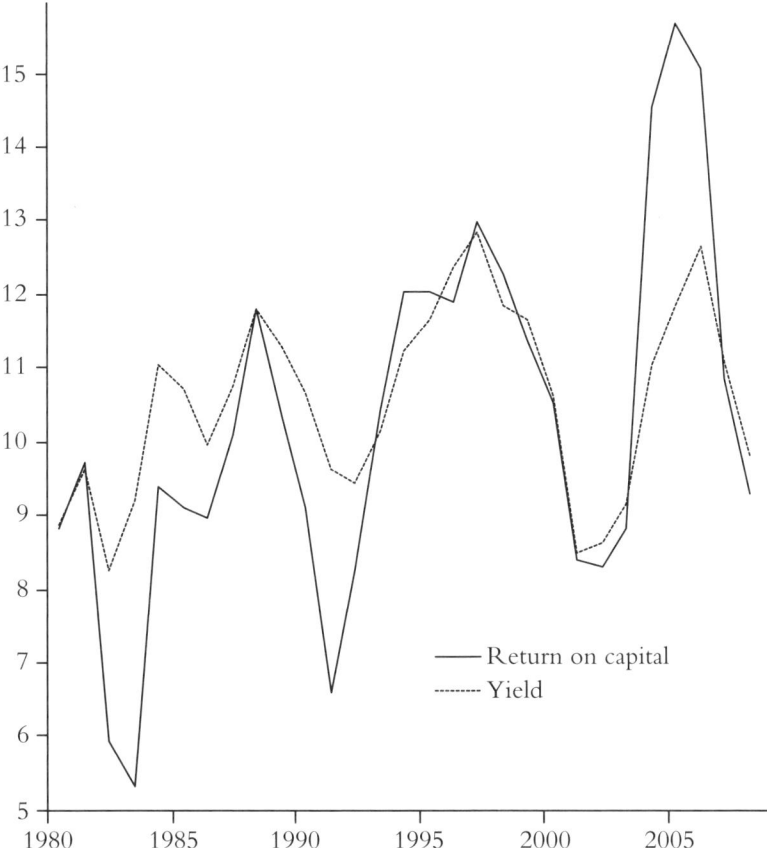

References

Callinicos, Alex, 2009, "An Apologist with Insights", *International Socialism 122* (spring 2009), www.isj.org.uk/?id=532

Choonara, Joseph, 2009, "Marxist Accounts of the Current Crisis", *International Socialism 123* (summer 2009), www.isj.org.uk/?id=557

Daly, Kevin, and Ben Broadbent, 2009, "The Savings Glut, the Return on Capital and the Rise in Risk Aversion", Global Economics Paper No 185, Goldman Sachs Global Economics, Commodities and Strategy Research.

Harman, Chris, 2007, "The Rate of Profit and the World Today", *International Socialism 115* (summer 2007), www.isj.org.uk/?id=340

Harman, Chris, 2008, "From the Credit Crunch to the Spectre of Global Crisis", *International Socialism 118* (spring 2008), www.isj.org.uk/?id=421

Tribunals and tribulations

David Renton

In January 2009 a health worker and Unison activist, Karen Reissmann, brought a claim of unfair dismissal to the Employment Tribunal.[1] She complained that she had been dismissed for publicly criticising cuts at her trust. After her dismissal 700 of her fellow workers struck for 14 days in an attempt to save her job. Her battle then entered a legal stage, culminating in a tribunal hearing that lasted for two days. The employment judge made rulings that narrowed the scope of Reissmann's claim. On the third day the case was compromised, with the settlement agreement including a confidentiality clause. *Socialist Worker* took up the story:

> In a statement...Karen said that she was "happy with the outcome of the case". She also pointed out that, in general, employment tribunals reflect a system that benefits employers. She said, "About 87 percent of cases brought to tribunal are won by employers"... The problems in the tribunal system are a matter for the whole trade union movement.[2]

In the decision to bring a claim, in its settlement and in the sense that no more could be achieved at tribunal than a partial victory, the events of

---

1:   Many thanks to Anne Alexander, Sukhmani Bawa, Simon Behrman and Keith Flett for comments.
2:   *Socialist Worker*, 7 February 2009.

Karen Reissmann's hearing mirror the experiences of thousands of workers every year.

The past 20 years have witnessed a dramatic rise in the number of Employment Tribunal cases in the UK, from about 29,000 per year at the end of the 1980s to 189,000 in 2007-8,[3] with every expectation that this figure will increase further in 2008-9 and 2009-10 as a result of increasing redundancies during the recession.

The tribunal system

Much of the rise in tribunal claims has taken place over the past four years (table 1). The main claims brought are currently: equal pay claims (62,706), working time claims (55,712), unfair dismissal claims (40,941) and wages claims (34,583).[4] Where claims actually make it to a hearing the claimant's chances are, on the face of it, relatively high: 72 percent of wages claims that made it to a full hearing in 2007-8 were successful, as were 53 percent of unfair dismissal claims, although this figure fell to 19 percent for race claims and 15 percent for claims for religious discrimination.

A total of 63 percent of all cases submitted to tribunal were settled in 2007-8.[5] The reason employers compromise is that it usually costs them more to defend a hearing than a successful claimant stands to win in compensation. In 2007 the average tribunal case was estimated to cost an employer £9,000 to defend,[6] more than twice the median amount paid in compensation to successful claimants (£4,000).[7] Thus the employer will usually be able to offer the employee, say, 50 percent of their maximum possible winnings in a settlement agreement, and, where the employee agrees, finish the claim with less losses than if they had fought on and won.

In so far as there is a literature on the long-term increase in tribunals, the trend is only explained in the shallowest fashion. The recent government-commissioned Gibbons report[8] seems to accept that in an industrial society with a population the size of the UK there is a natural

---

3:    House of Commons, 2003, p80; BIS, 2009, p2.

4:    BIS, 2009, p3. Equal pay claims are an exceptional group, which take up only a small proportion of the total workload of the tribunal. In contrast to most other tribunal cases, they are usually joint claims by often large numbers of workers. The claims were pioneered in the middle years of this decade by a few firms, based in the north east of England, which have promoted them as a cheap alternative to trade union membership. See McKenna, 2008.

5:    BIS, 2009, p3.

6:    DTI, 2007, p7. Claimants face an average bill of £3,000—DTI, 2007, p22.

7:    BIS, 2009, p5.

8:    DTI, 2007.

level of tribunal claims. Reforms, it follows, should be aimed at reducing the number of claims to this level. But 20 years ago the number of claims was less than a sixth of what it is today. Fifteen years before that, in the early and mid-1970s, the normal level of claims stood at just 13,000 to 14,000 per year.[9] Before 1964 there were no Employment Tribunals at all.

Table 1: Total Employment Tribunal claims, 2002–3 to 2007–8[10]

April 2002 – March 2003	98,617
April 2003 – March 2004	115,042
April 2004 – March 2005	86,189
April 2005 – March 2006	115,039
April 2006 – March 2007	132,577
April 2007 – March 2008	189,303

Where tribunals come from

The Employment Tribunals (previously Industrial Tribunals) were created in 1964 and for the first seven years of their existence they had the power to hear only a relatively small group of cases involving disputes between employers and the state. The Industrial Relations Act 1971 brought the present system into being, allowing tribunals to hear claims of unfair dismissal. At this point they became the UK's main employment court, and most new categories of employment disputes created since then are heard before the Employment Tribunals.

The 1971 act was adopted by Edward Heath's Conservative government as a result of the Donovan Commission (1965-8). One participant, labour lawyer Otto Kahn-Freund, told his fellow commissioners that increasing strike figures in the 1960s could be explained by workers' growing feeling that they had a right to their job—a right not dissimilar to that felt by the owner of a piece of property. He suggested that the creation of a system of industrial courts would bring these disputes into the legal sphere, ensuring that they could be settled without strikes. He wrote:

9:   LRD, 1998, p2.
10:   BIS, 2009, p3; ETS, 2006, p27.

Friction caused by dismissals is a contributory and considerable cause of (mainly unofficial) strikes and other stoppages. It would be rash to predict that legislation of the kind under discussion would remove this cause of industrial unrest, but if the procedure is manifestly fair and, above all, very speedy, it can reduce the number of stoppages at least to some extent.[11]

Is it true, as Kahn-Freund suggested it might, that an expanded tribunal system resulted in greater industrial peace? It would be possible to place on a single graph two lines showing the increase in the number of tribunal claims since 1971 and the decrease in the number of strikes over the same period, and to conclude mechanically from this graph that the rising number of legal claims explains the falling number of strikes. But such a simplistic approach must be wrong. People are not the prisoners of legal relationships; they respond flexibly to legal opportunities according to a judgment of their interest and in the context of longer historical, political and class dynamics that make litigation appear more or less sensible at different times.

One document submitted to the Donovan Commission was a survey of unofficial strikes categorised by cause (table 2). Looking at these categories now, it is clear that many of them—wages, hours of work and even working arrangements—continue to be taken up as issues by unions in a fashion that has not changed much since the 1960s.[12] Other areas—redundancy, disciplinary and "other individual" cases—have entered the legal sphere over the past 40 years, and in the majority of workplaces are now entirely dealt with as legal matters rather than by strikes.

By far the most important reasons for the decline in the number of strikes are those advanced previously in this journal: the legacy of the unions' defeat in the major battles of the 1980s; the anti-union laws introduced by the Thatcher and Major governments, and continued without reform under New Labour; and the residual loyalty of union leaders to the Labour Party and their unwillingness to take industrial action that might embarrass it.[13] If the use of the law to resolve individual employment disputes can be added to this picture, it remains a subsidiary explanation.

11:   Kahn-Freund, 1967, paragraph 7.
12:   The partial exception is equal pay, but for the reasons given at footnote 4, equal pay claims are isolated geographically and by sector.
13:   Kimber, 2009.

Table 2: Number of unofficial strikes in 1965, by cause[14]

Wages	1,173
Hours of work	22
Demarcation	59
Redundancy	51
Individual disciplinary	131
Other individual	150
Working arrangements	761
Trade union recognition	28
Closed shop	32
Victimisation for union membership	13
Trade union status	8
Sympathy disputes	26
Total	2,454

The extension of the law

In 1973 it was possible for an astute observer to write:

> There are some people for whom the prospect of litigation, of appearing in court, holds no terrors. The average Englishman, and in particular the average English employee, is not one of these people: if the pursuit of his legal rights involves an appearance in the court, it is quite likely that he will forego his rights rather than take those distasteful steps.[15]

This is no longer true in employment or in other areas of law. The law today appears more accessible not just to the millionaires, who have always retained family solicitors, but also to thousands of working class people.

While it is possible to see the increasing number of tribunal claims in the UK as an isolated trend, the rise can also be seen as part of a wider pattern in which the law has become more pervasive in people's lives. Between 1973 and 2005, for example, the number of personal injury claims

---

14: Kahn-Freund, 1967, appendix 1.
15: Greenhalgh, 1973, p20.

in England and Wales rose from 250,000 to 700,000 per year. Most personal injury claims (as with a growing number of employment cases) are now taken on a "no win no fee" basis, a means of funding which at first glance can appear to reduce the risks of litigation for claimants.

Under New Labour there has also been a dramatic increase in the number of criminal offences. Over 3,000 new criminal offences were created between 1997 and 2006.[16] The government has also given the courts the power to hear cases arising out of disputes previously considered too mundane to justify legal claims. The clearest example of this has been the adoption of anti-social behavioural orders (Asbos). These operate by giving a civil court the power to issue orders banning behaviour which would otherwise be considered bad but not criminal. If the order is breached, it may be enforced by a criminal court which can jail the breaching party for up to five years.[17]

The law is also increasingly being used to determine the outcome of political debates. For example, in summer 2009 a number of terrorism suspects brought a case to the House of Lords. The suspects complained that although they were not in jail and had never been subject to criminal trials they were being held in conditions akin to criminal detention. They were held at home on 16-hour curfews; any personal visitors had to be approved in advance by the Home Office; their calls were monitored and they could not use the internet or mobile phones. The suspects added that after having been placed on "control orders" by the Home Office they had complained to lower courts and the courts had allowed these orders to be made after the state had given evidence which the suspects had not been allowed to hear. The suspects said that this was unfair and the Lords agreed.[18]

The interesting point of the story is not the relatively benign outcome but how the result was achieved—by litigation in the courts. With good reason, neither the suspects nor any of the human rights lobbyists who supported them (including Amnesty International) believed that the laws enabling control orders to be made could be overturned in parliament.[19]

16: Morris, 2006. Many "new" offences, such as terrorist weapons training, using nuclear weapons for terrorism, etc, were in reality covered by existing law.

17: Examples of Asbos have included orders given to a depressed woman to stop jumping into rivers or canals; to a drug user, not to sniff petrol in Teesside; to children to stop being sarcastic; and so on. See Foot, 2005.

18: Secretary of State for the Home Department v AF (No 3) [2009] UKHL 28.

19: Other cases heard by the Lords in the first six months of 2009 included cases on whether the police are allowed to "kettle" protesters into confined spaces, on the legality of

Similarly, at the start of the US-led invasion of Iraq in 2003 countless journalists, lawyers and other critics of the war based their objections on the assertion that the war in Iraq was contrary to international law. As China Miéville points out in the most important rejoinder; this assumes, in effect, that, if the war had been totally lawful, the peace movement should have withdrawn its political opposition to the invasion.[20]

The limits of the law

The central problem with tribunals is that litigation tends to result in bad outcomes for workers. The problems begin before the hearing. An employee will approach a lawyer for legal advice. Sometimes they are told that their case has no merits, which is sometimes untrue, or, where it is true, it is unwelcome. Other lawyers will be much more encouraging at the initial meeting, only to lose interest in a case as soon as it encounters an initial difficulty.[21] As we have seen, most Employment Tribunal claims settle. Many employees find that their case is being settled too fast or for less than they had been led to expect was likely. One recent survey of tribunal claimants found many instances of lawyers applying what it termed "robust" (for which we may read "unwelcome") pressure on their clients to settle.[22]

It can take a long time to bring an employment claim to a resolution. Even a simple unfair dismissal case will usually be heard six months or so after the employee submits their claim form. Several categories of case (for example discrimination claims) often require two or even three pre-hearings. Where preliminary hearings are appealed by either side, the full merits hearing may take place as much as two years after the employee left employment. Where a full merits decision is appealed to a higher court, the delay between claim and resolution can be as much as a decade. Where a claimant leaves their employment with a strong sense of injustice, the delays add to their stress and can prevent the claimant from fully recovering, as well as making it harder for them to find a new job.

Tribunal hearings are environments in which employers usually (but not always) get a much more sympathetic hearing than employees.

---

assisted suicide and whether an employee on sick leave can accrue annual leave. For the last two decades the relationship between law and politics in the UK has been getting closer to the American model, in which such issues are the subject of repeated litigation.

20: Miéville, 2005.

21: Trade union solicitors, having no incentive to take on a large number of cases, are usually more cautious at an initial meeting than no win no fee solicitors. Both groups of solicitors tend to become more cautious the longer a case continues.

22: Moorhead and Cumming, 2009, p1.

Employers have spent more on their representation and usually have a clearer idea of what to expect. In addition, various legal doctrines have the effect of tilting proceedings in favour of employers. For example, the tribunals have recently invented a rule whereby if an employment agency drafts a contract with an agency worker stating that they are not an employee, the contract takes precedence unless something makes it "necessary" to ignore it.[23] This has the effect of making most of the UK's 1.4 million agency workers ineligible to claim unfair dismissal.[24] Of course where a worker has no power to complain about a dismissal they are more likely to suffer low pay, bullying and so on.

Another hostile legal doctrine, dating back to Lord Denning and the early years of the Thatcher government, is that where an employer dismisses an employee, and a tribunal must decide whether the dismissal was fair or not, the tribunal approaches the question not by asking what it would have done in the employer's place, but whether the decision to dismiss was so bad that no reasonable employer would have done it.[25] In effect the presumption is that a dismissal was fair.

Tribunals tend to disregard workers' priorities. Interviews with tribunal claimants have repeatedly found that what motivate claimants are "notions of justice".[26] Workers who have been humiliated at work want to see their bosses criticised publicly in turn. Yet in most cases this is exactly what a tribunal does not do. It confines its findings to a narrow reading of the facts. It does not make a public declaration that an employer has been acting inappropriately. Moreover, while the tribunals have the power to order the reinstatement or re-engagement of a dismissed employee, this power is hardly ever used in practice. Of the 40,000-plus unfair dismissal claims before tribunals in 2007-8 only eight led to orders to reinstate or re-engage the employee.[27]

The main power of tribunals is to grant awards of financial compensation. Tribunal awards are low because of hostile statutory rules and the unwillingness of employment judges to make awards outside a narrow band that they consider reasonable. For example, compensation for unfair dismissal combines two elements: a basic award calculated in a fixed statutory ratio and a compensatory award which is intended to reflect

---

23: James v Greenwich Council EAT case number 0006/06; also see James v London Borough of Greenwich [2008] IRLR 302, CA.
24: Renton, 2007; Renton, 2008a.
25: British Leyland (UK) Ltd v Swift [1981] IRLR 91, CA.
26: Moorhead and Cumming, 2009, p iv.
27: BIS, 2009, p4.

the financial loss an employee has suffered as a result of dismissal. Under the basic award employees are compensated for dismissal at the rate of one week's salary for every year that they have been continuously employed. For no obvious reason at all, when calculating the basic award it is limited to £350 per week.

In addition, tribunals start from the actual losses of an employee and then reduce this figure for various potential reasons. The most important reasons are: that the worker has contributed to their own dismissal; that it would be "just and equitable" to do so; or that the worker has failed to remedy their loss (eg by not taking sufficient steps after dismissal to find a new job). Many tribunal panels routinely make more than one such reduction.

The cumulative injustice can be seen by imagining a worker who was previously employed on £20,000 a year whose tribunal case comes to a hearing 12 months after dismissal, and who the tribunal accepts was unfairly dismissed, but who has not subsequently found a new post. Where the tribunal finds that the employee contributed to her dismissal it will routinely reduce her award by 25 percent under each of the first two powers, and in addition cap her award to (say) six months (a period in which a tribunal may decide she could reasonably have found a new post). On these facts, an employee will be £20,000 poorer as a result of her dismissal. Her actual award, however, will be just £5,625 (before tax).

The final challenge facing a successful claimant, armed with an order from the tribunal requiring the employer to pay compensation to them, is actually to secure payment. A recent study estimated that about 39 percent of claimants who won their case were paid nothing by their employer, while a further 18 percent or so were only paid part of the sum ordered.[28]

Tribunals against unions
The use of tribunals as a system to resolve disputes tends to weaken unions. In general, legal argument is a poor restraint on employer power because it always requires the employee to go outside the workplace for protection and in our current legal system it usually requires the employee to undergo dismissal in order later to be vindicated. Moreover, legal knowledge is the favoured preserve of a caste of trained professionals who are only ever weakly subject to any democratic control.

A further concern is cost. Where a union brings a case, the costs are not dissimilar to those for the employer (an average of £9,000). The

---

28: Adams and others, 2009, p i.

average conceals a wide range of different legal costs, depending on the complexity of the case. Employment Tribunals hear very many one-hour or half-day hearings to decide wage cases. In cases of middling complexity (eg an ordinary race or disability discrimination claim) it is not unusual for an employer to spend £50,000 defending a claim. It is worth comparing this to the legal budgets of most unions, typically between £2 and £12 per member per year (table 3).

Table 3: Legal expenditure of selected unions, 2008[29]

Union	Members	Expenditure	Expenditure per member
CWU	230,968	£322,373	£1.40
Unite	1,635,483	£4,814,000	£2.94
GMB	601,131	£2,089,000	£3.48
Equity	36,441	£135,994	£3.73
NUJ	36,081	£401,789	£11.14

Crucially, over-reliance on legal advice tends to diminish the power of the rank and file within any given union. In a context where the most important powers of the unions (including the power to strike) remain bounded by hostile legislation, legal advice is likely to concern matters where the law can be of least help. Lawyers are conservative by their nature. Who wants to be the solicitor whose advice caused a union to have its funds sequestered? And the nature of union organisation means that it tends to be the full-time officials who are charged with the administrative task of asking lawyers for their advice. Lawyers in their initial advice tend to give encouragement to whoever it is who asked for their opinion. There are several recent examples of lawyers' advice being sought in internal union debates and bolstering the position of full-time officials (eg in the lecturers' union UCU union over the question of whether the union's annual conference could lawfully vote in 2009 to boycott Israeli institutions).

29: Derived from union annual reports for 2008, published on www.certoffice.org Larger unions such as the CWU typically employ a full-time legal team whose salary costs do not appear in these figures. Legal expenses of smaller unions such as the NUJ tend to be higher, and in any event any one year's figures can be made artificially high by even small numbers of complex cases.

Escaping the law

When Marxists have criticised the law they have tended to do so by reference to classes and modes of production. The Employment Tribunal is well suited to this form of analysis because it clearly and directly pits workers on one side against employers on the other. As a first stage of analysis we can say that under capitalism the law is a hostile terrain in which workers' complaints are never fully satisfied. As Karl Marx himself wrote, "Legislation, whether political or civil, never does more than proclaim, express in words, the will of economic relations".[30] The main reason why workers lose at Employment Tribunals is because they take place under capitalism, and just as bosses have every economic advantage in capitalist society so too they have the tacit backing of the legal system.

The problem with such explanations is that the ruling class must also seek to retain the consent of the majority. One way this is achieved is by ensuring that laws are seen to be neutral and fair, thus encouraging workers to bring to the law complaints that would otherwise be settled in more unruly ways.[31] In a letter written in 1890 Engels made the obvious point that if justice really did favour the employer in every single case it would cease to be attractive to the poor:

> Law must not only correspond to the general economic condition and be its expression, but must also be an internally coherent expression which does not, owing to internal conflicts, contradict itself. And in order to do this, the faithful reflection of economic conditions suffers increasingly.[32]

It should be clear that there are plenty of ways in which Employment Tribunals confirm this more nuanced picture. I have already referred to workers' relatively high chances of success in many tribunal jurisdictions. Moreover, claimants at the tribunal are often encouraged to feel that they have access to high standards indeed of procedural fairness.

In Employment Tribunals, for this reason, there is relatively little problem of individual bias by judges against claimants. The worst that can be said is that too many judges reach decisions prematurely based on a kind of lethargy, seeking the simplest way to resolve a decision, which generally means a finding against the employee. The problem for claimants

---

30: Cain and Hunt, 1979: p59.
31: See Cain and Hunt, 1979; Beirne and Quinney, 1981; Collins, 1982. Thompson, 1975, in particular argues that in so far as the law is neutral between classes, this neutrality was the product of struggle and should be defended by the workers' movement.
32: Quoted in Cain and Hunt, 1979, p57.

is that high procedural fairness is often matched by substantive unfairness. This can only really be demonstrated by examples of tribunal practice. Here are three:

In a case where an unrepresented claimant was cross-examining a witness (his former manager), the claimant stopped the witness from answering questions and spoke over him. It felt almost as if the claimant was bullying the witness. The manager was represented by a barrister who rose eventually to her feet and attempted to intervene. The employment judge turned to the barrister and barked at her: "Sit down right now Ms X-." The barrister sat back down. The judge allowed the claimant's questions to continue.

At a pre-hearing review a claimant's claim barely made any sense at all. Moreover, she appeared to have submitted the key parts of it so late that on a proper application of the tribunal rules it was out of time and could not be heard. The judge allowed the claimant to continue, advising her that she really should sort out the defects in her case, giving her a fortnight to do so.

A claimant wanted to raise new allegations at his hearing that the real reason for his dismissal was that he had been tortured by another country's secret police; that his employers (a UK-based subsidiary of a foreign state) had given the police his details and facilitated his torture; and that they had dismissed him immediately afterwards. The employer said that as a matter of natural justice it was unfair to be expected to respond to such serious allegations, when the claimant had done nothing to warn that he would make them at a hearing. The judge allowed the allegations to be put in full.

Had any of these three claimants been interviewed afterwards for their thoughts on the merits of the tribunal system, each would have probably said that they had been lucky to have a scrupulously fair judge, while each respondent might have had genuine grounds for complaint. But in each of the three cases the tribunal ultimately found on the merits in favour of the employer and against the employee.

To understand contradictory, day to day experiences of this character requires something deeper than economic categories that determine the outcomes of litigation (but do so mediated by the needs of the legal system to retain an appearance of neutrality). An analysis that proceeds in these terms can usefully be complemented by the further insight that in any capitalist society there is a specific legal culture that will cause legal disputes to have certain outcomes.

As the emphasis of this article is on employment litigation in the UK, I will concentrate on the legal tradition in England, Wales and Northern Ireland: the common law.[33] The most distinctive feature of the common law system, as opposed, for example, to constitutional legal systems, is that decisions are made on the basis of the authority of previous judgments, rather than by working from first principles from a list of constitutional precepts. Explaining the system to an audience of German socialists, Engels characterised common law in the following terms:

> English law is either common law, in other words, unwritten law such as existed at the time when statutes were first gathered and later collated by legal authorities—on the most important points this law is naturally uncertain and ambiguous—or else it is statute law, which consists of an infinite number of individual acts of parliament gathered over 500 years, which contradict each other and represent not a "state of law", but a state of complete lawlessness.[34]

Common law logic starts from previous legal decisions and asks what principles are compatible with a host of contradictory previous cases. In such a system there is always bound to be more at work than mere respect for the authority of past judgments. Again, at a level of great generality, common law is a tradition which:
(a) Tends to protect property rights.
(b) In particular encourages contractual disputes to be settled primarily on the basis of the terms actually contained within a contract (rather than by reference to, say, general values of fairness or reasonableness).
(c) Offers to the litigant in a civil dispute, or the defendant in a criminal case, a high level of fairness in procedure (if not in substance).
As an example of point (a), until parliament created environmental standards, which occurred over the past 30 years, there was no common law right for a person to bring a claim for losses arising from environmental harm. The only equivalent right was a right of property holders to bring claims over "nuisance", ie when their personal right in a property was diminished by environmental damage. Also, in this area of law, there was and remains to this day a common law assumption that environmental damage is not actionable where the property damaged belongs to the poor (hence the legal maxim, "What would be a nuisance in Belgrave Square

---

33: It is not suggested here that civil law or other legal systems produce more favourable outcomes for workers.
34: Engels, 1844.

would not necessarily be so in Bermondsey").[35] The same logic can also be seen also in the ease with which the courts found that the first attempts of socialists in the UK to pass municipal reforms were unlawful.[36]

Point (b) has been repeatedly affirmed, and was given a judicial gloss by Lord Jessel, in the case of Printing and Numerical Registering Co v Sampson, when he said, "Contracts when entered into voluntarily shall be held sacred".[37] In a decision of the House of Lords, made as recently as 2003, Lord Hobhouse explained the same principle but eschewed religious language, relying instead on patriotism and economic benefit:

> When the parties have deliberately put their agreement into writing, it is conclusively presumed…that they intend the writing to form a full and final statement of their intentions, and one which should be placed beyond the reach of future controversy, bad faith or treacherous memory… This rule is one of the great strengths of English commercial law and is one of the main reasons for the international success of English law in preference to laxer systems which do not provide the same certainty.[38]

Eighty years ago the Soviet jurist Evgeny Pashukanis suggested that how the law deals with contracts is not a secondary concern. Whenever a lawyer or judge thinks about how the law operates, they start from the relationship between two owners of commodities engaged in a contractual relationship:

> The legal subject is thus an abstract owner of commodities raised to the heavens. His will in the legal sense has its real basis in the desire to alienate through acquisition and to profit through alienating. For this desire to be fulfilled, it is absolutely essential that the wishes of commodity owners meet each other halfway. This relationship is expressed in legal terms as a contract or an agreement concluded between autonomous wills.

Pashukanis concluded, "The contract is a concept central to law".[39]

35: Sturges v Bridgman (1879), 11 Ch.D 852 at 865; also see the discussion of nuisance, "the pale green tort", in Conaghan and Mansell, 1999, pp124-159.
36: Roberts v Hopwood [1925] AC 578, where decisions of the Poplar councillors to pay fair wages, including equal pay to men and women, were held to be a waste of municipal taxpayers' money and therefore unlawful.
37: LR 19 Eq. 462 (1875).
38: Shogun Finance Limited v Hudson (FC) [2003] UKHL 62.
39: Pashukanis, 1989, p21.

The main approach of common law is to read contracts carefully, closely, and only look with extreme reluctance outside the contract for a reason to disregard any particular term. For workers, the vast majority of whom have no power to negotiate the terms of their employment contract, this creates a constant situation of disadvantage. Should a contract allow an employer to relocate an employee's work to a town anywhere else in England, the worker will get little satisfaction from the court if she claims later that the term was unreasonable. There is a standard judicial answer: "But you signed the contract, didn't you?"[40]

As to point (c), this is the benign face of common law, the tradition of jury trial and the assumption of innocence for criminal defendants. One reason why there has been such an extraordinary rewriting of criminal law in the past decade is precisely because common law has come to offer defendants a high standard of procedural fairness. In an era of terrorism trials these standards act as a rebuke to government.

Precepts such as these dominate even in courts such as Employment Tribunals, which were set up in the modern era and are the product of statute rather than tradition, because the lawyers and judges involved are all schooled in a common law tradition in which these values dominate. The force of common law also obstructs reform, so if a hypothetical reform-minded government came to power and set out to reform tribunals, it would discover that many of the worst barriers for claimants are not the product of statute but are the work of common law judges, and are in these terms barely capable of repeal.[41]

As an example of the impact of judicial decision making, the rule that agency workers are in general not employees was made by the courts as recently as 2006. The decision was justified by an appeal to common law principles. Justice Elias said, "Agency workers are highly vulnerable and need to be protected from the abuse of economic power by the end users. The common law can only tinker with the problem on the margins".[42] Were parliament to legislate that agency workers should be assumed to be employees, judges would be incapable of escaping their common law training, with its emphasis on the need to follow the strict wording of

---

40: See, for example, White v Reflecting Roadstuds Ltd [1991] IRLR 331, EAT.

41: In strict legal theory, common law recognises parliament as sovereign and there is no limit to the ability of parliament to pass any law that it likes. Yet this doctrine is of diminishing force. The trend in recent years has been for parliament to pass laws limiting the power of future parliaments. And judges have always tended to read legislation how they choose. For some examples of this habit in early 20th century employment law, see Renton, 2008b.

42: James v Greenwich Council EAT case number 0006/06.

contracts, and would continue to find that many or most agency workers were not employees.

Another feature of tribunals that I have mentioned, their hostility to the reinstatement of employees, even though they have the power to do so, flows from the tradition of respecting the property rights of the employer within common law. The common sentiment of judges is that forcing an employer to take back an employee would infringe the employer's right to manage. There must be some limit to the power of the courts, and the courts choose to set it here. No legislation would be capable of transforming this antipathy, deep set as it is in our legal system.

Other possible reforms, for example an increase in compensation rates, are stymied by the comparison with common law (ie judge-made) limits on compensation in parallel jurisdictions of civil law. For example, the reason why awards for injuries to feelings in workplace discrimination claims are effectively capped at £25,000[43] is that judges in personal injury law, working from common law principles, limit the compensation for a psychiatric injury brought on by an accident to roughly that figure.

Conclusion

What then should socialists have as their programme for reform of the tribunal system? Workers, at present, bring claims to tribunal because on a realistic evaluation of the opportunities provided, for example, by strike action they judge tribunals, bad as they are, as their best option. The Karen Reissmann case given at the start of this article is a good example. It is not that Reissmann and her allies were unaware of the potential of strike action. They pushed industrial action as far as it would go. A strategy of litigation was adopted relatively late, when it became clear that strikes alone would not in fact win her job back.

Where there is an increase in rank and file confidence, socialists should argue for the removal of legal cases from tribunals and their resolution by the more effective means of industrial democracy. After all, if the shop stewards of the 1960s had been told that they were about to see the birth of a legal system in which most workers who were sacked would go to the courts rather than strike, and only one in 5,000 who did so would be reinstated, it is likely that they would have put up an even stronger fight against tribunals than they did.

Some reforms are conceivable that might go a modest way towards reversing the worst features of the tribunal system. Tribunal panels consist

---

43: Chief Constable of West Yorkshire v Vento [2002] EWCA Civ 1871.

of three member—a lay member nominated by a union, a lay member nominated by an employers' organisation and an employment judge who must be an experienced lawyer. Lay panel members have been complaining for years of marginalisation.[44] Were the judges removed from the panel, or held in reserve for a second appellate court, it is likely that different notions of justice would become apparent.

Even under the present system trade unions could go a modest step towards holding union appointed panellists accountable by the simple expedient of, for example, inviting them to publish at the end of each year a list of the number of cases on which they have sat and a summary of how they have voted.

In a revolutionary society a system of worker dominated tribunals would be almost bound to make better decisions than our existing employment courts. During the Portuguese Revolution of 1974-5 embryonic popular courts were formed to hear housing and criminal cases where it was believed that ordinary courts would be biased against poor litigants.[45] It was the repeated experience of injustice, combined with the general raising of expectations that came from participating in revolutionary upheavals that led workers to see a possibility beyond the existing court system.

In the Employment Tribunals that the UK has at present workers face a constant problem of institutional hostility. When bringing a claim, it often feels as if there exists a constant systemic assumption that employers are basically right and claimants wrong. Challenging this systemic injustice will ultimately take a complete transformation of economics, society and the law.

44: Dickens et al, 1985, p67.
45: Santos, 1982.

References

Adams, Lorna, Ashley Moore, Katie Gore and Joni Browne, 2009, "Research into Enforcement of Employment Tribunal Awards in England and Wales", Ministry of Justice, www.justice.gov.uk/publications/docs/employment-tribunal-awards.pdf

Beirne, Piers, and Richard Quinney, 1981, *Marxism and Law* (Wiley).

BIS, 2009, "Employment Tribunal and EAT Statistics (GB) 1 April 2007 to 31 March 2008", Department of Business, Innovation and Skills, www.employmenttribunals.gov.uk/Documents/Publications/EmploymentTribunal_and_EAT_Statistics_v9.pdf

Cain, Maureen, and Alan Hunt, 1979, *Marx and Engels on Law* (Academic Press).

Collins, Hugh, 1982, *Marxism and Law* (Oxford University).

Conaghan, Joanne, and Wade Mansell, 1999, *The Wrongs of Tort* (Pluto).

DTI, 2007, "Better Dispute Resolution: A Review of Employment Dispute Resolution in Great Britain", Department of Trade and Industry, www.berr.gov.uk/files/file38516.pdf

Dickens, Linda, Michael Jones, Brian Weeke and Moira Hart, 1985, *Dismissed: A study of Unfair Dismissal and the Industrial Tribunal System* (Blackwell).

ETS, 2007, Annual Report and Accounts 2005-06, Employment Tribunal Service, www.employmenttribunals.gov.uk/Documents/Publications/ARA0506.pdf

Engels, Frederick, 1844, "The English Constitution", *Vorwärts*, 18 September 1844, www.marxists.org/archive/marx/works/1844/condition-england/ch02.htm

Foot, Matt, 2005, "Asbo-lutely Farcical", the *Guardian*, 5 April 2005.

Gramsci, Antonio, 1971, *Selections from Prison Notebooks* (Lawrence and Wishart).

Greenhalgh, Roger M, 1973, *Industrial Tribunals, a Practical Guide* (Institute of Personnel Managers).

House of Commons, 2003, Research Paper 03/87: "Employment Tribunals", www.parliament.uk/commons/lib/research/rp2003/rp03-087.pdf

Kahn-Freund, Otto, 1967, "Protection Against Arbitrary Dismissal", National Archives LAB 28/26.

Kimber, Charlie, 2009, "In the Balance: The Class Struggle in Britain", *International Socialism 122* (spring 2009), www.isj.org.uk/?id=529

LRD, 1998, *Employment Tribunals: LRD's Guide to the New Procedures* (Labour Research Department).

McKenna, Bronwyn, 2008, "The Union Perspective on Equal Pay", *Equal Opportunities Review*, 1 March 2008.

Miéville, China, 2005, *Between Equal Rights: A Marxist Theory of International Law* (Brill).

Moorhead, Richard, and Rebecca Cumming, 2009, "Something for Nothing? Employment Tribunal Claimants' Perspectives on Legal Funding, Department of Business, Innovation and Skills, www.berr.gov.uk/files/file51880.pdf

Morris, Nigel, 2006, "Blair's 'Frenzied Law-making'", the *Independent*, 16 August 2006.

NHSLA, 2009, "Key Facts about our Work", National Health Service Litigation Authority.

Pashukanis, Evgeny, 1989 [1924], *Law and Marxism: A General Theory* (Pluto).

Pritt, DN ["A Barrister"], 1938, *Justice in England* (Gollancz).

Renton, David, 2007, "No Protection", *Red Pepper*, October/November 2007.

Renton, David, 2008a, "Agency Workers: Second Class?", *Socialist Lawyer*, April 2008.

Renton, David, 2008b, "Six Employment Cases Brought by Teachers (1906-1919)", *History of Education Researcher 82*.

Santos, B Boaventura De Sousa, 1982, "Popular Justice, Dual Power and Socialist Strategy", in Beirne and Quinney, 1981.

Thompson Edward P, 1975, *Whigs and Hunters: Origin of the Black Act* (Penguin).

Book reviews

International rescue

Ian Birchall

Jan Willem Stutje, **Ernest Mandel:**
A Rebel's Dream Deferred *(Verso,*
2007), £19.99

Ernest Mandel was a tireless socialist
activist over five decades. He wrote
prolifically on economics, history and
contemporary politics, and was an
impressive lecturer and debater in several
languages. He was one of the most influential figures on the revolutionary left in
the second half of the 20th century, and
certainly deserves an intelligent biography. Stutje has done him justice with
this account, which is both readable and
scholarly, based on over 40 interviews
with those who knew Mandel and on the
20 metres of Mandel archives stored in
Amsterdam. (There are a few slips, such
as the bizarre claim that British publisher
Victor Gollancz was in Buchenwald.)

So Stutje's account can be recommended,
both to those who remember Mandel
and to those who do not. Stutje achieves
a good balance between the personal, the
political and the intellectual. The story of
Mandel's love life—two marriages and an
unrequited youthful passion—is sometimes touching but not sensational. The
revelation that he might have lived ten
years longer but for overeating and indul-
gence in diet pills is a warning to us all.

However, the dour readers of *International
Socialism* will doubtless be mainly interested in Mandel's political evolution.

The most inspiring part of the story is the
opening section devoted to Mandel in the
Second World War. Though only 16 at
the outbreak of war, he was involved in
the Trotskyist movement from the outset
(his father was a Trotskyist activist). The
essence of the Trotskyist position was
to reject the nationalism which con-
taminated all other sections of the left,
and to insist that German soldiers were
"workers in uniform", to be approached
on a class basis.

Mandel worked closely with Abram Leon,
author of *The Jewish Question*, and with
Paul Widelin, who produced the journal
Arbeiter und Soldat (*Worker and Soldier*),
distributed to occupying German troops
in France. Mandel was the only one
of the three to survive the war. He was
himself involved in producing a pamphlet
in German, which told soldiers: "You are
being sacrificed as cannon fodder while
your masters negotiate to save their possessions." He also showed great personal
courage, escaping from a German work
camp by climbing over the fence during
the few moments when the electricity was
switched off. This section confirms the
view that the Second World War was the
golden age of the Fourth International,
when its militants combined heroic
actions with theoretical clarity.

Internationalism was always central to
Mandel's politics. Not only was he, in
Isaac Deutscher's phrase, a "non-Jewish
Jew", he was also a "non-Belgian
Belgian"—born in Germany with a
Polish father, he obtained Belgian citi-
zenship only in 1956. He was a Fleming

in a country where most militant workers were French speaking Walloons. He also—unlike the "Western Marxists" beloved of Perry Anderson—believed passionately in the unity of theory and practice, and he knew well that such unity could only be achieved through organisation. This explains his lifelong commitment to the Fourth International. And that is where the problems start.

Stutje writes from a stance of "critical admiration" for Mandel. His account is far from hagiography, and provides the information needed for a serious assessment of Mandel's politics. This needs to be done in a measured fashion. In the 1960s and 1970s Mandel inspired a generation of activists in several countries, and was undoubtedly an asset to the socialist cause, whatever tactical differences we might have had with him. And since none of us have made the revolution, there can be no question of counterposing Mandel's "errors" to the allegedly "correct" line followed by someone else. Nonetheless Stutje's account suggests certain reservations from which there may be lessons to be learned.

The first paradox that strikes a reader is that while Mandel was totally committed to Marxism, a theory of working class self-emancipation, there is relatively little in the narrative about actual workers. There are "workers' states" and "workers' parties" aplenty, but few actual workers in mines, factories or offices. Certainly Mandel enthused about the great explosions of mass working class struggle in the Belgian General Strike of 1960-1, France 1968 and Portugal 1974-5—he participated in all of them. But his orientation was generally towards radicalised youth, especially students.

As he said in Paris on 9 May 1968, "When this universal struggle succeeds in enlisting the adult workers, then we can remake today's vanguard into a powerful revolutionary party that can take its place at the forefront of the masses." The implication was clear: students today, workers tomorrow.

In 1956 Mandel took the initiative in launching the weekly paper *La Gauche* (*Left*), which represented the broad left within the Belgian Socialist Party—though Stutje records that during the 1960-1 General Strike it had "no decisive influence". But even here we hear far more about Mandel's relations with senior party figures and trade union leaders such as André Renard than about building in the working class rank and file of the party.

Likewise Mandel maintained close links with a number of the most important left intellectuals of his day—Ernst Bloch, Roman Rosdolsky, Lucien Goldmann, and among the younger generation Perry Anderson, Tariq Ali, Robin Blackburn, Rudi Dutschke, Michael Löwy, and Daniel Bensaïd. These are figures of some importance, and it is certainly to be hoped that parts of his voluminous correspondence with such people will eventually be published. But there is no indication of any similar contacts with worker militants.

After the Cuban Revolution, Mandel believed that its "revolutionary leaders have unconsciously resorted to Trotskyism". So in 1964 he was pleased to be invited to visit Cuba, where he stayed for seven weeks and had a long discussion with Che Guevara. In the economic debates then taking place between Che's friends and the more Stalinist elements, Mandel advocated "a management by the workers at the workplace, subject to strict discipline on the part of a central authority that is directly chosen by workers' councils". There is something decidedly odd about this. Historically workers' councils have been the product of working class struggle, not of the decrees of governments, however left their rhetoric. Mandel's enthusiasm for the Cuban Revolution seems to have led him into advocacy of socialism from above.

Mandel's whole life was bound up with the tangled history of the Fourth International. The many polemics and interminable splits may seem marginal to serious politics. Yet often the issues raised were of great importance. As Stutje notes briefly, in 1947 Mandel first came into conflict with Tony Cliff. Mandel was arguing that amid capitalist decadence an economic revival was impossible; Cliff argued the contrary. Of course neither man had as yet the remotest idea of how long the post-war boom was to last, but Cliff certainly seems to have had a superior ability to look the facts in the face.

Mandel was initially resistant to the idea that the Russian satellite states in Eastern Europe had become workers' states themselves despite the absence of working class self-activity and independent revolutionary parties. Only in 1951 did he finally give way on this question, probably more out of concern to hold the Fourth International together than from any conviction that the basic principles had changed. But it was a slippery slope.

In the early 1950s Michel Pablo argued that since world war was impending there was no time to build revolutionary parties and that the Trotskyists should therefore "enter" the mass Communist parties to intervene in a new situation in which the class struggle would acquire the form of a conflict between blocs of states. Mandel clearly had serious reservations about this but apparently told a comrade he would "rather serve unity than get his own way". The fact that the leaders of the opposing camp contained at least one unprincipled thug (Gerry Healy) was doubtless a factor in the argument.

In the early 1970s some of the Latin American sections, backed by the more Guevarist elements in Europe, launched a strategy of guerrilla warfare, which led to defeat and the death of numerous militants. Mandel seems to have had reservations about this disastrous course, but not to have fought for his position so as not to fall out with the pro-guerrilla comrades, especially in France.

The upsurge in struggle that began in 1968 gave the Fourth International a new lease of life. On Stutje's figures, which seem plausible, the International had about 10,000 members by the early 1980s, the bulk of them in France, Spain, Mexico and the US. Mandel now devoted his attention to building an international leadership team. (Britain was represented by John Ross who was later to enthuse about the contribution of hedge funds to London's economy.) A Paris office was opened with some 20 full timers. Wasn't this somewhat top-heavy—an attempt to build the International from the summit downwards rather than by the patient construction of local sections with real roots in the class?

For Mandel it meant that he was required to pronounce on the situation in countries around the world, often on the basis of secondhand information. I recall a meeting in 1986 where I ventured to criticise the Fourth International position on the Labour Party. Mandel howled at me scornfully that the Labour Party had ten million members. (Neil Kinnock would have been delighted at the news.)

By the early 1980s it was clear to many that the upturn in struggle begun in 1968 had come to an end. But Mandel refused to face the facts, insisting that the movement was still going forward. As Tariq Ali puts it in his foreword, Mandel's motto was "Optimism of the will, optimism of the intellect". The result could only be serious tensions within the International. Here it seems fair to contrast Mandel with Cliff, who, in 1979, argued that the Socialist Workers Party (SWP) must face up to a period of "downturn". Certainly the SWP suffered losses but Cliff was far more successful than Mandel in holding his organisation together.

Mandel rightly identified Trotskyism as embodying the healthy essence of Marxism and of Leninism. But this led to the attitude that anything that called itself "Trotskyist" deserved to be taken seriously. One of the saddest episodes in this story occurred in 1994 when Mandel, old and in declining health, took part, against the advice of his own comrades, in a public debate in New York with the Spartacist League, a bunch of buffoonish provocateurs. Would he have debated with Screaming Lord Sutch if he had called himself a Trotskyist?

Yet perhaps all this is too harsh. Since 1945 it has been a hard task to keep the flame of revolutionary socialism alight in a world system that has become progressively more rotten, corrupt, violent and self-destructive. Mandel was one of those who tried to do so, and he deserves to be remembered.

A welcome overview
Christakis Georgiou

Bill Dunn, **Global Political Economy: A Marxist Critique** *(Pluto, 2008),* £19.99

Political economy is as old as capitalism itself. It emerged in the late 18th century and its object of study was the way capitalist production and exchange were to be organised on a national scale—hence its name, derived from the Greek word *oikos* meaning the household and *polity* to denote the state's central role in the organisation of these activities. Originally, then, thinkers such as Adam Smith—one of the founding figures of economic liberalism—did not distinguish between the spheres of economics and politics in the way that contemporary neoclassical economics and rational choice theories of political science do.

With the development of industrial capitalism in the 19th century and the subsequent development of an organised labour movement, some of the central tenets of classical political economy such as the labour theory of value, especially the version of it developed by Marx, became ideological weapons in the hands of those who were challenging the existing order.

In the face of this, a new school of thought emerged in the 1870s—the marginalists, whose aim was to rid the study of capitalism from its associations with politics and to give it an apparently objective and scientific character. Their main representatives, such as Eugen von Bohm-Bawerk, Frank Fetter or Stanley Jevons (who recommended replacing the term political economy with "economics"), each made the point that classical political economy had evolved to become a potential weapon in the hands of radical critics of capitalism.

The legacy of the "marginalist revolution" is the fragmentation of the academic study of society. This legacy is so powerful that for a long time little space existed in universities for alternative or critical approaches. This was reinforced during the post-war period by the long spell of economic expansion of the 1950s and 1960s.

The end of the boom, however, created new space for approaches that sought to reintegrate politics and economics, not least because the crisis seemed to have been caused by overtly political events such as the creation of Opec and the oil price spikes. Political economy regained ground in the 1970s. The argument about the separation of politics and economics is not simply an academic one. Neoliberal policy-making has been legitimised by such arguments. Perhaps the most striking example is the argument for the virtue of independent central banks because of the alleged necessity to protect "technical" decisions from "political" influence. The counter-arguments have a political importance, therefore, because they attack one of the foundations on which neoliberalism has been developed.

Bill Dunn's book attempts to provide a Marxist overview of the debates that have punctuated the development of this discipline during the past 30 years or so. The book's scope is vast and this is both its strength and its weakness. It covers a huge amount of material and addresses a large number of debates. As such, it is a brilliant introduction to the debates raised by the study of capitalism. However, for the same reason, some of the issues are only insufficiently covered or are discussed in a way that requires some familiarity with the subject.

In the first of the three sections in the book, Dunn starts off with a discussion

of the shortcomings of liberalism both in terms of the discrepancy between its theoretical models and the world as it really exists, and the methodological individualism on which it is founded. Dunn shows how liberalism managed to adapt to changing social circumstances, especially during periods of crisis, and how each time it served to legitimise the status quo.

Dunn then considers realism and institutionalism—two traditions that challenge liberalism's claim that capitalism is a harmonious system of self-regulating markets by trying to incorporate power into their analyses. But both of these traditions fail to integrate questions of class and class antagonism in a consistent way. The following chapter is dedicated to more critical approaches such as constructivism, green political economy and feminism, whose main contribution has been to push political economy beyond the simplistic dualism of states versus markets and to bring under examination issues that traditionally would not feature in economic or political analysis.

The final chapter in this section deals with "Marxisms", with the plural referring to debates that have divided Marxists. The chapter's main concern is to refute the accusation of structural determinism that has so frequently been thrown at Marxists.

The second section of the book deals first with the transition from feudalism to capitalism and the historical development of the system. It shows how the various stages of development were the product of the dynamic of capitalist development. The last chapter of this part discusses the post-war boom and US hegemony.

The third section deals with some of contemporary political economy's favourite themes and deconstructs many myths about the world economy.* So, for example, concerning production, "the evidence does not support characterisations of a runaway world of manufacturing relocation from rich to poorer countries". Regarding international trade, Dunn shows that "neither openness nor closure are unqualified goods" and that global poverty cannot simply be attributed to free trade and hence that "opposition to free trade alone does not adequately challenge the roots of global inequalities and poverty".

The chapter on finance provides evidence to counter-claims that "finance trashes state powers to tax and provide welfare" and argues that "financial globalisation should be seen firstly as a political achievement". The role of labour in the "new economy" is also considered and Dunn argues that "recent transformations do not require new conceptualisations nor do political strategies have to be re-imagined from scratch". In a particularly interesting chapter entitled "The Political Economy of the Non-Economic" Dunn considers a series of issues that are excluded by mainstream economics because they escape commodification, such as the natural environment, non-commodified forms of work or the alienation generated by the organisation of the labour process.

It is the third section that forms the lengthiest and in many respects the most valuable part of the book. The patterns of inter-imperialist rivalry that have emerged since the mid-1970s and the collapse of Stalinism could have been covered in more detail in this section. The final chapter of the book is dedicated to debates about "global governance" and the "new imperialism" but it only considers the various Marxist theories

without providing the same breadth of empirical material given in other chapters.

Despite some weaknesses stemming from the vast amount of material that the author engages with, this book is a brilliant introduction to debates that have animated Marxists and provides a strong critique of alternative approaches to the study of capitalism. It is recommended reading to anyone, student of political economy or otherwise, who wishes to gain an overall understanding of the way capitalism has developed and of the position it finds itself in.

An Engels for the bourgeoisie
Katherine Connelly

Tristram Hunt, **The Frock-Coated Communist: The Revolutionary Life of Friedrich Engels** (Allen Lane, 2009), £25.00

Ten years ago Paul Foot wrote a review of Francis Wheen's engaging and jovial, if somewhat lightweight, biography of Karl Marx. In the review he commented that while most dead left wingers are patronised and rehabilitated by the establishment, "detestation of Karl Marx...has persisted for over a hundred years". Not so now. A systemic and global crisis of capitalism is so profound that previously smug free-marketeers are looking desperately for answers in the writings of two 19th century communists who said that capitalism is inherently unstable, that crisis is inevitable. The spectre of Marx, which for so long faced an academic wall of silence, is haunting the press, the universities, financial institutions and

---

* As he did in his article in *International Socialism* 121—www.isj.org.uk/?id=509

booklist. For one reviewer of Hunt's book "the faddish return to Marx visible in sales of some of his books is mostly just a sign of loss of nerve"—embarrassing evidence of his class failing to keep a stiff upper lip.

Just as governments have turned to state intervention (albeit to bail out the rich) after years of the mantra "there is no alternative" to laissez-faire capitalism, so we face an ideological somersault from establishment figures who are now writing about Marxism.

Tristram Hunt is a product of this contradiction, and perhaps this is why the "contradictions of Hegelian proportions" in the public and private lives of Frederick Engels appeal to him and lie at the heart of his biography. "This was where the eye of the storm and stress really lay," writes Hunt, "in squaring his two diametrically opposed public and private lives as exploitative cotton lord and revolutionary socialist, as frock-coated member of the upper middle class and ardent disciple of the low life".

Engels was the gentleman in the club and the communist in the beer hall; the fine living wealthy manufacturer who lived in secret with his love, an Irish factory worker; the adrenaline-fuelled young man hunting foxes and, just a few years before, shooting from the barricades. This provides Hunt with the perfect medium to explore one of his own passions—the socio-geography of the 19th century city. Engels had unique equality of access to the two nations contained within entirely segregated cities. Hunt emphasises the influence of Engels's lover, Mary Burns, "his underworld Persephone" who was his guide into the realm of the Mancunian working class. This allows Hunt to demonstrate that the pioneering work *The Condition of the Working Class in England* was not just the product of one brilliant

man. Engels's insight at the age of 24—that the working class was the class with the potential power to transform society—was a product of his real experience:

"Friedrich Engels's two worlds—of the mill owner and Mary Burns—profoundly influenced his journey from philosophy to political economy and, in turn, had a marked effect on the emergent shape of Marxism. Uniquely, Engels was able to fuse his real experience of industrial capitalism and working class Chartist politics with the Young Hegelian tradition."

This skilful exploration of the origins of Engels's work avoids a "great man" narrative by emphasising his intellectual debts—both to acknowledged political thinkers (Georg Hegel, Thomas Carlyle, etc) and to working class agitators including Mary Burns and the Chartists. This allows us to see what was truly creative and original in the works of Marx and Engels. By the same treatment, Hunt is able to show the immense debt that Marx owed to Engels. It is evident not just in the works that they formally co-authored. Hunt quotes Marx asking Engels the manufacturer about the practical dynamics of capitalism: "Engels's grafting at Ermen & Engels helped to construct the empirical foundations of *Das Kapital*."

Also refreshing is Hunt's refusal to write hagiography. Engels's sexist and racist assumptions, and his homophobia, are discussed frankly. In fact this effectively vindicates the Marxist idea that "being creates consciousness", and also that it is engagement with class struggle that enables people to throw off the "muck of ages"— Hunt acknowledges that Engels rejected most of his racist ideas and revised his earlier contradictory attitudes to women. Indeed he subjected women's oppression to the same method with which he explored class society and not only railed in fury against it but argued that this oppression emerged in particular historical conditions, concluding that it could also, like class society, be swept away.

All this is valuable, but there are serious flaws in Hunt's book that impoverish his analysis. While Engels overcame his early prejudices about Irish people, Hunt continues throughout the book to apply the adjective "earthy" to the Burns sisters or, as he sometimes calls them, the "earthy Irish sisters". More disturbing is his use of the poor journalistic trick of deciding for his readers what the best story is, rather than presenting the more uncertain but human narrative.

He has made extensive use of Yvonne Kapp's superb biography of Eleanor Marx* and he references this book when he describes the fate of Frederick Demuth, the illegitimate son of Karl Marx and the family servant Helene Demuth. Frederick was fostered but Engels allowed everyone to assume he was the father. Hunt describes the "impoverished life" Frederick Demuth lived, which, reflecting the author's own social prejudices, includes "his professional life as a skilled fitter and turner and member of the Associated Society of Engineers".

Hunt adds that "Freddy [Demuth] and his son Harry used the tradesman's entrance to visit... Engels, however, was always careful to absent himself on such occasions." Kapp also tells this story but there is an important difference. She conducted the interview with Harry Demuth and she wrote that he and his father went on a Sunday to have dinner with Eleanor Marx in Engels's house where Helene Demuth "reigned". The "tradesman entrance" story has an entirely different genesis (unacknowledged by

Hunt), which Kapp explores in a footnote. It originates in a letter by Louise Kautsky, who had a turbulent relationship with the Marx family and who was writing of an event that took place before her arrival in the Engels household. Kapp's extensive research concludes:

"There is but a single occasion when he [Frederick Demuth] can be known for certain to have been there: on 1 July 1894 he was one of 13 signatories to a postcard sent from the Engels's address to Mrs Liebknecht saying they were all drinking German beer while they awaited the telegram announcing the Reichstag election results."

To reference another author and deliberately distort their meaning is dishonest and lazy history. Furthermore, at times, the cost of the good yarn is a superficial analysis. However, where Hunt is weakest is in conveying the experience of workers' struggle. This is not merely stylistic; it is ideological. In the vivid, intimate portraits in Kapp's work lies the same sense of excitement and attention to detail that her subject, Eleanor Marx, infused her life with during her deep involvement with the New Unionism strikes in the East End of London.

Hunt, by contrast, fails to take working class subjects seriously and it produces a poor historical analysis. He dismisses the demise of Chartism as the product of "public inertia, government repression and rain". The growth of reformism, the European context and the change in the economic climate were all apparently unimportant—or perhaps just less amusing. The 1871 Paris Commune provided Marx and Engels with some of their most concrete ideas about workers' power and the role of the state. The Commune was, in Marx's words, "a harbinger" but it remained isolated and the cost was

* Published in two volumes as *Eleanor Marx: Family Life, 1855-83* and *Eleanor Marx: The Crowded Years, 1884-98.*

horrific—a counter-revolution slaughtered tens of thousands of ordinary Parisians in just seven days.

Marx and Engels's writings on the Commune, their contact with the survivors who fled and their celebrations of the anniversary of the birth of the Commune are dismissed by Hunt who writes that the diverse strands of socialism and anarchism in the Commune "proved a relief for Marx and Engels: when it all went wrong, there was someone else to blame". This is cheap and dishonest. The point of analysis was, for Marx and Engels, not simply to interpret the world but to change it. Their analysis therefore reflected the actual experience of working class struggle. The Paris Commune enabled them to argue for practical aspects of proletarian dictatorship, for example the right to recall elected representatives. To insist, then, that they were interested in preserving an analysis at the expense of working class struggle is to devalue the entire point of their live's work.

And it is precisely this, removing the element of revolution, that is distinctive in the popular resort to Marx that is taking place now. What Hunt fails to understand is that the contradictions in Engels's life, which he finds so attractive, were created by the absence of proletarian revolution. Engels knew there was no bourgeois answer to resolve the contradictions of capitalism. He returned to business after the defeat of the 1848 revolutions and he hated it. Such contradictions were forced on Engels. They were not an integrated part of his character and certainly were not celebrated by him.

This surely is why Hunt is so bitter about the Russian Revolution and again there is dishonesty in his analysis here. Hunt effectively refutes the charge from both bourgeois critics and Stalinist apologists that Engels was the architect of Stalinist determinism. He writes, "There lies an unconscionable philosophical chasm between Engelism and Stalinism." This is an analysis developed in this journal specifically in regard to Engels.* While borrowing from this strand of Marxism, Hunt refuses even to engage with its analysis of October 1917, which he contends represents the distortion of Marxism into "an irreproachable dogma" and was led by "power-hungry" Lenin.

This is a biography for a bourgeoisie in crisis. "It is recent events in the world's stock markets and banking sector which bring Engels's criticisms so readily to the fore," writes Hunt. But as such it is the biography of only half of Engels's life. Ten years ago Marxism was frozen out of the mainstream. Now they are attempting to rehabilitate Marx and Engels while removing the driving force behind their ideas. It is material circumstances—the crisis of capitalism—that has caused this. It will be working class resistance to the crisis that will bring the practical application of Marxism to serious attention. It is time to listen to the gravediggers.

---

* See for instance, *International Socialism* 65—a special collection on Engels's Marxism.

A beardless monument

Owen Hatherley

Norbert Lynton, **Tatlin's Tower: Monument to Revolution** *(Yale University, 2009), £35*

Vladimir Tatlin's "Monument to the Third International" is the most famous building never built. Designed from 1919 to 1920 by a collective, led by the futurist painter and sculptor, it was initially a response to the Bolsheviks' call for "monumental propaganda"—a plan to replace the statues of Tsars and saints that littered Russian cities with monuments to revolutionary heroes. Over a couple of years a variety of strange edifices arose, from neoclassical busts of Karl Marx and Frederick Engels to a figure of Mikhail Bakunin. Most were fairly traditional in form. Yet Tatlin's project, initially rather secretive but publicly exhibited in Petrograd in 1920, broke entirely with these attempts to put new wine in old bottles.

His monument was both dedicated to, and the headquarters of, an idea, not an individual, however revolutionary. The idea was the International, specifically the Third (Communist) International, known as the Comintern, that would restore honour to an ideal sullied by the nationalist treachery of its social democratic predecessor.

Encased by a spiralling, leaning iron frame that would rise taller than the Eiffel Tower were glass volumes housing the operations of the Comintern. The lowest, a cube, would be for conferences of the international, and would rotate "at a speed of one revolution a year". Above it a pyramid would revolve on its axis for one revolution per month, and would house the International's executive committee, and

an upper cylinder would hold "an information bureau, a newspaper, offices for public proclamations, pamphlets, and manifestos—in short, all the various mass media for the international proletariat". Elevators would connect all three. At least three scale models were made in Tatlin's lifetime, but no date was ever set for its construction.

This non-structure has taken on a second existence as the spectral symbol of the unfulfilled promises of the 20th century, of the world revolution that never happened. This is particularly so since the 1960s, when the tower was reclaimed from the Stalinist dungeons into which it had disappeared, with new models erected in art galleries from Moscow to New York.

Even in Britain the tower reappeared, here and there, most often as a symbol of the anti-Stalinist left. In the 1970s a schematic silhouette of it was the logo of New Left Books, which later became Verso; a red plastic model shelters the books in Bookmarks; and on the tube a few years ago posters promoted "Tatlin's Tower and the World", a quixotic initiative to build the entire 1,300 foot tower piece by piece in different countries, fulfilling the internationalist dream of the early Comintern in the absence of the International itself.

Norbert Lynton's *Tatlin's Tower: Monument to Revolution* is not the first book-length study in English on this "building". That accolade was swiped by the Russian-American theorist and artist Svetlana Boym's elliptical *Architecture of the Off-Modern*, an attempt to re-imagine the monument to the Third International as a monument to a glorious failure, a provocative art project rather than a viable structure.

Lynton was a curator and writer who died in 2007, soon after his book's completion. In 1971 he curated Art and Revolution, the first major exhibition in the West of the Constructivist art, design, film and architecture that marked the first decade or so of Soviet rule. The exhibition's catalogue featured an invaluable quantity of translated texts, revealing the theoretical and political sophistication of these artists so often dismissed as dreamy dilettantes out of their depth in practical politics. Hence it provided the foundation for the works that would finally let the Constructivists speak for themselves, rather than through garbled Western interpretations.

Tatlin's Tower is usually slotted into the story of Constructivism—a gigantic machine, "made", in Viktor Shklovsky's oft-quoted words, "of iron, glass and revolution", a modernist monument, something utilitarian. Yet Tatlin's Tower is here a far from merely "useful" structure. Instead Lynton constructs a grandiose, and frequently rather peculiar edifice of theological and art-historical speculation, with relatively little reference to the political or even artistic context of the time.

The actual tower itself takes up a surprisingly small proportion of the book's contents, with much exposition on Tatlin's life, his connections with the avant-garde poet Velimir Khlebnikov, and on subsequent projects such as his "Letatlin" flying machine. Lynton's central thesis is almost lost among this fairly extraneous material, but it is a fascinating and audacious idea. In essence, it is that the monument to the Third International is the (inadvertent, unofficial) artistic embodiment of "god-building"—that is, the attempt to create a sort of "religion of socialism" undertaken by the Russian Marxists Alexander Bogdanov, Maxim Gorky, and Tatlin's later patron as head of the Soviet Commissariat of Enlightenment, Anatoly Lunacharsky.

Lynton explains this "god-building" as an attempt to connect with the Russian peasantry by creating a form of socialism that would resonate with the biblical language and references to which they were accustomed. This notion was mocked by Lenin: "It is one thing if an agitator [uses religious language] in order to find a starting point for his argument, and a mode of expression familiar to the under-developed masses, so that his views may make more impact. But it is quite another if a writer actually starts preaching the 'construction of god' or a 'god-constructing' socialism...in the former case the thesis 'socialism as religion' serves as a bridge from religion to socialism; in the latter it passes from socialism to religion."

In Lynton's account, the tower certainly used a religious formal language, and did so for a quasi-mystical conception of socialism as the fulfilment of all humanity's wishes, after centuries of striving to transcend gods and oppressors. The tower is literally, in Marx's phrase, "storming heaven".

So in his pre-history of the tower Lynton fixes upon both the Malwiyya mosque in Samarra, Iraq, with a similar spiralling form and, more pointedly, a 17th century woodcut by Athanasius Kircher of the Tower of Babel. With its dual spirals, its god-threatening height and its barred structure, this tower is indeed enormously akin to Tatlin's, though there is absolutely no proof Tatlin was aware of either.

Meanwhile, the forms within the spiralling metal skeleton were themselves elemental, primal—cube, cylinder and most of all pyramid, now transformed from the geometry of dynastic power into buildings for the promotion of human emancipation. There is some evidence that the tower was intended to straddle the river Neva, with its iron legs on each side—which leads Lynton into a comparison both to the Colossus of Rhodes and to *The Bolshevik*, a then well known painting by Boris

Kustodiev showing a gigantic worker, red flag in hand, striding across the crowded streets of Petrograd.

The argument that the tower was inspired by ancient forms, a product of collective memory as much as of the Eiffel Tower and industrial cranes, is extraordinary enough. It starts to become rather curious when the author embarks, seemingly at random, upon a long excursus on a work of 19th century Russian Orthodox "history painting", Alexander Ivanov's *Christ's First Appearance Before the People*. In this image semi-clad figures crowd about John the Baptist, who gestures to the figure of Christ in the far distance.

One wonders what the significance of this is, until Lynton claims that the figure of John the Baptist, the angle of his leg, the jut of his staff, is in silhouette fundamentally identical to the form of the monument to the Third International. For Lynton this makes perfect sense. In Russian Orthodoxy John the Baptist is a highly important figure, "the forerunner" who points the way towards the messiah. The monument does the same, as forerunner for Communism, for what Ernst Bloch called "concrete Utopia". Again Lynton offers no proof but does aver that "any Russian artist" of the time would have known Ivanov's painting intimately.

Aside from this intriguing and peculiar venture into theological aesthetics, Lynton reminds us that Tatlin's Tower has much to do with the other elements in the thought of Alexander Bogdanov—the Proletkult or "Proletarian Culture" movement that followed the revolution, to which Tatlin had some connections, and utopian science fiction, embodied in Bogdanov's novel of a Martian Marxism, *Red Star*. Certainly Russia's Communist Futurists frequently spoke of their kinship with the Martians, representatives of a new red planet. But

even on the level of architecture, the tower was a work of science fiction, something recognised by Leon Trotsky, who visited the tower's first model in Petrograd during the Russian Civil War. Though he applauded Tatlin's break with architectural tradition, this was, he claimed, "not a building, but an exercise".

At the time there would not have been enough steel in Russia to erect a metal model (the original was in wood), let alone to build the structure itself. This was a speculative structure and no doubt Tatlin knew it. Accordingly, two subsequent models, both of them different from the original, emerged in the early years of the Soviet Union. One, by Tatlin himself, was exported to the Soviet Pavilion at the 1925 Paris Exposition, in which, alongside Konstantin Melnikov's temporary pavilion and Alexander Rodchenko's *Workers' Club*, it promised a distinctively socialist new architecture. This model was less complex, more streamlined and, Lynton suggests, buildable.

The last model was a schematic, ad hoc wooden tower carried on a May Day festival in the same year, reminding us that this was also to be a deeply festive, celebratory building, formally akin to a helter-skelter. Lynton reminds us that public festivals were key to the revolution's early years, with Tatlin himself helming the firework display in May 1918. If, in Mayakovsky's words, this was the "first monument without a beard", it was also the first monument to be intentionally funny.

This is a strange and cranky book, and its anti-theoretical, anti-Leninist perspective is at times a problem. Lynton devotes many pages to describing the books in Tatlin's library, looking for clues, yet ignores the presence there of a volume of Lenin's philosophical writings. If he had investigated them, he would have found a definition of dialectics as "a development that proceeds in spirals, not in a straight line" that would perhaps explain the tower as well as, if not better than, his excursions into the esoteric.

Nonetheless, the approach manages to catch the sheer elemental force of the tower as emancipatory idea and object. He writes, "Petrograd, Russia, Earth, shall have a super-tower from which to guide the human race into world comradeship and space exploration...it would have altered the path of modern architecture and just possibly modern politics", a socialist dream-image to transcend capitalism's Eiffel Towers, Statues of Liberty and Empire State Buildings. It is unbuilt because the society which would deserve such a tower is unbuilt.

Not so smooth criminologist

Simon Behrman

Mark Cowling, **Marxism and Criminological Theory: A Critique and a Toolkit** *(Palgrave Macmillan, 2008), £50*

Two periods of history have witnessed a serious and sustained Marxist engagement with the study of law. The first, not surprisingly, was in Russia in the years following the 1917 Revolution. The high point is represented in the work of Evgeny Pashukanis.* By applying the method developed by Marx in his analysis of the commodity in *Capital*, Pashukanis argued that the legal form was itself an expression of relations of capital. His conclusion was that law would, along with the state, wither away with the advent of a communist society.

Tragically, Pashukanis perished in Stalin's purges of the 1930s and his work was almost unknown outside Russia until the late 1970s. However, it remained an article of faith among Marxists that law was not a neutral concept. At best law represented a series of fictions behind which the reality of ruling class power continued to be deployed; at worst the law was an instrument of class domination, pure and simple.

The second significant period of Marxist writings on law began with an attack on this longstanding hostility held by the radical left towards law. In the closing pages of *Whigs and Hunters* E P Thompson argued that the rule of law represented a historical advance against the arbitrary exercise of power under absolutism. Moreover, the rule of law was "an unqualified good" that transcended social forms, be they feudal, capitalist or socialist.[†] Law was a weapon that time and again the oppressed had looked to and wielded with success in their struggles. From being a shockingly unorthodox Marxist approach to law, Thompson's defence of the rule of law became over the next two decades the received orthodoxy among Marxist legal academics.[‡] This, of course, was against

---

* Evgeny Pashukanis, *Law and Marxism: A General Theory* (Pluto, 1989).

† E P Thompson, *Whigs and Hunters: The Origin of the Black Act* (Peregrine, 1977).
‡ See, for example, Tom Campbell, *The Left and Rights: A Conceptual Analysis of the Idea of Socialist Rights* (Routledge, 1983); Christine Sypnowich, *The Concept of Socialist Law* (Oxford University, 1990); Alan Hunt, "A Socialist Interest in Law" in *New Left Review 192*; and Bob Fine, *Democracy and the Rule of Law: Marx's Critique of the Legal Form* (Blackburn Press, 2002). Indeed Sypnowich states explicitly that the collapse of Communism means that socialists must accept the liberal tradition of the rule of law.

the background of a generalised retreat by the working class and the left.

Unfortunately Mark Cowling's *Marxism and Criminological Theory* continues in the Thompson mould by defending law, in this case specifically criminal law, as a transcendent and necessary form of social regulation. Cowling begins his defence of law from the pessimistic view that the possibility of a working class led revolution "can now be regarded as dead". It is no accident that Thompson's argument likewise begins with the pessimistic premise that "it is not possible to conceive of any complex society without law".

Cowling argues that there are "crimes" that clearly reflect ruling class interests; a prime example is the way in which the US government has created a plethora of drug offences as part of a strategy, following the civil rights movement, to repress militancy within the black inner-cities. But equally, he argues, we cannot dismiss law in its totality as a tool of reaction, for how else can we explain the fact that many of the demands for civil rights were achieved by force of law?

But this can easily be explained by the fact that law must retain a certain appearance of balance in order to be effective as an ideological and not merely repressive tool of class power. Also this argument misses the key fact that in almost all cases progressive advances in the law reflect high points of extra-legal struggle, which are then incorporated into law as a mechanism for diverting militant action into constitutional dead ends. The plight of the civil rights movement once it had achieved many of its legislative aims and retreated from the streets is a case in point.

Cowling goes on to argue that there are crimes that have no role in the exercise of class power. These are what he calls "consensus crimes" that transcend social class as recognised harms, namely killing, assaults or taking other people's possessions "without good reason". How one can abstract a universal notion of a "good reason" in the context of a society based on exploitation and oppression escapes me.

To take just one example, does the nationalisation of a firm without compensation in the interests of protecting jobs constitute a "good reason" for depriving shareholders of their property? There is no one objective answer to this question, and there cannot be in a society divided between those who own the means of production and those who don't. This is the ABC of Marxism. Indeed, the one thing that the law consistently seeks to avoid is any contextualising of cases beyond the law itself. Any discussion of motive (as opposed to mitigating circumstances such as self-defence, provocation or insanity), for example, is excluded in most jurisdictions in a trial for murder.

I have many other such disagreements with the book, but I believe that they are mostly related to some key methodological problems. First, he follows Louis Althusser in dismissing Marx's early work on alienation as mere juvenilia. As István Mészáros has pointed out, to dismiss the theory of alienation is tantamount to destroying the foundations of Marxism itself.* Further, it seems to me that without the concept of alienation one is left with the question as to why the oppressed accept law as an institution when it is so frequently used against them. Moreover, Cowling devotes just seven pages to a discussion of alienation, while immediately preceding this he spends eight pages weighing up the contribution of Charles Murray's right wing theory of the underclass.

---

* István Mészáros, *Marx's Theory of Alienation* (Merlin, 1975).

It could be argued that the reason the oppressed look to the law is that it is genuinely a neutral vessel within which a struggle for justice can be waged. Cowling clearly takes this view and is quite open in accepting the reformist conclusions it implies. Fair enough, but the idea that a political strategy that seeks redress primarily through legal constitutional means can be found in Marx, as Cowling argues, is completely false.

The second major flaw in this book, in any claim for it as a serious contribution to the Marxist tradition, is the almost complete absence of class struggle. Cowling discusses changes in the laws on homosexuality, civil rights, drugs, etc, without once mentioning the political struggles that led to these changes. For Cowling the working class is divided and passive and thus the idea of revolution is utopian. The best hope for social justice is trade union "campaigning", lobbying by NGOs and social democratic reforms. Yet Marxism is nothing without the notion of the primacy of class struggle as the engine of progressive change.

This book certainly has some use as a survey of left literature on crime over the last hundred years. A whole series of authors and schools of thought are presented in easily digestible portions, which is useful as a starting point for academic research. But in no sense is this, as the title suggests, a serious account of Marxism and criminal law. Given the meagre tradition of Marxist writings on law this book promises much and delivers little. Anyone interested in pursuing the question of law in general would be better off starting elsewhere.*

---

* Pashukanis remains the best application of Marxist analysis to the question of law in general. Alan Norrie, *Crime, Reason and History* (Butterworths, 2001), offers an excellent introductory socio-historical account of crime.

A forgotten fighter
Christian Høgsbjerg

*Fitzroy Baptiste and Rupert Lewis (eds), **George Padmore: Pan-African Revolutionary** (Ian Randle, 2009), £14.95*

This collection of essays on the Trinidadian Pan-Africanist George Padmore (1902-59), appearing on the fiftieth anniversary of his death, is a timely tribute to the life and work of a fascinating but forgotten anti-colonial activist and intellectual. The appearance of such a volume is to be welcomed, not simply because Padmore stands as a towering figure of the 20th century "black Atlantic" who fully deserves more critical appreciation in his own right, but also because the question of why he has remained so overlooked for so long, despite the rise of postcolonial studies, is in itself illuminating.

George Padmore was the pseudonym of Malcolm Nurse, who was born in 1902 in Trinidad, then a British crown colony. After leaving school Nurse went into journalism before leaving the Caribbean to study law at university in the United States in 1924. Yet instead of returning home to become a respected professional among the small black middle class of Trinidad (indeed he never returned to the Caribbean), he became a student radical and soon joined the Communist Party of the USA, becoming George Padmore in the process.

Padmore's talents as an organiser and writer meant he was soon appointed head of the Communist International's "Negro Bureau", and from 1929 to 1933 he threw himself into agitating for black liberation and colonial revolution, residing for periods in Moscow, Hamburg, Vienna, London and Paris, and undertaking daring underground work in colonial Africa. As well as editing the *Negro Worker*, Padmore wrote prolifically, and his pamphlet *The Life and Struggles of Negro Toilers* (1931) became something of a classic.*

However, when Russia's Stalinist rulers, threatened by the rise of Nazi Germany, sought new diplomatic and military ties with the "democratic" empires of Britain and France, anti-colonialism ceased to be the critical issue it once was for the Communist International. Padmore, a principled anti-imperialist, resigned from his position in disgust in 1933 and was vilified by the Stalinist bureaucracy. In 1935 he moved to London, the "dark heart" of the British Empire, and joined forces with his boyhood friend from Trinidad, the Trotskyist C L R James.

For the next 20 years or so Padmore devoted all his energies to the struggle to liberate Africa and the Caribbean from colonial rule. In 1937 he formed the International African Service Bureau, later the Pan-African Federation, and in 1945 was central to organising the historic Fifth Pan-African Congress in Manchester. Matthew Quest offers a useful discussion of the "class struggle Pan-Africanism" of the bureau's journal *International African Opinion*, while Hakim Adi and the late Fitzroy Baptiste examine respectively how the fifth congress was built and how its potential impact was somewhat blunted by the realpolitik of British colonial officials.

Besides writing several books from his London home, from *How Britain Rules Africa* (1936) to *Pan-Africanism or Communism?* (1956), Padmore's greatest triumph undoubtedly came when one of his African disciples, Kwame Nkrumah, led the Gold Coast to independence in 1957. Nkrumah had met C L R James in America during the Second World War and when Nkrumah moved to Britain in 1945 James referred him to Padmore as a matter of course.

Marika Sherwood discusses Padmore's relationship as mentor to Nkrumah, quoting one of Padmore's letters, from 1955, in which he notes that James "introduced [Nkrumah] to Trotskyism and I knocked that nonsense out of him before his return [to the Gold Coast]. And put in its place Pan-Africanism (black nationalism and socialism)."

The extent to which Padmore, who ended his life working as adviser to Nkrumah in Ghana, bears responsibility for the manifest failings of Nkrumah and Pan-Africanism generally is perhaps a moot question, but it is certainly one avoided in this volume due to the Pan-Africanist perspective and hagiographic tone of some of the contributors.

Fitzroy Baptiste's fine contribution does, however, note important continuities between the Stalinist "two-stage theory" of colonial liberation (first political independence then socialism) that formed part of Padmore's training while in Moscow and his later strategic vision for achieving "Pan-African Socialism". Baptiste also quotes from a British Foreign Office document from December 1959 entitled "Africa: The Next Ten Years", which, with what Baptiste notes was the "typical smugness" of those wielding imperial power, concluded that "Pan-Africanism, in itself, is not necessarily a force that we need regard with suspicion and fear". This statement stands as an epitaph to the limitations of the "Pan-African Socialism" envisioned by Nkrumah and Padmore (and for that matter by James).

That said, George Padmore's extraordinary lived experience as an "organic

---

* For this pamphlet and more of Padmore's wrting, go to www.marxists.org/archive/padmore/

intellectual" of anti-colonial movements in Africa and the Caribbean is well brought out in this volume and remains in many ways inspiring for anti-imperialists today. Moreover, his relentless work exposing and denouncing what Karl Marx called "the profound hypocrisy and inherent barbarism of bourgeois civilisation" is of course relevant today.

Indeed, as a new "Scramble for Africa" centred around oil unfolds, the memory of anti-colonialists such as Padmore becomes particularly poignant. His fate was to be largely ignored by postcolonial studies, never forgiven by Stalinists, regarded as a "problem" by the British Labour Party and, after his death, turned into a "harmless icon" by the new Pan-Africanist rulers of post-colonial Africa. Anyone interested in the past, present and future of revolutionary socialist politics in Africa and the Caribbean can learn much from a critical engagement with his life, work and legacy.

Seeds of Canadian radicalism
G Francis Hodge

Ian McKay, **Reasoning Otherwise:
Leftists and the People's
Enlightenment in Canada 1890-1920**
(Between the Lines, 2008), £26.87

Ian McKay begins *Reasoning Otherwise* with the frank acknowledgement that there exists little published scholarship relating to the development of the Canadian left prior to 1914. The book is a first attempt to make up this lack. McKay describes his method as a "reconnaissance" of this history, rather than an attempt to polemicise or judge.

By this McKay means both a preliminary survey of the ground and an attempt to gain information about an enemy. He does not pretend to have written a definitive argument, but rather sees *Reasoning Otherwise* as "one step in a co-operative struggle to understand contested terrain".

The Canadian left prior to the First World War was neither homogeneous nor united. McKay describes this "first formation" of the left as a milieu of many different small groups, discussion circles, cultural associations and craft unions. These groups often knew little of each other. Coal miners in Nova Scotia likely knew little of what loggers in British Columbia were doing. Groups were often further divided by language and ethnicity. What these groups had in common, however, was a package of ideas derived from the social sciences of the 19th century. Socialism was seen not as a mystical utopia but as a scientific possibility, even probability.

Marx's labour theory of value, which holds that all wealth is the creation of human labour, was a key for these "first formationists". Also central to the thought of these early leftists was the notion that social progress and socialism were part of a Darwinian process of social evolution. Just as humanity had physiologically evolved from earlier species, these early leftists held that socialism was a natural evolutionary progression from class society.

Though these early socialists have been dismissed simply as positivists or vulgar Marxists, McKay does not do so. He sees them as a product of the Victorian and Edwardian world, shaped by positivist science and Eurocentric nationalism. He stresses that many of Marx's writings were not yet available in Canada. Though the first formationists were indeed guilty of misusing the ideas of natural science in their theorising of human society, McKay argues that they were "doing original and important things in Canada with an unavoidably abbreviated 'Marx' whom they often read with discernment and adapted with intelligence".

However, McKay does not ignore their failings. He points out that many of them assumed the existence of different "races" and some of them felt that some races were inferior to others. He highlights the deterministic cast of much of their thought but points out that a great deal of science at the time was still described in deterministic language. The acceptance of probability over certainty as a useful way to frame scientific theory was "as yet unconsolidated".

McKay, then, sees this first formation of left politics in Canada as "not a toxic waste dump" of mistakes and shoddy theory, "but a freshly planted field" that laid the basis for a more organised, united and coherent left politics after the First World War. He also argues that what some might construe as the greatest weakness of this early left—its looseness and lack of coherence—was in fact a strength. This allowed it to withstand state repression and survive to lay the basis for the fighting left that emerged during the 1920s.

Readers are given some opportunity to decide for themselves how true this contention might be in the chapter on the month long Winnipeg general strike that took place in the summer of 1919. The chapter makes for gripping reading. The strike was described by Antonio Gramsci as part of an international revolutionary movement of workers at the time and "a bid to install a soviet regime". McKay presents this material in as neutral a fashion as possible, attempting to show both what he considers the strengths of these early leftists in Winnipeg and their shortcomings. However, the reader looking for an analysis of the lessons of the strike will have to look elsewhere.

That said, McKay does an excellent job of situating the emergent Canadian left of the early 20th century in a wider context of political developments in Britain, the United States and Europe. Though the language used is occasionally ponderous or overly academic, *Reasoning Otherwise* is nevertheless an excellent resource for anyone interested in left politics before the First World War, whether in Canada or internationally.

Sub-Saharan nightmares
Claire Ceruti

Joseph Mensah (ed), **Neoliberalism and Globalisation in Africa: Contestations from the Embattled Continent** *(Palgrave Macmillan, 2009), £40*

This collection examines Africa's special place in globalisation. Africa south of the Sahara often appears in cheery UN and World Bank reports after the phrase "the sole exception". Its wealth has declined in the last 20 years, against the trend for other regions.* Globalisation skipped chunks of Africa, whether the issue is electricity, "space-compressing" technologies such as the internet or tourism. What Africa has more of is death—life expectancy here is regressing. The authors of this collection

---

* Which is not to say that everyone was getting richer in the rest of the world—the gap between the richest and the poorest also increased over this period, and Mensah notes islands of wealth within the poorest puddles.

expose the "Washington consensus" that Africa's special predatory and protectionist states cause all its problems, while also avoiding bland generalisations about contemporary globalisation.

Joseph Mensah explores culture. Globalisation has not made everywhere identical. Africa has always acted back upon the rest of the world culturally as much as it has been acted on. Modern transport and communication have intensified the exchange between global and local, embodied in Asian rap, Chinese tacos, Irish bagels, dreadlocks and African music crossing the world. Mensah is no romantic. He knows this integration is deeply unequal. Not everyone's world is getting closer. The woman collecting water on foot connects to the world differently from a jet-setter with a wi-fi laptop, although things going on in the jet-setter's world might be directly responsible for the water-bearer having no water on tap.

Globalisation in the era of neoliberalism amplifies both integration and the inequality in an "overarching process that makes exclusion an integral part of globalisation". A century ago Leon Trotsky called this uneven and combined development. Only Patrick Bond calls it by this name in this volume but the concept appears in other chapters.

In fact the new scramble for Africa's resources creates predatory states. "Managing large-scale resource extraction requires strong geopolitical and military capacity, and given the failure of many Pentagon missions in Africa, local strongmen are required," writes Bond. He recounts a memorable measure of international looting, from a World Bank report called "Where is the Wealth of Nations?". The report compared the existing productive capacity of various African countries with the capacity they could have had if

the oil and mineral revenues had been reinvested, not extracted to distant headquarters. Nigeria could have had five times more productive stock than it has now, and it would have been less dependent on oil. On a personal scale the losses translated to more than $2,000 for each Gabonese person in 2000.*

Unequal integration produces new kinds of criminal survivalism, described in William Tettey's chapters, such as those emails from Kabila's son who needs your bank details to help him secretly move millions from the country. Some young people in Ghana also try to exploit the power imbalance, hoping to escape dead-end situations by hooking up with an *Obroni* (a white person) from a richer country over the internet. Frequently, the power imbalance chews them up and spits them out.

Blair Rutherford's chapter on land redistribution in Zimbabwe marries the local and the global to transcend the false dichotomy of either absolving the Western powers or of regarding Mugabe as anti-imperialist. Zimbabwe's structural adjustment programme, begun in the late 1980s, kept the loans coming but impoverished most black Zimbabweans. It also enriched the mainly white commercial farmers who replaced food production with flowers and tobacco grown for export. Hence the land invasions. Many were later hijacked by Mugabe's cronies, but even before that they failed to link up with the farm workers who were excluded from wealth grabbed by the white farmers.

---

* A weakness in several chapters is an absolutely uncritical use of David Harvey's phrase "accumulation by dispossession". It is not wrong as a description of the daylight robbery of Africa but as several contributors to this journal have pointed out it is more problematic to see it as a form of primitive accumulation rather than some bonus loot on the side.

I was shocked to learn that this is partly rooted in the fact that black farm workers could not vote in local elections until 17 years after Zimbabwe's liberation and therefore were assumed to be with the white farmers. When their vote was debated in 1988 the minister of local government objected it might allow them to vote out their bosses and employers.

Most of the authors are healthily sceptical of existing African elites. Eunice Sahle's chapter on "The New Economic Partnership for Africa's Development" shows up the African leaders who drafted it staking their claim to be doorkeepers to neoliberalism on their continent. I was therefore astonished by the claim in the closing paragraphs of the book that "internal leadership" is the problem; the West "can only operate on the continent with the tacit agreement of local leaders" and therefore perhaps what Africa needs is "visionary, tech-savvy…philosopher-kings" who "understand the power geometries of the world", acccording to Mensah and Roger Oppong-Koranteng. Of course solutions must come from within Africa but "false diagnoses and dangerous prescriptions" such as those from the World Bank may also flow from the self-interest of Africa's rulers.

Julius Kiiza's discussion of protectionism vs deregulation observes that globalisation is not the opposite of economic nationalism but the economic nationalism of the dominant economies. Yet his solutions barely peek past the existing top-down order. "We need to recruit the best and brightest national skills… We also need to reclaim the state from neoliberal state elites and transform government into a key strategic player in the economy," he writes.

Carolyn Basset is much better. She observes that the people's budget campaign in South Africa failed to challenge neoliberal budgeting because it relied on lobbying government rather than mobilising people. Bond outlines a set of responses a "genuinely left government" could take (including defaulting on the debt, refusing tied aid and import-substitution) but acknowledges that no government is "genuinely left", so "bottom-up social movements have to intensify their work".

Bond's measures could be an early bulwark for a Chavezista-type mass movement in Africa putting its foot down on looting, but it has to start out powerfully to outweigh the benefits politicans get and the international punishments they avoid when they play along with globalisation. It would eventually need to overturn all existing government. Real independence requires a movement powerful enough to take back mining interests, land rights, and workplaces from big corporations like Shell, De Beers and Anglo.

Africans need equal access to all the world's riches, no more and no less. We could not afford to remain confined in an import substitution ghetto. The movement will have to reach into the very heart of the West's shiniest financial districts and into the very heart of people like itself in every part of the globe. Such a movement could not long be limited to the ghetto of capitalism.

A sketchy chapter on mass resistance outlines social movements and social forums, but skims or misses the waves of democracy movements, "IMF riots" and mass strikes that Bond mentions. These tidbits are important because all the way through the book what I missed was more discussion of how these forms of resistance can grow into a power able to overturn entirely the current order of things.

Pick of the quarter

Many on the left viewed last year's food crisis and price rises as a blip, a delayed by-product of the debt-induced boom of the mid-2000s aggravated by speculation. According to this argument, concerns over the ability of capitalism to feed the world's people in the long term are severely misplaced. But articles in recent issues of *New Left Review* and *Monthly Review* challenge such complacency.

A *New Left Review* article by Kenneth Pomeranz in the July-August issue considers the chronic problem of providing enough water for the agricultural systems of China and northern India. He shows how the methods associated with the "Green Revolution", which have allowed food output to keep ahead of population growth over the past three decades, are also leading to a fall in the level of the water table. This is happening just as global warming threatens the annual input into water systems from the Himalayas where "glaciers and annual snowmelts feed rivers serving just under half of the world's population".[*]

Monthly Review devoted most of its July-August issue to articles on the issue of food. The quality of the articles is uneven, but some are very good indeed and contain important arguments. Deborah Fahy Bryceson writes well on the problems faced by Africa's peasant farmers.[†] And there is an outstanding piece by Utsa Patnaik which shows how the growth figures normally quoted for India—and probably China as well—hide a fall in average consumption of food, along with a growing inequality in its distribution.[‡]

Not everyone on the left has yet heard the about *The Wire*, recently repeated on BBC and now available on DVD. This is a "cops and robbers" TV series with a difference—the cops often turn out to be robbers and the robbers to be victims of the wider system. *Jumpcut*, "a review of contemporary media", contains a long and very readable Marxist analysis of the series by Helena Sheehan and Sheamus Sweeney.[§]

A year after the credit crunch turned into a full-blooded crisis, the discussion on its origins is now well under way on the Marxist left. Andrew Kliman (who reviews Chris Harman's *Zombie Capitalism* in this journal) provides his analysis of crises and the destruction of capital in the July issue of *Socialism and Democracy* (volume 23, number 2). The most recent issue of *Historical Materialism* (volume 17, number 2) contains a detailed analysis by David McNally, whose views were among those discussed by Joseph Choonara in our previous issue, and a piece by Costas Lapavitsas, who roots the crisis in changes in the banking system and its technology, leading to what he calls (in our view

[*] www.newleftreview.org/?page=article&view=2788

[†] www.monthlyreview.org/090720bryceson.php

[‡] www.monthlyreview.org/090727patnaik.php

[§] www.ejumpcut.org/currentissue/Wire/

misleadingly) "financial expropriation". In the same issue Richard Seymour, a regular contributor to *International Socialism*, has written on John Spargo—a socialist who defected to the right and became an early architect of neoconservatism.

Soon after the Indian elections some of us were lucky enough to receive a widely circulated email containing an excellent analysis by two Calcutta-based Marxists, Kunal Chattopadhyay and Soma Marik. Now it is readily available on the *International Socialist Review* website, the best article to appear in that publication for a long time.*

Finally, most issues of *Work Organisation, Labour and Globalisation* are required reading for anyone who wants to know what is really happening to the world's workers. The latest issue, "Working at the Interface", contains a series of articles looking at the call centre industry.

JC and *CH*

---

* www.isreview.org/issues/66/feat-india.shtml